# DRACULA

### THE
### CONNOISSEUR'S
### GUIDE

ALSO BY LEONARD WOLF

*A Dream of Dracula (1972)*
*Wolf's Complete Book of Terror (1979, 1994)*
*Bluebeard: The Life and Crimes of Gilles de Rais (1980)*
*The False Messiah (1984), a novel*
*Horror: A Connoisseur's Guide to Literature and Film (1989)*
*The Glass Mountain (1993), a novel*
*The Essential Dracula (1993)*
*The Essential Frankenstein (1993)*
*The Essential Dr. Jekyll & Mr. Hyde (1995)*
*The Essential Phantom of the Opera (1996)*

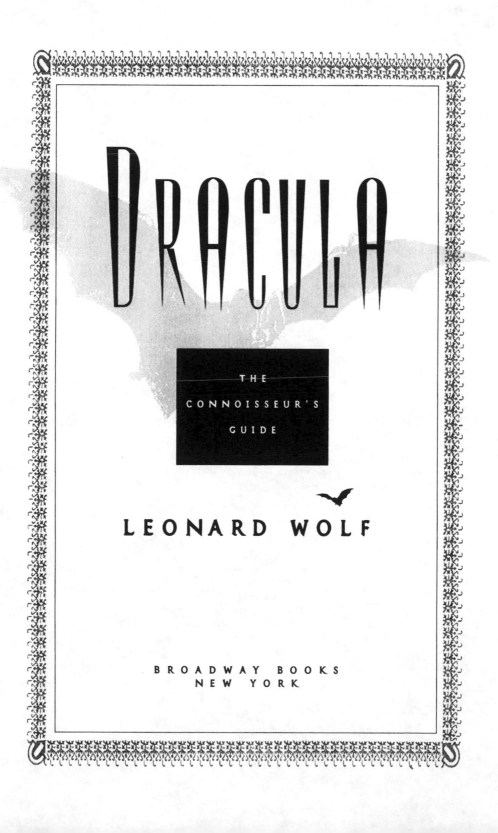

# DRACULA

### THE CONNOISSEUR'S GUIDE

# LEONARD WOLF

BROADWAY BOOKS
NEW YORK

Broadway Books titles may be purchased for business or promotional use or for special sales. For information, please write to: Special Markets Department, Bantam Doubleday Dell Publishing Group, Inc., 1540 Broadway, New York, NY 10036.

BROADWAY BOOKS and its logo, a letter B bisected on the diagonal, are trademarks of Broadway Books, a division of Bantam Doubleday Dell Publishing Group, Inc.

Library of Congress Cataloging-in-Publication Data
Wolf, Leonard.
Dracula : the connoisseur's guide / Leonard Wolf.
p.   cm.
Includes bibliographical references.
ISBN 0-553-06907-1 (pbk. : alk. paper)
1. Vampires in literature.   2. Dracula (Fictitious character)   3. Horror tales—History and criticism.   4. Horror films—History and criticism.   I. Title.
PN56.V3W65   1997
809'.93351—dc21                                                                          96-37538
                                                                                          CIP

*Designed by Chris Welch*

EXAMINE, ANALYZE EVERYTHING THAT IS NATURAL, ALL THE ACTIONS AND DESIRES OF THE PURELY NATURAL MAN; YOU WILL FIND NOTHING BUT THE HORRIBLE. EVERYTHING THAT IS BEAUTIFUL AND NOBLE IS THE RESULT OF REASON AND THOUGHT. CRIME, FOR WHICH THE HUMAN ANIMAL ACQUIRES A TASTE IN HIS MOTHER'S WOMB, IS OF NATURAL ORIGIN.

—CHARLES BAUDELAIRE


THE UNRULY POWER OF SEX, THE WILD CARD OF OUR EXISTENCE. THE ELEMENT IN US THAT IS BOTH INSTINCTIVE AND ENCRUSTED WITH SYMBOLIC MEANINGS. ITS PHYSIOLOGY IS IMPLACABLE—AND METAPHORIC: RISING ACTION, CLIMAX, FALLING ACTION.

—LUDOVIC FLOW


THE EXPENSE OF SPIRIT IN A WASTE OF SHAME
IS LUST IN ACTION; AND TILL ACTION, LUST
IS PERJUR'D, MURD'ROUS, BLOODY, FULL OF BLAME,
SAVAGE, EXTREME, RUDE, CRUEL, NOT TO TRUST.
ENJOYED NO SOONER BUT DESPISED STRAIGHT;
PAST REASON HUNTED AND NO SOONER HAD,
PAST REASON HATED, AS A SWALLOWED BAIT,
ON PURPOSE LAID TO MAKE THE TAKER MAD . . .

—WILLIAM SHAKESPEARE, "SONNET 130"

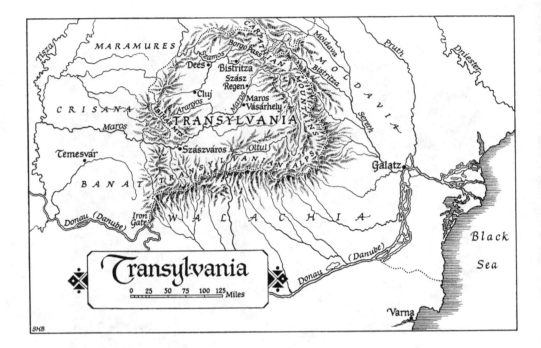

# Contents

........................................

# Acknowledgments

.......................................................................

s always, a great many people have helped me in the making of this work. I cannot acknowledge them all, but special thanks go to James V. Hart, David J. Skal, Barbara Steele, Ann Sachs, and Morgan Rice, who were interviewed for this book.

I want to thank Arthur Greenhall, who knows more about vampire bats than anyone in the world; David Del Valle, who once again provided film stills and horror-film knowledge when I needed them; Mary Corliss of the Museum of Modern Art Film Stills Archives; the librarians in the public libraries of New York City, and of Columbia University and New York University.

This book would be much poorer if I had not the advantage of the insights and the scholarship of several recent books. Most notably, there is Barbara Belford's new biography, *Bram Stoker: A Biography of the Man Who Wrote Dracula*; David Skal's *Hollywood Gothic*; Nina Auerbach's *Our Vampires, Ourselves*; and Christopher Craft's *Another Kind of Love*. I do not always agree with my colleagues' conclusions, but their work has always proved invaluable.

My thanks go to Lauren Marino, my editor at Broadway Books for her intransigent insights, which often made me think again. And to John Thornton, my agent.

Finally, my thanks go to Faith Groesbeck, my research assistant and colleague, who did so much to bring the manuscript to its final form.

# PICTURE CREDITS

........................................................

# In Which the Author Greets His Readers

*"It grew colder and colder still. . . . All at once the wolves began to howl."*

IN THE PSYCHOLOGICAL NOVEL . . . THE AUTHOR HIMSELF
ATTEMPTS TO RESHAPE HIS MATERIAL SO AS TO RAISE IT FROM THE
LEVEL OF CRUDE CONTINGENCY TO THAT OF PSYCHOLOGICAL EXPO-
SITION AND ILLUMINATION. . . . THE PSYCHOLOGICAL MODE DEALS
WITH MATERIALS DRAWN FROM THE REALM OF HUMAN CONSCIOUS-
NESS. . . . THIS MATERIAL IS PSYCHICALLY ASSIMILATED BY THE
POET, . . . EVERYTHING THAT IT EMBRACES . . . BELONGS TO THE
REALM OF THE UNDERSTANDABLE.

THE VISIONARY NOVEL, ON THE OTHER HAND, DERIVES ITS EXIS-
TENCE FROM THE HINTERLAND OF MAN'S MIND. . . . IT IS A PRI-
MORDIAL EXPERIENCE WHICH SURPASSES MAN'S UNDERSTANDING,
AND TO WHICH HE IS THEREFORE IN DANGER OF SUCCUMBING. . . .
THE PRIMORDIAL EXPERIENCES REND FROM TOP TO BOTTOM THE
CURTAIN UPON WHICH IS PAINTED THE PICTURE OF AN ORDERED
WORLD, AND ALLOW A GLIMPSE INTO THE UNFATHOMED ABYSS OF
WHAT HAS NOT YET BECOME."

—FROM C. G. JUNG, MODERN MAN IN SEARCH OF A SOUL

This book, *Dracula: The Connoisseur's Guide*, marks one more stage in my twenty-five-year fascination with Bram Stoker's novel, *Dracula,* and the myth that he turned loose into the world in 1897. By now, the name Dracula has become a household word. With very little encouragement, an unlettered child of five or six who has never seen a vampire movie can tell you about vampires (Ugh! He drinks blood . . . hates garlic) and imitate Bela Lugosi, saying, "Welcome to my house . . ." or "I do not drink . . . wine," or, even though the statement never appeared in a film or in the book, "I vant to suck your blohd." The world of commerce has taken Dracula's name to heart and has used it or its associations to sell an endless variety of products, beginning with Dracula dolls, Dracula masks, fake fangs, and fake blood meant to be daubed onto children's necks. For a while, the Gillette Company sold a hair tonic praised by "Dracula's son" because with it he was able to achieve the "dry look" instead of the greasy hair his father sported. A Lugosi-voiced announcer has sold Jell-O; a Dracula brand of furniture has been marketed; recently, a wine shop in Greenwich Village, New York, displayed a Vampire Wine in its window. Some years ago, Smirnoff encouraged the use of its vodka in making a Vampire Gimlet. Its slick magazine advertisement showed a seated woman wearing a black band around her neck. Her hands were folded in her lap as she looked longingly out of a window. Above her head was printed the message: "Hurry sundown . . ." The gimlet's recipe, which served two, called for:

Six ounces 100 proof Smirnoff
One ounce Rose's lime juice
Three quarters teaspoon sugar

Shake or mix in blender with ice. Serve with a black olive up or on
the rocks.

Children with a slightly cannibalistic bent could devour a break-
fast cereal called Count Chocula which, I used to think, should
have been sold with the injunction "Add milk and it clots," because
the resulting glop looked very suspicious.

James Twitchell's extensive roll of Dracula-inspired products
lists:

> coloring books, . . . figurines, masks, bath mittens, erasers, stamps
> and decals, plastic model kits, wallets, bubble bath, bracelets . . .
> pencil sharpeners . . . popcorn and lunch boxes.[1]

Finally, even in a place as innocent as the TV show "Sesame Street"
there is a vampire count who teaches children—what else?—how
to count.

For some twenty-five years, the span of an entire generation, the
phenomenon of Dracula has been on my mind. I have watched the
cultural and film interest in his name and legend expanding outward in ever-widening circles. With each passing year, the puzzle-
ment increases: Why, in a century, has Stoker's book never been
out of print? What is it about this monster who drinks human blood
that has so caught the imagination of the West that it has created
both a feared and a beloved icon? Why has the film industry been
so charmed by him that, since 1921, when the first film based on the
novel appeared, there has been no decade that has not seen the
release of one or more Dracula films, not to mention the literally
hundreds that are based on vampire legends?

Such questions fascinated me twenty-five years ago and they
were to lead, in 1972, to the publication of my first book about
Dracula, *A Dream of Dracula.*[2] That was followed two years later by
*The Annotated Dracula,* an edition of Stoker's novel in which, on the
belief that it is true that God hides in the details, I subjected
Stoker's text to the very closest of close textual, historical, and literary critical readings.

One may well ask, as I have been many times, how I came to be
interested in the Dracula Matter. The answer is simple. In 1967 I
was teaching at San Francisco State University. It was a period of
great social unrest, particularly for young people, because of America's involvement in the Vietnam War. Antiwar protests erupted on

campuses around the country, including, in 1968, San Francisco State University where there was a huge student strike that led to bloody confrontations with the police.

In addition to being affected by the antiwar political turmoil of the time, thousands of students around the country found themselves caught up in the hippie movement, whose ecstatic optimism was fueled largely by the widespread use of mind-expanding drugs like LSD and marijuana. The combination of hatred for the war and a vision of a coming period of blissful enlightenment in which, in the words of Richard Brautigan, we would live "all watched over by machines of loving grace" produced profound changes not only on college campuses but on America's young people everywhere. Students took seriously Timothy Leary's tidy and irresponsible call to "Turn on, tune in, and drop out."

The response to that invitation was particularly visible in the streets of San Francisco where the movement was born. Middle-class young people in colorful garments stood on street corners, their hands out for "spare change." Refugees from Des Moines and Steubenville lived in overcrowded communes, where they pursued enlightenment and ate bowls of gummy rice. In Golden Gate Park, there were free rock concerts, where the music tried to create the auditory equivalent of a mystical fusion with the universe. Meanwhile, police were rounding up and jailing runaways or teenagers so blissed out that they could not remember their names.

Soon my colleagues and I noticed that we were losing our best students. Those who remained on campus were irritable, given to asking disturbing questions about the relevance to their lives of the education we were offering them.

One of the functions of a university is to be a place where such questions are asked. To get at the answers, to maintain a dialogue, required the presence of students as well as faculty. At the rate at which our students were dropping out, we would soon be talking to ourselves.

Worried by the empty seats in my classrooms, and touched by the students' criticism that our college offerings were irrelevant, several of my colleagues and I, with financial help from sympathetic San Franciscans, tried to reach out to our dropouts by creating a sort of parallel university called Happening House where courses undreamed of in academia—macramé, candle making, meditation—were offered. Mostly, Happening House provided harassed young seekers with a hassle-free environment, where they could sit quietly and, in the language of the times, "get their shit together."

Happening House worked quite well until I was myself arrested. I had just come back from lunch and, walking into the Straight Theater, where Happening House was sponsoring a conference on runaways, I saw that a group of dancers was performing naked on stage. I had just enough time to say to Terence Hallinan, an attorney friend who was standing in the entryway, "These kids are going to get busted," when almost immediately, scores of police swarmed all over the place while the young people, on stage and in the audience, disappeared like magic. Baffled, the police ran about asking, "Who's in charge here?" As the administrative head of Happening House, it was up to me to say "I am," and I did.

I was charged with contributing to the delinquency of minors despite a sworn deposition by the dancers that I had had no knowledge of their plans. After an expensive trial that lasted three weeks, I was acquitted.

Perhaps it was my time at Happening House that in 1969 put the idea into my head of proposing to my publishers a freshman-composition reader (in those days they were called "casebooks") based on Bram Stoker's novel, *Dracula*. A textbook containing essays about *Dracula* might be more appealing to our students than the usual anthology of essays by approved writers whose excellent prose students were supposed to use as models for their own writing.

Harry Sions, my editor at Little, Brown, a man with impeccable taste and shrewd judgment, thought my proposal was silly; but when he was done laughing, he asked a critical question: "Could you write a serious book about *Dracula?*"

The thought had not occurred to me. At the time, I had no special interest in scary literature or film and only the most passing interest in *Dracula*. I had based my casebook idea on nothing more than my happy memory of how terrified I had been as a twelve-year-old reading Stoker's novel and on the hope that the students still on campus would find a collection of essays about the King Vampire more fun to read than those culled from *The New Yorker, Harper's Magazine*, the *Nation*, and the *Atlantic*. I could not answer Harry Sions's question on the spot. I had to do some library work first.

In the cool stacks of San Francisco State University's library, I caught my first glimpse of the Dracula Matter. A fresh reading of the novel showed that *Dracula* is a very great work of fiction, an opinion that, in 1969, was not shared widely by my academic colleagues, either at San Francisco State University or elsewhere. Even more surprising, this marvelous, petrifying novel had been written by a second- or a third- or fourth-rate hack none of whose fiction, before or after *Dracula,* had ever risen above the level of the most pedestrian adventure fiction. More than that, the life of the author of this amazing work seemed to be a riddle enclosed in a mystery and wrapped in an enigma. In short, I had a conundrum on my hands, and who can resist a conundrum? I was well and truly hooked, and Harry Sions got his answer: Yes, I could—and would—write a serious book about *Dracula.*

That book, *A Dream of Dracula* (Little, Brown, 1972), was my first effort at dealing in print with Stoker's novel; and, as I have just confessed, writing it had nothing to do with the fact (proclaimed, naturally, by my publishers on dust jackets ever since) that I was born in Transylvania.

*A Dream of Dracula* is a strange book. Because writers harbor the illusion that they are writing for the ages instead of being affected by their times I find it embarrassing now to see just how much I let the emotional and intellectual climate of the 1960s and early 1970s influence me. I made *A Dream of Dracula* into a very personal book in which I cast myself as a sort of stunned observer of an American society which had appropriated to itself certain vampiric characteristics. To illustrate the impact of the Vietnam War, for example, I described how a young man outwitted his draft board by drinking a pint of his own blood three hours before his medical exam. I wrote: "The busy draft board doctors had no complicated diagnosis to make. Courteously, sympathetically, they sent Mark home. A young man with a bleeding ulcer cannot, and should not, serve in the American army." Between chapters of literary critical analysis and history, I interspersed brief essays on the blood rites practiced by the Hell's Angels, on the psychological vampirism of encounter groups. I went to some trouble to make a universal experience of my own sense of uprootedness as someone born in Transylvania who, from an early age, was raised in America.

I called attention to the ways in which Americans are drawn to power, and to youth. How they resolutely refuse to face the issue of death and, finally, to the degree to which vampire imagery reflected our still-endemic anxieties about our sexuality.

*Dracula: The Connoisseur's Guide* does not pretend to be either a social commentary nor a disguised autobiography. *A Dream of Dracula* was an inner-directed work, one of whose goals was to show that, to a remarkable degree, the image of the vampire represented American culture in the 1970s. *Dracula: The Connoisseur's Guide* is both other-directed and narrower in scope. It is addressed to readers who know, and who care about, the phenomenon of Dracula and who, like connoisseurs everywhere, want to enlarge their knowledge and refine their appreciation. With them in mind, I have seized on the making of this book as one more opportunity to get at Stoker's profoundly enigmatic, always-powerful novel.

Like any great work of art, Stoker's *Dracula* has refused to hold still. With each decade since 1897, it has presented a new Dracula for the scrutiny of a new set of readers. The book that in 1897 seemed to be a first-rate shilling shocker has become, as the twentieth century ends, the symbolic repository of an astonishing array of anxieties, passions, and dreams. Above all, and for good reason, the novel has been seen to reflect the sexual confusions which, despite every reasonable supposition that in this liberated century they would go away, continue to haunt us.

There is much more Dracula still left to consider. What is even better, from my point of view, is that I now get to talk about Dracula to a new generation of readers, many of them the children of those students who sent me to the library so long ago to find my Dracula.

I have not written *A Skeleton Key to Dracula*. My ambitions are more modest. A guidebook can, and should, take you where you want to go. It is not expected to define, circumscribe, or circumvent your experience. The whole point of this book is to illuminate, not to explain. To shed light on Stoker's novel as well as on the social and psychological questions raised by its complexity and by the ubiquity in our lives of the symbolism it has generated.

Let me describe briefly what resources I have tried to make available for my readers: I will pay attention to the varieties of folklore from which Stoker drew. The surface of his novel has a remarkable resemblance to a plum pudding: there is a substantive narrative that is studded all over with folkloric elements. For example, Jonathan Harker's Transylvania experience in Dracula's castle neatly replicates the story of Jack and the Beanstalk, with Dracula in the role of the angry giant who comes out of the depths of his castle growling, "Fee, fi, fo, fum, I smell the blood of an Englishman." One catches glimpses of other folk and fairy tales at intervals throughout the book: the tale of St. George and the Dragon; the story of Bluebeard, or Sleeping Beauty, or Pandora. Other elements which lurk in the fiction are the folklore of blood, of death and dying. And, of course, the folklore of vampirism.

Dracula is a shape shifter. In the novel, the favorite shape into which he shifts is that of a bat. Rather cavalierly, Stoker allows us to suppose that the bats we see are vampire bats. To correct and to prevent any further misperception about the little creatures, I have taken time out to give my readers an account of how *Desmodus rotundis*, the real New World vampire bat lives. *Desmodus* actually has rather decent family values; but for reasons I cannot explain, we, who are carnivores, cannot forgive *Desmodus* its liquid diet and have hung around its neck the opprobrious name of "vampire," taken from one of our most feared monsters.

Archetypal though Dracula is, he did not spring from Stoker's brain as a pure invention. He is based cursorily on Stoker's reading about the historical figure, Vlad Dracula, or Vlad the Impaler, a fifteenth-century Prince of Wallachia whose career of cruelty we will examine.

From Vlad, I'll move on to the Gothic novel, a genre of fiction which appeared in England in the middle of the eighteenth century. Though *Dracula* appeared one hundred years after the genre had reached its peak of popularity, it is still recognizably a Gothic novel.

From the Gothic tradition to the tradition of vampire fiction is an easy step. In the section on vampire fiction, I have tried to point to those works which, like John Polidori's *The Vampyre* and Sheridan Le Fanu's *Carmilla* actually influenced Stoker's work as well as to those on the Continent, which since they were in the mainstream of this genre, may have influenced his thought.

The chapter in which I have dealt with Bram Stoker's life has given me—and I trust will give my readers—pause; because Stoker, for whatever self-destructive reason, worked hard to create the impression that he was a man without qualities. This leaves a writer who has only one chapter in which to survey his subject's life, baffled. Fortunately, since I last had to deal with Stoker, Barbara Belford's informative *Bram Stoker: A Biography of the Author of Dracula*[3] has appeared and it has armed me with details I had not previously known. Still, my take on Stoker, though I would like to believe it is inspired speculation is, finally and irreducibly, speculation.

My critical reading of Stoker's *Dracula* rests on firmer ground. Obviously, it is the product of long familiarity. Despite that, I make no claim that the analysis I have made of it is intended to be anything more than a guide for readers.

Long years spent in classrooms teaching literature have convinced me that the most important way to illuminate a text is to make sure that it has been read accurately, a task that is harder than one may suppose. In order to deal with the most abstruse, the most ambiguous matters, one must establish unambiguously who is doing what to whom, when, where, why, and how. In Robert Frost's poem, "Stopping by Woods on a Snowy Evening," the "little horse" must be seen as little. Otherwise, literary criticism floats about in what T. E. Hulme called "the circumambient gas."

Here's what can happen. A historian of Gothic fiction as reputable as Sir Devendra P. Varma cites in print an image of Dracula that is nowhere to be found in Stoker's novel:

> "His [Dracula's] movements are deft and amazingly graceful. Even within the folds of his dark, flowing cape, every gesture is rich with command. His broad shoulders are framed in the glare of the candles, his pointed cane, whose ferrule is of hammered silver, reflected flashes of lightning in the night sky or sparkled like a star . . . and what a faded splendor his clothes have: his swallow-tail coat of dark serge worn out and shiny; the edges of his cuffs and shirt collar wilted; the purple cravat at his throat bravely affecting a swirl no longer natural to fine silk."[4]

Professor Varma's Dracula is purely a figment of his imagination. Nowhere in *Dracula* does the Count appear with a cane, with or without a silver ferrule, and there is never any indication that his clothes have "a faded splendor" or that he is wearing "dark serge worn out and shiny." As for the purple cravat at his throat which bravely affects a swirl, Professor Varma is dreaming away.

While Varma's is the most blatant nonreading from *Dracula* that I know, there have been other, less egregious ones. In *The Tale of Terror*, Edith Birkhead, an otherwise trustworthy scholar, says: "No one who has read the book *[Dracula]* will fail to remember the picture of Dracula climbing up the front of the castle in Transylvania." What is mesmerizing about that scene is that Stoker's Dracula is climbing "face down, with his cloak spreading out around him like great wings."

More recently, Christopher Craft, the author of "Just Another Kiss," a provocative, if narrowly focused essay, refers persistently to the three beautiful, but loathsome women who surround Harker in the castle as Dracula's daughters, though only two of them, according to Stoker, bear any family resemblance to Dracula. Given Stoker's text, all we are authorized to say about the women is that they *may* be related to him, not that they are. There is no textual basis for calling them his daughters.[5] Once he has called them that, Craft has no trouble referring to, as if it were a fact, as "the incestuous vampire daughters who share Castle Dracula with the Count."[6] In passing, let me be petulant for a moment about the way any number of recent critics have taken to referring to Dracula's castle as Castle Dracula. It is not a term that Stoker ever uses. It is entirely an invention of the movies.

It must be clear by now that I value close textual reading. That I want to see the book steady, and to see it whole, which is why, in Chapter 6, there is a careful summary of Stoker's plot.

From Stoker's novels, I go on to consider Dracula's descendants, the vampire tales that have been published over the century since *Dracula*.

Then I'll review the evolution of the Dracula theme in the movies and will follow the fortunes of the Count or his incarnations, beginning with F. W. Murnau's 1921 *Nosferatu* and ending with Francis Ford Coppola's 1992 *Bram Stoker's Dracula*.

The movies, which in our century have become the art form in which our nightmares find their most congenial expression, have endlessly unwound and rewound Stoker's story, to make it appealing to the filmgoers of the decade in which their films appeared. We have had Draculas who are macabre, coldly handsome, hilarious, romantic, sad, lonely, tragic, or downright ridiculous. It says much for the immortality of Stoker's conception that no single film has ever given the Count either his full due or his quietus, once and for all.

Finally, I will sum up, in the form of a reappraisal, as we move into the twenty-first century, the sociological, psychological and cultural implications of this literary figure that has ensconced himself in our consciousness. We stare at him; he stares at us. In the process, the myth keeps changing.

# In Which the Lore and Lure of Death and Vampirism Are Displayed

*"In the gloom, the courtyard looked of considerable size."*

—AND THAT WHITE SUSTENANCE, DESPAIR.

　　——EMILY DICKINSON (POEM #266)


AS HAS BEEN REMARKED, THE EARLIEST KNOWN REPRESENTATION OF
A VAMPIRE SHOWS HER IN THE ACT OF COPULATION WITH A MAN.

　　——MONTAGUE SUMMERS (*THE VAMPIRE: HIS KITH AND KIN*)

Leaving all folklore aside, what might have originally prompted rational people to believe in the possibility of vampires? The answer is near, and it has to do with such simple matters as the state of the soil in which a body is buried, the climatic conditions prevailing at the time of the burial, and even on the diet on which the deceased was nourished. Each of these variables can have some influence on the rate of a body's decomposition, which means that not all bodies decompose at an absolutely predictable rate.

The matter is put before us comically enough in Hamlet's exchange with the First Clown:

*Hamlet:* How long will a man lie i' the earth ere he rot?
*First Clown:* I' faith, if a' be not rotten before a' die — as we have
    many pocky corpses now-a-days, that will scarce hold the laying
    in — a' will last you some eight or nine year: a tanner will last you
    nine year.
*Hamlet:* Why he more than another?
*First Clown:* Why, sir, his hide is so tanned with his trade that a' will
    keep out water a great while; and your water is a sore decayer of
    your whoreson dead body.[1]

The body of St. Cuthbert, who died in A.D. 687, staved off decay until the nineteenth century when, inexplicably, like a movie vampire after it has been staked, it was suddenly "reduced to a skeleton."[2]

If, then, in a community where there was reason to believe that there was a vampire loose, a suspected body was dug up and found not to be decayed, it is not surprising that a superstition-prone populace would conclude that it had a vampire on its hands. Commenting on the willingness of the diggers to believe in the vampirism of such corpses, Paul Barber writes:

> Note that what is being said here is that if the body remains as it was, then it is a vampire, whereas if it changes—then it is a vampire.[3]

He tells us:

> . . . that most of the material on the subject was collected in past centuries and shows a natural bias for the dramatic and the exotic, so that an exhumation that did *not* yield a vampire could be expected to be an early dropout from the folklore and hence from the literature.[4]

One more evidence that a body had been vampirized was the groan uttered by the corpse as a stake was driven through its body. The scientific explanation is that in the course of decomposition, gases build up in the body cavity so that the entire body can take on a plump appearance. The groan "uttered by the corpse" is merely a consequence of the gas either escaping from the point of entry of the stake or being shoved upward into the throat.

In *Dracula,* we read that as Lucy's body was being staked, "the blood from the pierced heart welled and spurted up around it." We may wonder how blood from a corpse can possibly spurt. In a normal death, the blood in the body coagulates very quickly. However, when the death is the result of "a sudden end to the functions of either the heart or the central nervous system," the blood can reliquefy.[5] This fact has some bearing on the folklore of the vampire because one of the ways in which one can become a vampire is by committing suicide, and the deaths of suicides are likely to be violent or sudden.

If only corpses would behave as they should, there would be less vampire legendry in the world. The trouble is that dropping dead is only the most immediate signal that the end has come. At that moment, the body has experienced "somatic death." It's what we see crumpled in a heap against the base of the wall after the members of the firing squad have pulled their triggers; or when, as we sit at their bedside, we see those we love closing their eyes for the last time.

Visually, somatic death is more tolerable than the "molecular" death that begins moments later. In a peaceful death, it's the look that undertakers strive to preserve: a calm stillness, eyes closed, with a vague serenity inhabiting the features. An inanimate version of the departed self. If the death has been violent or for some other reason disfiguring, it's the look the funeral directors try to re-create. Molecular death on the other hand, has nothing to do with society, with culture or mores, with vanity or pride. It's what happens when the body is taken over by the natural processes that, by means of teeming billions of bacteria, transform all that was human, all that was made in God's image, back again into the soil from which we have been made.

It is an unsightly process, and there are plenty of good reasons for getting the body out of sight as soon as possible as death gives way to decay.

In "A Carcass *(Une Charogne)"* Charles Baudelaire puts the matter cruelly:

> *Rappelez-vous l'objet que vous vîmes, mon âme,*
> *Ce beau matin d'été si doux:*
> *Au détour d'un sentier une charogne infâme*
> *Sur un lit semé de cailloux.*

> *Les jambes en l'air, comme une femme lubrique,*
> *Brûlante et suant les poisons,*
> *Ouvrait d'une façon nonchalante et cynique*
> *Son ventre plein d'exhalaisons . . .*

> *Les mouches bourdonnaient sur ce ventre putride,*
> *D'où sortaient de noirs bataillons*
> *De larves, qui coulaient comme un épais liquide*
> *Le long de ces vivants haillons.*

> Do you remember the object you saw, my soul,
>     That lovely morning in summer?
> At the turn of the path, a foul corpse
>     On a bed, strewn with stones.

> Its legs in the air, like a woman in lust,
>     Aflame, and sweating its poisons,
> Opening cynically, nonchalantly,
>     Its bellyful of gases . . .

> The flies buzzed over this putrid belly
>   From which battalions of black larvae
> Emerged, streaming like a thick liquid
>   Over the living rags . . .[6]

Put less lyrically, the signs of molecular death include a greenish color over the abdomen; swelling and discoloration of the face, scrotum or vulva; abdominal swelling produced by gas; blood seepages; and the bursting open of body cavities.[7] While all of these processes are going on, the body stinks.

There is a point to this grim listing, and that is to emphasize how, in the face of a destiny that will turn us into a massive putrefaction, we can hardly wonder at the attraction of a mode of life-in-death that the vampire's immortality promises. In Anne Rice's *Vampire Chronicles,* the Vampire Lestat never tires of telling the reader how beautiful he is and how much he loves being beautiful, century after century. Of course one wants to outwit both somatic and molecular death. With Baudelaire's "The Carcass" in mind, the temptation of immortality, even at the cost of one's immortal soul, must prove irresistible—especially in a secularized world.

Our real decomposing carcass continues to do things that could lead one to believe that it belonged to a vampire. Blood can appear in the vicinity of the mouth. The appearance of such blood leaking from pools of it in the intestinal cavity, was further evidence "that the vampire has been gorging on blood." Paul Barber adds, "here again we have a remarkably close fit with the folklore of vampirism, for . . . the putative vampire was typically buried face down."[8]

The most famous undecomposed bodies in the world are those of the bog people. These were the bodies of Iron Age people whose tissues, acted upon by the tannic acid of the bogs in which they were buried, acquired the toughness and the flexibility of leather. The fact that their stomach contents uniformly consisted only of seeds has suggested that these people were killed as sacrifices in a religious ritual. It is unnerving to see photographs of the faces of these preserved people who seem so deeply, so peacefuly at rest. They give the impression that they are waiting for us to raise our voices only a little, so that they might respond.[9]

When we are trying to account for the willingness of people to believe in vampires, another factor to be considered has to do with the authentic and pervasive fear that the dead whom we have buried may not be truly dead. Edgar Allan Poe's story "The Fall of

the House of Usher" has, as its climactic moment, the scene in
which Lady Madeline of Usher, who had been believed dead and
entombed, appears suddenly in the doorway:

> There was blood upon her white robes, and the evidence of some bit-
> ter struggle upon every portion of her emaciated frame. For a
> moment she remained trembling and reeling to and fro upon the
> threshold, then, with a low moaning cry, fell heavily inward upon the
> person of her brother, and in her violent and now final death-
> agonies, bore him to the floor a corpse, and a victim to the terrors he
> had anticipated.[10]

In the millennia preceding our own, when death was ascertained
by holding a feather or a mirror to the mouth of the dead to see
whether the feather would stir or the mirror cloud up, there must
have been many occasions when someone was buried prematurely.
Sufferers of catalepsy or drug-induced low metabolic rates were no
doubt mistaken for dead.

In the nineteenth century, bodies were sometimes buried with a
string attached to the big toe. If the body should come alive, it had
only to wiggle its toe to make a bell ring in the watchman's hut. In
America, in 1882, John G. Krichbaum patented a device built into

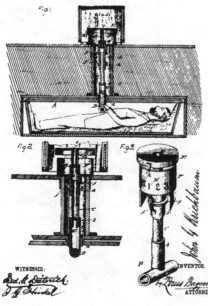

*Krichbaum's device for indicating
life in buried persons. Patent
Sketch, 1882.*

a coffin that would enable a person buried prematurely to turn a handle that would set off a signal aboveground that would bring help running.

## THE LORE OF THE VAMPIRE

In *The Phantom World*,[11] the eighteenth-century Catholic cleric Dom Calmet early documented what he believed to be the existence of vampires in Europe, though Voltaire remarked sneeringly that the true European vampires were the oppressors of the poor. Montague Summers, perhaps the most enthusiastic searcher into vampire lore, scatters citations of vampiric events in his classic, *The Vampire: His Kith and Kin*,[12] and while he is willing to accept the most fleeting and least substantiated reports as authentic, he is certainly the most industrious researcher we have and since, as Dr. Van Helsing points out, all we have to go on are traditions, Summers is a useful preliminary guide. He quotes John Heinrich Zopfius, who gives us an early definition of the vampire, which hardly differs from the one which we take for granted now. Zopfius writes:

> Vampires issue forth from their graves in the night, attack people sleeping quietly in their beds, suck out all their blood from their bodies and destroy them. They beset men, women and children alike, sparing neither age nor sex.[13]

The work that Stoker consulted and which gave him most of the folklore he used in constructing his *Dracula* was Emily Gerard's book, *The Land Beyond the Forest* (1888).[14] Hers is one of those astonishing travel books written by hardy Englishwomen who seemed not to have known fatigue or inconvenience as they traveled from one difficult place to another, wearing long, cumbersome dresses, eating inedible food, braving unpaved, rutted roads and squalid inns, all the while taking accurate notes of all they saw and heard. Emily Gerard had a particular advantage in this case: she was married to a Rumanian army officer, which gave her entry to the life of Transylvania not usually accessible to foreigners. Her book, *The Land Beyond the Forest*, which is what the word "Transylvania" means, was and is a gold mine of information about what was then an obscure part of Europe, and Stoker had the good sense to use it

Capricho 45 *by Francisco de Goya*

well. She tells us how the nineteenth-century Transylvanians regarded the vampire:

> More decidedly evil is the *nosferatu,* or vampire, in which every Rou-manian peasant believes as firmly as he does in heaven or hell. There

are two sorts of vampires, living and dead. The living vampire is generally the illegitimate offspring of two illegitimate persons; but even a flawless pedigree will not insure any one against the intrusion of a vampire into their family vault, since every person killed by a nosferatu becomes likewise a vampire after death, and will continue to suck the blood of other innocent persons till the spirit has been exorcised by opening the grave of the suspected person, and either driving a stake through the corpse, or else firing a pistol-shot into the coffin. To walk smoking round the grave on each anniversary of the death is supposed to be effective in confining the vampire. In very obstinate cases of vampirism it is recommended to cut off the head, and replace it in the coffin with the mouth filled with garlic, or to extract the heart and burn it, strewing its ashes over the grave.

That such remedies are often resorted to even now is a well-attested fact, and there are probably few Roumanian villages where such have not taken place within the memory of its inhabitants. There is likewise no Roumanian village which does not count among its inhabitants some old woman (usually a midwife) versed in the precautions to be taken in order to counteract vampires, and who makes of this science a flourishing trade. She is frequently called in by the family who has lost a member, and requested to "settle" the corpse securely in its coffin, so as to insure it against wandering. The means by which she endeavors to counteract any vampire-like instincts which may be lurking are various. Sometimes she drives a nail through the forehead of the deceased, or else rubs the body with the fat of a pig which has been killed on the feast of St. Ignatius, five days before Christmas. It is also very usual to lay a thorny branch of a wild-rose bush across the body to prevent it leaving the coffin.[15]

Folklore sanctions other ways of keeping the vampire away. Since the nosferatu can make newlyweds impotent or sterile, they are advised to sprinkle holy water on the sheets of the marriage bed. Or to sprinkle poppy seeds or leave a ball of tangled yarn before a dwelling on the premise that the vampire will feel compelled to count the seeds or untangle the knots.

Writing in *Les Vampires*, Tony Faivre tells us that a sure way to find the grave of a vampire is to hire a Dhampire who, being a vampire's son, will know instinctively where his father or mother are buried.[16] Still another way to locate a vampire's grave is to turn a white horse loose in the burial ground where the monster is buried.

In the 1979 film *Dracula*, starring Frank Langella, we are shown vampire hunters following the peregrinations of a white horse in a cemetery.

*Les Vampires* tells us

> that a vampire could continue to sleep with his still-living wife at night, and that such a woman, made pregnant by the cadaver, could give birth to children whose peculiarity was that they had no bones at all.[17]

While I am laying out such bits of bizarrerie, I may as well add this one: because the vampire is a creature of Satan who, on occasion, has dallied with mortal women, those women have reported that Satan's sperm is as cold as ice.

Later in this book, I'll have more to say about the varieties of eroticism that the vampire's embrace can imply. In the vampire folklore, there are accounts of revenants who were extremely sexually active, combining with their vampire characteristics the behavior of succubi who, not content with draining their victims' blood, also wore them down with their insatiable sexual attentions. A possible explanation for this belief may be the fact that the sexual organs of some male corpses sometimes bloat in the course of decomposition.[18] Nor is that all. When rigor mortis sets in, it can produce an oozing of sperm from the dead penis.

The joke in America is that garlic will keep vampires—and people—away. We remember that Dr. Van Helsing hangs garlic flowers all around Lucy's room to ward off the vampire. According to Montague Summers, in China "to wet a child's forehead with garlic is a sure protection against vampires." In the Philippines, the armpit is the appropriate place to rub the garlic. In the Middle Ages, it was believed that garlic could ward off the plague. To prevent the reanimation of a vampire, garlic stuffed into the mouth of the corpse was often recommended.

Surpassing himself as a collector of fascinating vampire lore, Montague Summers reports that in Bulgaria

> There is yet another method of abolishing a Vampire—that of *bottling* him. There are certain persons who make a profession of this; and their method of procedure is as follows: The sorcerer, armed with a picture of some saint, lies in ambush until he sees the Vampire

pass, when he pursues him with his *Eikon:* the poor Obour [vampire] takes refuge on a tree or on the roof of a house, but his persecutor follows him up with the talisman, driving him away from all shelter, in the direction of a bottle specially prepared, in which is placed some of the vampire's favourite food. Having no other resource, he enters this prison, and is immediately fastened down with a cork, on the interior of which is a fragment of the *Eikon.* The bottle is then thrown into the fire, and the Vampire disappears for ever.[19]

Forever has a nice sound. But there is a fetching mystery in the paragraph above. Summers fails to tell us what the vampire's favorite food might be that is put into the bottle to entice the vampire. Blood? Blood pudding? Blood sausage? Or some more usual human food. In any case, of all the ways of dealing with a vampire, bottling seems the most humane.

The folklore of the vampire is not confined to the Western world. There is vampire lore in China, in Africa, and among the Native Americans of the New World. Vampiric creatures make their appearance in Tibet, in Borneo, and Japan.

The lore of the Chinese vampire, the Kiang-si, is predicated on the notion that humans have two souls: the Hun, the superior soul, and the P'o, the inferior, malignant one. The Chinese believed that, after death, the P'o, in the form of the vampire Kiang-si, would seek to reinhabit its corpse, after which it would nourish itself on the blood of the living. To prevent the return of the Kiang-si, the body was exposed to the air so that it would decay, or it was destroyed by fire.

The Kiang-si described by Montague Summers is anything but the suave vampire who inhabits our movies:

> In appearance, the Chinese monster is very like the European vampire, for he has red staring eyes, huge sharp talons or crooked nails, but he is also often represented as having his body covered with white or greenish white hair.[20]

Like his Western counterparts, the Chinese vampire is inert by day and rises at night to drink the blood of the living. However, the Kiang-si is merely a physical enemy to its victims. There is no hint at all that his bite can affect the soul.

The first hint Jonathan Harker has that his host, Count Dracula, is not like other men is the moment when Jonathan, looking into his shaving mirror, cannot see the Count's reflection in it, though the Count is standing directly behind him.

In his novel, *The Student of Prague* (1912), Hans Heinz Ewers also makes use of the idea that the damned are not reflected in mirrors. In that novel, there is a scene in which the student, Balduin, who has made a Faustian contract with the devil, dances before a mirror with his naked mistress in his arms. What the mistress sees there as she is being whirled about sends her screaming from the room.

Mirrors have aroused fear in many cultures. Zulus will not look at their reflections in pools of water because they believe that a beast will kill them by drinking their reflected image. Otto Wilhelm von Vacano says:

> Among mankind throughout the world a fear of reflections — in water or in shining disks — and of their power to cast a spell over the soul used to be common; in ancient popular customs we find many and various precautionary measures designed to shield an embryonic life, an unborn or newly born child, and its mother, from mirrors.[21]

A mirror is an uncanny object. It renders absurd our comfortable notion that we can can believe what we see; because, though we see ourselves *in* a mirror, we are not in it. Not only that, but a mirror possesses vexing properties: rendering you to yourself in reverse so that your right hand is the left hand of your image. Hold a page of print up to the mirror, and you become dyslexic instantly. A photographer who tries to photograph distant-appearing images in a mirror and focuses on them instead of on the surface of the glass is in trouble. Not to mention the trouble we feel facing a fun-house mirror that turns us fat or thin, or tiny or tall; or when we are trapped in a mirror maze with no way of knowing which of the six doorways we face is real. No wonder Alice was drawn to the Looking Glass. As she says to her cat, "it may be quite different on beyond. Oh, Kitty! how nice it would be if we could only get through into Looking-glass House." Nice, and weird!

Mirrors have so much power implicit in them that we know that breaking one will bring us seven years of bad luck. Jews cover mirrors in a home where a death has occurred to avoid the temptation of vanity by looking into a mirror at a time of grief or, as some believe, to prevent the spirit of the dead from taking up residence in the mirror. James G. Frazer, who says that the custom is widespread, offers another explanation:

It is feared that the soul, projected out of the person in the shape of his reflection in the mirror, may be carried off by the ghost of the departed.[22]

Alchemists used black mirrors for divination, as do modern practitioners of the art of scrying and the Cabalists are said to have used seven mirrors, each one made of a different metal, in their divinations. In Matthew Lewis's Gothic novel, *The Monk*, the wicked Ambrosio uses a magic mirror in which he is able to see in her bath the beautiful Antonia, for whom he lusts.[23] We will remember that the wicked queen in the fairy tale, "Snow White and the Seven Dwarfs," has a magic mirror whose attribute is that it always tells the truth. A magic mirror said to have belonged to Catherine de Medici who consulted it about affairs of state is said to have disappeared from the Louvre in 1688. We know, too, about Narcissus' unfortunate adventure with the reflecting pool, which, when he looked in it, caused him fall madly in love with his image.

There is no persuasive explanation why the vampire has no image in a mirror. Most of those I have come upon cite Stoker as their authority, which leaves one uninstructed. I like the suggestion that an evil person has no soul. Therefore, he has no spiritual reality, which makes him invisible in a mirror. There is, however, nothing in *Dracula* to support the idea that the Count is soulless. Instead, he is a damned soul.

I have my own theory why we do not see Dracula in the mirror. The Introduction to *The Essential Dracula* concludes:

> Finally, Stoker's achievement is this: he makes us understand in our own experience why the vampire is said to be invisible in the mirror. He is there, but we fail to recognize him since our own faces get in the way.[24]

The religious component to Western vampire lore needs now to be considered. In Chapter 5 of this book, I point out that in Stoker's novel, Renfield's role in relation to the Count is analogous to that of John the Baptist, prophesying the coming of Christ. Renfield is the anti-John-the-Baptist to Dracula's Antichrist. The premise on which the analogy is based is that Christ's promise to believers is eternal life. Dracula offers his followers the same thing. But there is a difference. Christ demands nothing more from his followers than

Capricho 73 *by Francisco de Goya*

their belief in Him. As a creature of Satan, Dracula requires, as the price of immortality, the shedding of innocent blood as well as the tainting of their souls.

In the folklore derived from the Christian tradition, excommunicants who died without being reconciled to the church could become vampires. Suicides, too, ran the risk of turning into vampires because they had taken upon themselves the godlike power to choose life or death. It will be remembered that when Dracula lands on the Whitby coast, he takes refuge in the grave of a suicide, the "lammiter."

A parent's curse could create a vampire. Montague Summers writes:

> . . . for the hauntings of a Vampire, three things are necessary: the Vampire, the Devil, and the Permission of Almighty God. . . . Whether it be the Demon who is energizing the corpse or whether it be the dead man himself who by some dispensation of Divine Providence has returned is a particular which must be decided severally for each case.[25]

When asked how Dracula dies, the man or woman—or child—in the street, is likely to answer, "with a stake driven through his heart." But in *Dracula,* the stake is used only against female vampires, not against Dracula himself. It's an imposing weapon. Made of oak, it is three feet long, three inches around at its base and is fire-sharpened to a point.

It is apparent that Lucy's fiancé, Arthur Holmwood, had not read Summers's description of a proper staking. In the appalling scene in Lucy's tomb in which he drives the stake through her heart, he is described as striking

> with all his might. . . . Arthur never faltered. He looked like a figure of Thor as his untrembling arm rose and fell, driving deeper and deeper the mercy-bearing stake . . .[26]

But Summers says:

> It is highly important that the body of the Vampire should be transfixed by a single blow, for two blows or three would restore it to life.[27]

Oak is the wood authorized by folklore because it is the wood from which the cross on which Christ was crucified is said to have been made.

There is a tiny, very beautiful late-medieval poem that is apropos:

*Woe's me. Woe's me.*
   *The acorn's not yet fallen from the oak*
*That's to build the cross*
*That's to save me.*

Van Helsing has other holy weapons available to him to combat the vampire. At one point, he makes a paste made of the Host, with which he seals off Lucy's tomb.

He tells his accomplices that he has an Indulgence, which would grant him remission of temporal punishment for committing this sin. I have gone to the trouble of consulting the Canon Law Office of the Archdiocese of San Francisco, which informed me:

> This procedure is, in terms of church doctrine, absolutely inpermiss-able since, in Catholic belief, the sanctified wafer *is* the Body of Christ Himself. The Host, therefore, may not be used in any profane way, no matter how exalted the end in view.[28]

The rose and the wild rose, because of their association with Christ's life, are also said to be useful in keeping off vampires.[29]

Van Helsing and what I call his chivalric knights, also arm themselves against the vampire with holy water and crucifixes. Stoker himself gives us a scene in which Mina's forehead is burned by the touch of the Host. The film industry has seized upon these holy artifacts as marvelous opportunities for the creation of special effects. Holy water flung into the face of a vampire will set his face a-sizzling. The mere shadow of a cross has been enough to stop the vampire in his or her tracks. In film lore more than in folklore, the ordinary light of day is a sovereign destroyer of vampires. In *Blacula,* for instance, the sympathetic Blacula, rather than survive the loss of his beloved a second time, walks deliberately into the light of the sun. In *Nosferatu* and scores of subsequent films, the vampire overstays the nighttime hours allotted to him and is destroyed by sunlight.

For those of us who will be living at the end of the twentieth and the beginning of the twenty-first century, there is one further element that makes vampires fascinating to us: in the vampire, we see a creature who has said no to the divinely ordained order of things. To have a will to live so strong, to have energy so powerful as to overcome the limits of mortality seems at once admirable and evil.

Life is the issue whose assertion arouses our admiration. When Dylan Thomas exhorts us to "Rage, rage against the dying of the light," he joins his voice to those of the great—and criminal— refuseniks of God's right to put limits on human life. And when tracing the development of a vampire consciousness in Veronica, in the "Bloodstone" chapter of her novel *Bellefleur,* Joyce Carol Oates has her suddenly illuminated by the knowledge that "she wanted to be *on the side of life.*"[30]

## CHAPTER 2

# In Which the Author Talks of Blood

*"In the moonlight opposite me there were three young women. . . . I thought at the time that I must be dreaming. . . . I felt in my heart a wicked, burning desire that they would kiss me with those red lips."*

I WAS . . . RUMINATING WHAT I SHOULD DO, UNTIL A STRANGE
FEELING CREPT OVER ME THAT I SHOULD LIKE—WHAT? BLOOD!—RAW
BLOOD, REEKING AND HOT, BUBBLING AND JUICY, FROM THE VEINS
OF SOME GHASTLY VICTIM.

—JAMES MALCOLM RYMER, VARNEY THE VAMPYRE


THERE WILL BE BLOOD EVERYWHERE. THERE WILL BE BLOOD IN THE
STREETS, AND BLOOD IN THE RIVERS, FILLED TO OVERFLOWING,
LAKES OF BLOOD, RIVERS OF BLOOD, WITH GREAT HEADS FLOATING
THERE, I TELL YOU, FLOATING IN THE BLOOD . . . TWO MILLION
DEVILS LOOSED FROM HELL . . . MORE EVIL IN EIGHTEEN YEARS
THAN IN THE PAST FIVE THOUSAND.

—THE PROPHECY OF FRANCESCO DA MONTEPULCIANO (1513)


THERE IS SCARCELY ANY NATURAL OBJECT WITH SO PROFOUNDLY
EMOTIONAL AN EFFECT AS BLOOD.

—HAVELOCK ELLIS, STUDIES IN THE PSYCHOLOGY OF SEX

To the British, the word "bloody" was once deemed so powerful that it was used in speech only as an adjective meant to intensify truly dreadful feelings. In Chapter 24 of *Dracula*, in Mina Harker's journal entry of October 5, there are a couple of pages in which the "blood" word is used for seriocomic effect eight times in a little more than two paragraphs. Mina is recording Van Helsing's account of what happened when he and Quincey Morris visited Doolittle's Wharf. There they interviewed several rough-spoken fellows who "say much of blood and bloom" as they describe the conversation between the man we know to be Dracula and the captain of the *Czarina Catherine*. According to them:

> the captain tell him that he had better be quick—with blood—for that his ship will leave the place—of blood—before the tide.... Finally the captain ... tell him that he doesn't want no Frenchmen—with bloom upon them and also with blood—in his ship—with blood on her also. ...[1]

The text continues in this vein (no pun intended) for another longish paragraph, and Stoker clearly means for us to find it all very funny.

Renfield, the madman in Stoker's novel whom Dr. Seward has called his "zoophagous" patient, actually never drinks blood. Instead, Renfield contents himself with ingesting flies and spiders, though he does plead once for a kitten. But the controlling—if mad—vision he has of the relationship of blood to life is in no way different from the one that defines Dracula's existence: To live, life must feed on life.

Both Dracula and Renfield are fictional characters. In the real world, John Haigh, the last publicly confessed blood drinker to be executed in England, was hanged for his crimes not in the eighteenth or nineteenth centuries, but on August 10, 1949. Known as the acid-bath murderer, Haigh confessed at his trial to having murdered nine people from whom he had taken a cupful of blood each to drink. Although there is persuasive evidence that the blood-drinking confession might have been concocted to persuade the world that he was insane, the ploy did not work. With Stoker's *Dracula* before us, and the Christian allegory it contains, it is fascinating to read Haigh's descriptions of the dreams he claimed he had:

> Before each of my killings, I had a series of dreams, I saw a forest of crucifixes that changed into green trees dripping with blood . . . which I drank, and once more I awakened with a desire that demanded fulfillment.[2]

The fascination with blood is still with us. In 1971 I interviewed a young man who drank the blood of his lovers as he was having sexual intercourse with them. I gave him the pseudonym Alex.

Alex characterized his blood drinking:

> I like it when someone has enough to spare a little blood or . . . That's it! It's an energy exchange. The energy of blood is particularly strong because it usually involves some kind of pain. When you're with someone who's at the other end of the razor blade or whatever, it's a transaction. Whether it's in the neck, whether it's in the veins. It's energy you're going to be able to use. Beautiful. If somebody cares enough for you to suck your blood . . . I can't think of much more to ask.[3]

A little later, he made an observation that seemed (and seems) crammed with implication. He described what he did with his lover as

> . . . an accomplice entry into the other self. . . . For sure. It goes along really well when you're fucking. Just marvelous. *You* might call it blood lust. I don't know. All I know is that it goes particularly well with sodomy. An accomplice entry . . . Because, you know . . . the blood sucking is forbidden, and it's in the front, at the throat; the sodomy is at the back, and it's forbidden. It takes a contortionist to do them both at the same time. But it works out nicely. It's a real high. The blood and the balling. It works out well.[4]

Alex was not much more than a fairly amateur sadist who, I think, got his kicks from making horrific demands on his lovers, and yet he seems to me to have put his finger on the twofold attractions of blood drinking: the sense that one ingests power and that one penetrates into another self. His final words to me were

> Look. I'm not on any Dracula kick. . . . I'm just really hot on the idea of sucking blood. . . . Look. . . . A lot of guys are on a heavy M [masochist] trip. They have to split it up in some dark corner. And the darkest corner they can find is me.[5]

That interview was done twenty-five years ago. Since then, there has been a spate of Dracula movies, Stephen King has written *Salem's Lot,* Anne Rice her *Vampire Chronicles.* Now, in 1996, the *New York Times* reports the existence of a netherworld of blood drinkers, who may number as many as several thousand. It seems clear from the *New York Times* article that this population of self-confessed vampires is made up of people very much like Alex. Frank Bruni writes in the *Times* piece: "For many, vampirism is merely a kitschy game of dress-up, or an elegant style, not to be taken too seriously. For others, it is something deeper: a romantic fantasy, a sexual identity, even a religion." The *Times* reports an interview with a certain Ms. Brosky:

> Transfixed by horror films and literature as a teenager, Ms. Brosky later latched onto the Gothic nightclub scene, acquiring a black satin gown, antique silver jewelry and acrylic fangs. She says that with her boyfriend, whom she trusts to be free of the AIDS virus, she has dabbled in blood exchanges, nibbling on his neck or letting him nibble on hers.[6]

It is easy to dismiss the subculture of blood drinkers reported on by the *New York Times* as one more trendy manifestation, but it is hard not to notice the sinister phrase in the above quotation, where Ms. Brosky tells her interviewer that she trusts that her boyfriend is "free of the AIDS virus." For all of us, living at the end of the twentieth century, in the Age of AIDS, two things are inevitably true in any transaction involving blood: though the blood is the life, it can also be the death of you.

We are familiar with our own blood. When Shylock says, "If you prick us, do we not bleed?" we know the answer. We have had nosebleeds, cuts, and scrapes enough to know that there's a juice within our bodies on which our lives depend.

Technically, that juice is a "fluid circulating tissue," which is to say that it is made of living cells generated in the bone marrow. These cells carry nutrients to and remove soluble waste products from the body's other cells. The blood cell is composed mostly of water (90 percent), but the protein that constitutes 9 percent of the cell is the chemical basis of all life. The network of arteries, veins, and capillaries through which the heart pumps our blood is a sort of road system on which the blood cells travel, carrying the soluble sugar, amino acids, oxygen, fat, salts, and hormones which the body's cells need. The debris they carry away to the excretory system is made up of carbonic acid and compounds of nitrogen, ammonia and, from the liver, urea.

It is not hard to see how ordinary experience would create in us a readiness to believe that if blood is the juice of life, then ingesting it is revivifying. Since battle experiences, ordinary accidents, and various illnesses in which blood is lost demonstrated that loss of blood resulted in weakness or death, it seemed reasonable, if not scientific, to suppose that having blood, getting it, or drinking it, would do one good.

Among the ancient Egyptians, bathing in blood was prescribed as an aid to resuscitation. Later, in the days of the Roman Empire, spectators at the gladiatorial games hurried into the arena to dip their handkerchiefs in the blood of the dead or dying combatants.

Late in the eighteenth century, in the more sophisticated culture of France, when Louis XVI was about to be executed on January 21, 1793, he cried out from the scaffold, "I am ready to die for my people. May my blood save them from the horror I fear for them. . . . I pray God that the blood about to be spilled will never fall upon France."[7] When the guillotine had done its work the executioner, Samson, raised Louis' disembodied head and showed it to the people. The crowd rushed forward and soldiers and citizens alike dipped their lances and swords, their hands and their handkerchiefs in the king's spurting blood. One citizen took a handful of stones which, having dipped them in Louis' blood, he flung into the crowd, crying, "They have threatened that the blood of Louis Capet will fall upon our heads. Very well! Let it fall."[8]

There is a gorgeous couplet in Christopher Marlowe's play, *The Tragedy of Dr. Faustus*, in which the damned Faustus, before he is haled down to hell, cries:

*(See, see where Christ's blood streams in the firmamente!)*
*One drop of blood will save me. O, my Christ!*[9]

Faustus hopes to benefit from the salvational power of Christ's blood. Among Catholic Christians who take communion, the wine in the communion cup is literally the blood of Christ.

In John, 17:10–11 we read:

"Verily, verily, I say unto you, except ye eat the flesh of the Son of man, and drink his blood, ye have no life in you. Whoso eateth my flesh and drinketh my blood, hath eternal life; and I will raise him up at the last day."

From that image of divine transubstantiation, it is hard to turn to the ugly story of the sixteenth-century Hungarian countess, Elizabeth Bathory (1560–1614), who is said to have bathed in the blood of virgins, believed to be a youth-restoring cosmetic. In *Cannibalism and Human Sacrifice*, Henry Hogg describes the practice of eighteenth-century Bohemians who not only decapitated their prisoners, but hurried to drink the blood spurting from their wounds.[10]

A bloodstained garment is at the center of a well-known biblical tale. It is the coat of many colors, worn by that young prig, Joseph, the patriarch Jacob's favorite son. When Joseph's brothers could no longer stand his air of superiority, they sold him into slavery to the Egyptians. To persuade their father that Joseph was dead, they dipped his offensive coat of many colors in the blood of a goat, then showed it to their doting father.[11]

For Hindus, the goddess Kali symbolizes both fertility and destruction. The goddess is both the nurturing power of the earth and its destructive forces. Sir Richard Burton's translation of *The Baital-Pachisi (Vikram and the Vampire)* describes her:

naked . . . [her head] half-severed, partly cut and partly painted, resting on her shoulders, her tongue lolled out from her wide yawning mouth . . . her eyes . . . red like those of a drunkard . . . [she was] robed in an elephant's hide . . . with a belt composed of the hands of the giants whom she had slain in war: two dead bodies . . . for ear-rings . . . her necklace . . . of bleached skulls. Her four arms sup-ported a scimitar, a noose, a trident, and a ponderous mace.[12]

Burton goes on to tell us that Kali is so bloodthirsty that when she cannot drink the blood of a victim, she cuts her own throat and laps up the blood gushing from the wound. Parenthetically, in the description above, her necklace is composed of the skulls of her husbands.

In the Greek myth of Pyramus and Thisbe, the sight of blood is the occasion for the disaster that befell those lovers. One day, as Thisbe was waiting for Pyramus, she saw a lioness with blood-stained jaws. Frightened by what she had seen, Thisbe fled, leaving behind her scarf, which the lioness mauled and then abandoned. Finding the smeared scarf, Pyramus believed that Thisbe had been killed. Overwhelmed by grief, he slew himself. And when she learned of her lover's death, Thisbe committed suicide.

In the fairy tale "Sleeping Beauty," which children hear when they are very young, they learn how critical the shedding of a single drop of blood can be. At Beauty's birth, all the fairies were invited to celebrate with the court. That is, all the fairies but one. Feeling vindictive because she has been spurned, she shows up just the same and announces: "The king's daughter, when she is thirteen, will prick her finger with a spindle and die." Though she cannot undo the spell entirely, a good fairy who is present modifies it: Beauty will not die, but as a consequence of the spindle wound, she will fall asleep for a hundred years. And she does, only to be awak-ened by a kiss.

The folktale of Bluebeard also turns on the importance of a drop of blood. Charles Perrault's seventeenth-century version of the story is a cautionary tale about the evil effects of curiosity. In Perrault's tale, Bluebeard is a rich man who actually has a blue beard, which makes him so frightfully ugly "that all the women and girls ran away from him." In addition to being ugly, he has a bad reputation because he has been married several times, but nobody ever knew what became of his wives. But wealth can overcome even powerful preju-dices. The youngest daughter of his next-door neighbor allows her-self to be wooed and won by the man with the blue beard.

What happens next is well known. Bluebeard gives his wife the keys to his castle and tells her that she may use them to enter any of the rooms which hold his treasure. However, she is forbidden to use one key—the key to a small room that he showed her.

Of course, in the tradition of Eve and Pandora, she cannot resist the temptation of curiosity. She uses the forbidden key and opens the door of the little chamber. There she finds Bluebeard's former wives, covered with blood and leaning against the wall, like so many mannequins. Panicked by the sight, she drops the key with which she opened the door, then picks it up and hurries from the room. Moments later, she notices that the key is spotted with blood which, no matter how many times or how hard she washes and scrubs and rubs it, continues to cling to the metal as tenaciously as the damned spot that Lady Macbeth wanted out.

When Bluebeard returns, he examines his keys and discovers his wife's disobedience immediately. He pronounces her doom at once: "Madam, you shall go in and take your place amongst the ladies you saw there."

Now Perrault brilliantly manipulates the fictional tensions that follow. The final three or four paragraphs of the story are a triumph of theatricality as the young wife, who has been given fifteen minutes to say her prayers before she is to die, calls to her sister Anne at the top of the watchtower, "Anne, sister Anne, dost thou see nothing coming?"

Anne sees nothing and keeps on seeing nothing. From there on, we get a three-way dialogue with the wife calling to her sister; then Bluebeard threatening his wife; then Anne reporting the news that the brothers are not coming. At the penultimate moment, as Bluebeard is about to kill his wife, there is "such a loud knocking at the gate, that the Blue Beard stops short of a sudden," and in rush the lady's brothers on their way to a happy ending.

Lady Macbeth, who was prepared to unsex herself for the sake of ambition, was nevertheless tormented by guilt for the blood she caused to be shed. In the sleepwalking scene, the queen enters, carrying a taper. She keeps rubbing her hands as if she were washing them:

> Yet here's a spot. . . . Out, damn spot! Out, I say! One, two . . . Yet who would have thought the old man to have had so much blood in him? . . . What, will these hands ne'er be clean? . . . Here's the smell of the blood still. All the perfumes of Arabia will not sweeten this little hand . . . ![13]

There is no escaping the meanings of blood. We say of a murderer, or of anyone who is responsible for someone's death that he or she has bloodstained hands. While the mark of Cain is not described precisely, we know that he acquired it after he spilled his brother's blood. The bodies of murder victims are believed to bleed from their wounds when their killers are nearby.

If we speak of having blue blood, we are letting the world know that we are descended from the nobility. When we believe that we have worked especially hard, we speak of "sweating blood." Or, when we are overwhelmed by grief, we may speak of shedding tears of blood.

We say that blood is thicker than water when what we mean is that our first loyalty belongs to members of our own family. Or, if we say, "Blood will tell," we mean that someone has inherited good (or bad) traits from an ancestor.

In cultures based on tribal or clan relationships, blood feuds begin when someone in tribe A is killed by a member of tribe B. His son or nearest kinsman in tribe A must avenge that death, which then must be avenged by a son or kinsman of tribe B, and so on. Comic as well as tragic examples come to mind: the Hatfields and McCoys in America; the Montagues and the Capulets in Shakespeare's Verona. And, if the shedding of blood creates blood feuds, it can also serve to make "blood brothers," as when friends who are not related can choose to establish such a relationship by mingling the blood each of them sheds from self-made wounds.

A sinister use of the word "blood" is that to be found in what has come to be called "the blood libel." In the history of Europe, a common excuse for a pogrom against Jews was the charge that they had stolen a Christian child and murdered it to use its blood in a religious ritual.

One of the most moving of Chaucer's *Canterbury Tales* is based on the blood libel. "The Prioress's Tale" is fascinating as well as sadly instructive. Fascinating because of the skill with which Chaucer establishes the character of the prioress, who is so genteel that she would not dip her fingers too deeply into her sauce, and who is careful to wipe her lips so cleanly that no drop of grease ever falls from her mouth into her cup. She is a softly spoken, upwardly mobile woman who relishes court gossip and speaks provincial-accented French because "the French of Paris was unknown to her." And yet, with all her refinements, she is the teller of the ghastliest tale told by any of Chaucer's pilgrims. Not only that, her tale is most musical when she is describing its most horrifying moments.

This amiable nun tells the story of a Christian lad living somewhere in the East who walks daily through a Jewish ghetto, singing a song in praise of the Virgin Mary, *"Alma redemptoris Mater,* Hail, redemptress mother." The wicked Jews, outraged by what they consider an affront to their religion, hire a murderer who "cut his throat and cast him in a privy."

There, though his throat is cut and he is up to his chin in filth, the boy begins to sing

Alma redemptoris *so loud, that all the place began to ring.*[14]

The miraculous song is heard by the Christians, who take the child up intending to bury him, but when they sprinkle holy water on him, he sings again, *"O Alma redemptoris Mater."* When the abbot asks the boy to explain the miracle, the boy replies that at the moment when he should have died, the holy Virgin placed a grain of cardamom upon his tongue:

*Wherefor I sing and sing*
*Until that grain is taken from my tongue.*[15]

The enthusiasm with which the prioress describes the child singing away in the privy is more than matched by the delight with which she describes how the Jews are punished:

*To torture and to shameful death,*
*The Provost condemned these Jews . . .*
*Therefore he had their bodies torn apart by wild horses.*
*And after that, he hanged them according to the law.*[16]

Sadly instructive, the tale shows us that the work even of great writers is affected by the times in which it is written. Chaucer, one of the finest poets who ever put pen to paper, was also a medieval Catholic Christian who had no trouble accepting the folklore of anti-Semitism that pervaded the Christian world. Almost equally troubling to a contemporary reader is that, despite the anti-Semitism that drives the story, "The Prioress's Tale" is one of the world's most exquisite narrative poems.

Ironically enough, even in the Middle Ages, the literate Christian

world knew very well that Jews were—and are—strictly prohib-
ited from drinking blood. Noah and his sons, for example, are told
that they may eat anything that moves "but flesh with the life
thereof, which is the blood thereof, shall ye not eat."[17] Again: "Only
be sure that thou eat not the blood: for the blood is the life; and thou
mayest not eat the life with the flesh./Thou shalt not eat it; thou
shalt pour it upon the earth as water."[18] In the New Testament, too,
we are reminded "That ye abstain from meats offered to idols, and
from blood . . ."[19] It is clear from the frequency and the urgency of
these injunctions that the Hebrews were reacting against the idola-
trous practices of the peoples among whom they dwelled, and who
offered blood sacrifices to their gods.

Menstrual blood is profoundly totemic. Coming at the beginning of
a girl's adolescence, it is the outward and visible sign that she is
ready to bear children. The show of her blood, repeated monthly,
will continue to indicate that ability until she reaches menopause.

Menstrual blood is a mark of fertility; yet, everywhere in the
world, menstruation is surrounded by complex folklore and taboos.
In various parts of the world, menstruating women are believed to
wither plants, spoil wine, keep bread from rising, Among Orthodox
Jews, a menstruating women is not permitted to be near the ark of
the covenant, and it is strictly forbidden to have intercourse with a
woman during her menses. Similar prohibitions exist among Mus-
lims. Menstruating women cannot touch the Koran, which says of
them:

> They will ask thee also, concerning the courses of women: Answer,
> they are a pollution: therefore separate yourselves from women in
> their courses; and go not near them, until they be cleansed.[20]

A menstruating Hindu woman may not cook or visit temples. The
African Lele keep menstruating women from entering the huts of
warriors lest their condition spoil their hunting. In *Blood Magic*, by
Alma Gottlieb and Thomas Buckley, we are told that among the
Yurok women of California:

> Menstrual blood itself was thought by Yurok to be a dire poison,
> and menstruating women were believed to contaminate whatever
> they came into contact with. . . . Menstruating women, beyond cont-

aminating concrete objects, were perhaps most dangerous through their negative effects on men's psychic or spiritual life. These women spoiled men's "luck" *(heymoks)* — their ability to exercise power in, among other things, the accumulation of wealth.[21]

Even to some moderns, menstrual blood has been regarded as fearful. In *A Dream of Dracula,* I reported a Hell's Angels initiation rite in which a would-be member of the bikers' club had to prove his manhood by "going down on" a menstruating woman in the presence of the bikers.[22]

On the positive side, menstrual blood has been credited with making wheatfields ripen and with curing a variety of ailments, including epilepsy. Mixed with sweat and drunk, menstrual blood was believed to be an effective aphrodisiac.

A couple of modern researchers have recently discovered the genesis of Bram Stoker's *Dracula* in the effects of menstruation on Bram Stoker's wife:

> Stoker was married to the beautiful Florence Balcombe, who was much admired by Oscar Wilde, and who was also, according to authorities, frigid as a statue. It is likely that a woman with an unsatisfactory sex life will have very bad menstrual disturbances. Was it some image of these that gave Stoker's subliminal mind the hint that formulated a myth of formidable power, out of the ferocity of a frustrated bleeding woman, crackling with energy and unacknowledged sexuality?[23]

The authorities referred to above have their source in the mean-spirited speculations of Stoker's granddaughter,[24] which, repeated and embroidered by careless scholars have now taken on a life — but certainly no truth — of their own.

# In Which We Meet the Vampire Bat and Discover Its Family Values

*"There was no cry from the woman, and the howling of the wolves was but short."*

TWINKLE, TWINKLE, LITTLE BAT!
HOW I WONDER WHAT YOU'RE AT!
UP ABOVE THE WORLD YOU FLY,
LIKE A TEA-TRAY IN THE SKY.

—LEWIS CARROLL, ALICE IN WONDERLAND

REMOVED FROM OUR PREJUDICE, EVEN THE COMMON VAMPIRE [BAT]
IS A REMARKABLY ALTRUISTIC AND SOPHISTICATED ANIMAL. IT IS
ONE OF THE WORLD'S RELATIVELY FEW MAMMALS KNOWN TO ADOPT
ORPHANS AND TO CARE FOR UNRELATED INDIVIDUALS.

—ARTHUR M. GREENHALL, **NATURAL HISTORY OF VAMPIRE BATS**

In Stoker's *Dracula,* the Count appears several times in the form of a bat. Mina, in her August 13 diary entry, two days after Lucy's encounter with him at the suicide's seat, reports that on that particularly lovely moonlit night, she went to the window of Lucy's room where she saw that "between me and the moonlight flitted a great bat, coming and going in great, whirling circles."[1]

In Chapter 9, Dr. Seward describes finding an escaped Renfield crouching beside the chapel door at Carfax Abbey. Though Renfield is at first violent, he suddenly turns calm under the influence of

... a big bat, which was flapping its silent and ghostly way to the west. Bats usually wheel and flit about, but this one seemed to go straight on, as if it knew where it was bound ...[2]

Later in the novel, Lucy reports that before the wolf crashed through her window

... outside in the shrubbery [she] heard a sort of howl like a dog's, but more fierce and deeper. [She] went to the window and looked out, but could see nothing except a big bat, which had evidently been buffetting its wings against the window.[3]

Again, in Chapter 12, Quincey Morris says of Holmwood:

When I saw him four days ago ... he looked queer. I have not seen anything pulled down so quick since I was on the Pampas and had a mare ... go to grass all in a night. One of those big bats that they call vampires had got at her in the night.[4]

Quincey says she was so emptied of blood that he had to put a bullet through her as she lay.

Finally, in Chapter 18, Dr. Van Helsing is instructing the Holy Crew on what is known or is believed about vampires. In the course of his lecture, it will be recalled, Quincey Morris leaves the room. Moments later, he endangers them all by firing a pistol shot through the window. His excuse is that

> whilst the professor was talking there came a big bat and sat on the window-sill and I went out to have a shot . . . as I have been doing of late of evenings.[5]

---

Bats get a bad press among humans. Even in their natural state, they look like uncanny creatures. Part rodent and part bird, they seem to have flown out of a mythological zoo where composite creatures like minotaurs, cockatrices, were-tigers and centaurs dwell. Bats frighten us with their tight little grimacing faces, their hysterically chirping voices, their apparently wild and erratic flight, and their curved claws which, popular opinion has it, will certainly get entangled in our hair. Since they are creatures of the night, it is easy to imagine them as allied to all that lurks or prowls or hunts in the dark. Long associated with the devil, bats were nailed to barn doors to keep off bad luck. Francisco Goya invoked our repulsion by filling *Los Caprichos* with bats. When Gustave Doré wanted us to see Satan at his majestic worst, he depicted him with huge extended bat wings.

We are wary around bats, even benign or beneficent fruit- or insect-eating bats that live in our latitudes. And if we turn our attention to bats that drink blood—the vampire bats—we are likely to grow warier still.

But first let's deal with the word "vampire" itself. Montague Summers gives us the fullest etymology for the word:

> [It] is from the Magyar *vampir,* a word of Slavonic origin occuring in the same form in Russian, Polish, Czech, Serbian, and Bulgarian with such variants as Bulgarian, *vapir, vepir;* Ruthenian *vopyr, opyr;* Russian *upir, upyr;* South Russian *upuir;* Polish *upier . . .*[6]

The word existed long before the New World blood-drinking bats were discovered, and it was used to describe mythical human mon-

**Desmodus rotundis,** *Vampire Bat*

sters who, like Dracula, returned from the grave to prey upon the blood of the living. Part of the early folklore of the vampire describes him (as Dr. Van Helsing says) as a shape shifter, but bats were rarely mentioned as a one of the creatures whose shape a vampire could assume. A vampire might take the shapes of dogs, cats, birds, snakes, and horses. The vampire could also transform himself into inanimate forms like straw, fire, or smoke.

It was not until the sixteenth century, when the conquistadores in South America first encountered the most common of the vampire bats, *Desmodus rotundis*, that the word "vampire" was applied to the blood-drinking bats.

The vampire bat was known to the Pre-Columbian peoples of Central and South America who made totemic jade statues of them. The Aztecs worshiped a bat god named Tzinacan. The Mayans worshiped Zotz, a god who was said to be death's servant and the ruler of twilight. There was also a vampire-bat god named Camazotz, or death-bat whose image has been found depicted on glyphs.

Curiously enough, in the geographical range of the vampire bat, from Mexico in the north to Chile in the south, there is comparatively little vampire-bat folklore. In Trinidad, however, there is a folk legend about a "soucoyante," an evil blood-sucking spirit who is usually blamed for having made the wounds that a vampire bat has actually made.

> [The soucoyante] is usually an old woman, who at night sheds her skin ... and then flies off through the air as a ball of fire. ... There are several methods of trapping [her]. One is to locate the shed skin and sprinkle hot pepper on its underside, which may burn the soucoyante to death when she replaces her skin.[7]

One of the earliest descriptions we have of an encounter with vampire bats is that of de Oviedo y Valdes who reported in 1526:

> There are many bats which bite people during the night; they are found all along this coast to the Gulf of Paria and in other areas, but in no other part are they as pestiferous as in this province [Costa Rica]; they have gotten to me along this coast and especially at Nombre de Dios, where while I was sleeping they bit the toes of my feet so delicately that I felt nothing, and in the morning I found the sheets and mattresses with so much blood that it seemed that I had suffered some great injury.[8]

Not until 1890 did the first European, Charles Darwin, actually report seeing a vampire bat drawing blood. But even afterward, serious study of *Desmodus* did not take place until the 1930s, when it was discovered that the bat was the carrier of the virus for the outbreak of paralytic rabies in Trinidad that killed eighty-nine humans and thousands of cattle.

In Stoker's *Dracula*, the bats are always described as "great" or "big." In actual fact, *Desmodus rotundis* is quite small—not much larger than a laboratory mouse. Though it has a wingspan of as much as fourteen inches, the body of the bat can fit comfortably in the (gloved!) palm of an adult hand. Small and unthreatening though it may appear, it shares some characteristics with the vampire Count. Professor William A. Wimsatt tells us that the bat

> has a fixed gaze ... which ... follows ... every movement with uncanny watchfulness. ... [The creature] when newly caught is a savage, squealing animal which bites viciously, and is capable of inflicting painful bleeding wounds.[9]

Bats belong to the mammalian order of Chiroptera in the family *Phyllostomatidae*, which includes the three genuses of blood-drinking bats: *Desmodus rotundus*, *Diaemus youngi*, and the hairy-legged *Diphylla ecaudata*. *Diaemus* and *Diphylla* feed chiefly on bird blood. The most widespread of the three, and the one that concerns us here, is *Desmodus rotundus*.

In addition to its ability to fly, the vampire bat is an agile creature on land, capable of walking on all fours, running, and hopping. It has keen eyes and a highly developed sense of smell. In flight it has echolocator capabilities, which, like radar, bounce back sounds to help the bat position itself in relationship to its surroundings. Because of its exclusively liquid diet, the vampire has evolved still another adaptational capacity: it can urinate in flight.

Vampire bats are social animals that roost together in caves or hollow trees, in colonies that may have as few as twenty bats and as many as several thousand. The males and females do not roost together. The males may roost singly or form "bachelor" clusters near those formed by the females and their young. Among males,

*Vampire bat in flight*

access to the females is determined by the position in the cluster. As one might expect, the dominant male is the one at the top. There are occasionally fights between the dominant male and invading males who seek to drive the dominant male away.

Vampires have no fixed mating season, but they will mate in day roosts at any time of day. When coupling, the male clasps the female from behind with his folded wings while he grasps the back of her neck with his teeth. Copulation lasts from one to three minutes.

The females produce only one offspring at a time, and the gestation period is seven months—much longer than most lower order mammals. At birth, the young vampire clings to its mother's fur for about twenty minutes, being licked all the while by both its mother and any nearby females who pause to welcome it into the world. Meanwhile, the mother gently urges the infant to find her nipple by pushing it in the right direction.

The baby vampire's eyes are wide open, and it is quite agile. For its first four months, mother's milk is its only diet. It gets its milk not only from its mother, but from any lactating female. Not only that, nonlactating females that have adopted orphan infant bats can acquire the capacity to give them milk.

The infants do not drink blood until they are four months old, at which time their mothers regurgitate blood into their mouths. When they are five months old, they begin to be taken on foraging expeditions by their mothers so that they can learn the hunting and feeding skills they will need as adults. Even so, they are not completely weaned until they are nine or ten months old.

*Desmodus* is marvelously adapted to its life as a blood drinker. Its upper and lower teeth are razor sharp, and, though they have no enamel, nature has so arranged them in the bat's jaw so that the upper and lower teeth close against each other like the blades of a pair of scissors. When feeding, the vampire seizes the flesh of its prey with its two-lobed lower incisors while its upper incisors make an access wound in an area of its prey that is rich in capillaries.

The wound is not a mere scratch or puncture. The bat actually removes a triangular bit of flesh that has been called a "divot" because it resembles the plug of earth made by golfers when making a shot. When the divot has been removed, the bat applies its tongue to the wound. Its tongue is a marvel of engineering. There are two grooves on its underside, which, on contact with the wound create a "drinking-straw effect" which allows the bat to sip its meal with the underside of its tongue while anticoagulant in its saliva flows down its tongue's upper side into the wound. In addition to making the "divot" bite, the bat can create a wound with its rasping tongue. The story that Quincey Morris in *Dracula* tells about the bats' draining his horse is possible. Large animals can be killed by vampires, but only when the first wound a single vampire has made is revisited night after night at frequent intervals by several bats taking turns drinking from the wound.

Because the bats can walk, hop, or run, their range of biting areas in which they seek their prey is large. Arthur Greenhall tells us:

> Water buffalo may be bitten inside their nostrils when their bodies are immersed in mud or water. Pigs are bitten on the nose, ears, and teats. . . . Dogs may be bitten on the nose and poultry may be attacked on combs, neck, feet, and cloaca.[10]

Singularly equipped for what they do, *Desmodus* has even learned to get past the armored defenses of animals like armadillos and snakes.

Two final observations about vampire bats: the first, a jarring surprise to Draculaphiles, the bats are lunaphobic. They will not forage on full moon nights for several reasons. On such nights, the bats themselves become more visible to their predators. Also, because domestic cattle, which are the bats' chief prey, tend to

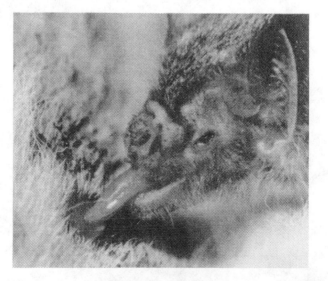

**Vampire bat feeding**

widen their own foraging distance when the moon is full, hunting takes more work then.

Second, I found a disturbing fact tucked away in a scholarly article. Had Quincey Morris lived in the Pleistocene age, he would certainly have seen giant vampire bats. Their fossils have been found and named *Desmodus draculae* by whimsical paleontologists.

And the matter doesn't end there. The scientists who describe the fossil record conclude their discussion on an eerie note:

> At the other end of the time scale, the occurrence of *Desmodus draculae* at surface in apparent association with living species, the absence of any immediately obvious cause of extinction, the vastness of relatively little-known territory in South America, and the recent discoveries of other "living fossils," all hold open at least the faint possibility that this giant vampire may be found living.[11]

Those fellows are holding their breath. Underneath their stiff academic prose lurks their hope that "this giant vampire may be found living." They *want* to see the thirsty *Desmodus draculae* leaving its roost on some moonless night, flapping its way toward us, "downward to darkness on extended wings."[12]

# In Which the Reader Meets the Horrible Vlad the Impaler: The Historical Dracula

*"I found myself in an old, ruined chapel."*

"AH, YES. MUSSOLINI. WELL, YOU MUST ADMIT THAT HE GOT THE TRAINS TO RUN ON TIME."

"WHO KNOWS WHAT EVIL LURKS IN THE HEARTS OF MEN? THE SHADOW KNOWS!"

*T*o those who know something of Bram Stoker's literary output before and after *Dracula,* it is an endless wonder how a man whose fictions were never much better than the penny-a-line shockers he was happy to imitate could write the masterpiece that for a century has engrossed its readers.

I have suggested that one source of Stoker's burst of focused creativity was his finding the protean symbol of the blood exchange with its sexual resonances singularly congenial. Working on *Dracula* enabled him to load onto the armature of his tale all the confusion and pain he suffered from because he could not acknowledge that he was in love with the famous actor Henry Irving.

Stoker had one other thing going for him. In addition to the liberating influence of his theme of blood, he had the good luck to stumble upon the infamous name and the history of Vlad Dracula, a fifteenth-century prince of Wallachia.

Here, then, is how Stoker's Count Dracula describes the history of his family as he paces the floor, "grasping anything on which he laid his hands as though he would crush it by main strength."[1]

"We Szekelys have a right to be proud, for in our veins flows the blood of many brave races who fought as the lion fights, for lordship. . . . What devil or what witch was ever so great as Attila, whose blood is in these veins? Is it a wonder that we were a conquering race; that we were proud, that when the Magyar, the Lombard, the Avar, the Bulgar, or the Turk poured his thousands on our frontiers, we drove them back . . . to us for centuries was trusted the guarding of the frontier of Turkey-land; . . . when the flags of the Wallach and the Magyar went down beneath the Crescent, who was it but one of my own race who as Voivode crossed the Danube and beat the Turk on his own ground? This was a Dracula indeed! Woe was it that his own unworthy brother, when he had fallen, sold his people to the Turk and brought the shame of slavery on them! . . . Ah, young sir, the Szekelys—and the Dracula as their heart's blood, their brains, and their swords—can boast a record that mushroom growths like the Hapsburgs and the Romanoffs can never reach. The warlike days are over. Blood is too precious a thing in these days of dishonorable peace; and the glories of the great races are as a tale that is told."[2]

I have condensed the speech, which in the novel runs to several pages. While accurate enough in many details, Dracula's monologue serves Stoker's fiction by providing an aristocratic pseudo-history for himself. It suffuses an aura of antiquity, nobility, and power around him and turns him into a larger-than-life figure at a point in the story where all we have seen him do is make Harker's bed and set the dinner table.

The "Voivode [who] crossed the Danube and beat the Turk" is Vlad Dracula, three times Prince of Wallachia in the fifteenth century. As will soon be clear, Stoker has sieved out all references to what Vlad, known as the Impaler, was famous for: a cruelty of monumental proportions. Here, early in the novel, all we get are Dracula's chivalric posturing.

Though the speech puts a patina of historicity and power over the Count, we should notice that we will never again see him as anything like the warriors he has described.

Instead, the Dracula we will come to know in Transylvania is such an impotent vampire that he can bring back no better prey to the three vampire women who depend on him, than a baby—and he must have his wolves kill the baby's unhappy mother. Once he leaves Transylvania, the best he can do is kill some hapless sailors in a storm he has generated. In England, this warrior numbers among his victims a dog, an innocent centenarian, and a couple of sleeping women. These are hardly the achievements of a prince whose line, descending from Attila the Hun, is superior to "mushroom growths like the Hapsburgs and the Romanoffs."[3]

The historical figure on whom Stoker based his Dracula, is infinitely fiercer. Known also as Vlad Tepes, the Impaler, his fame as a mass torture-murderer overshadows his achievements on the battlefield.

Though much has been made of the fact that Stoker had met Arminius Vambéry, the Hungarian scholar who, it has been suggested, told him about Vlad the Impaler, Barbara Belford says flatly, "There is no evidence that Vambéry initiated the vampire myth."[4] We do know that Stoker was in Whitby in 1890 for three weeks at which time he borrowed a book from the Whitby library. It was William Wilkinson's *Wallachia and Moldavia* from which he got the descriptions he used in his novel.

———◆———

Vlad Tepes, the historical Dracula, was born in Transylvania, sometime between 1428 and 1431. He was the son of Vlad Dracul, which translates as Vlad the Dragon, a sobriquet the father was given in 1431 when he received the Order of the Dragon from the Holy Roman Emperor, Sigismund of Luxembourg. Vlad Dracul, Prince of Wallachia, was given the task of defending the Transylvanian passes.

In 1442, suspecting Dracul's loyalty, Sultan Murad II imprisoned him and his sons, Dracula and Radu. Dracul managed to persuade the Turks that he was a loyal liegeman; as proof, he left his sons as hostages. At that time, the boy Dracula was twelve years old; Radu, his brother, was seven. The boys were held in captivity until 1448, when Dracula escaped. Radu remained a Turkish prisoner until 1462. Radu, known as The Handsome, was an early target of the amorous advances of Mehmed, the heir to the Turkish throne. As an adult, Radu would become a catspaw for the Turks in their battles against his brother.

We are told that during their captivity

> Dracula and Radu were brought up, tutored by the best minds and in the cultivated traditions of fifteenth-century Ottoman education. . . . Dracula's education was completed in the fine Byzantine tradition inherited by the Turks. Dracula's knowledge of the Turkish language was soon close to perfect.[5]

and that

> during those years [in captivity, Dracula] also developed a reputation for trickery, cunning, insubordination, and brutality, and inspired fright in his own guards.[6]

In 1447 Vlad Dracul was assassinated at the instigation of John Hunyadi, Prince of Transylvania. In 1448, with the help of the Turkish Pasha of Nicopolis, Dracula was made Prince of Wallachia. Dracula's rule lasted all of two months after which he was driven away by Vladislav II. Dracula found refuge first with the Turks in Adrianopole and then in Moldavia, at the court of Bogdan II, where he formed a friendship with Bogdan's son—Dracula's cousin—Stefan cel Mare. When Bogdan was assassinated, Dracula and Stefan were forced to flee to Transylvania where Dracula was reconciled to John Hunyadi, his father's murderer. In Transylvania, under Hunyadi's tutelage, Dracula received the military training that prepared him for his career as a warrior.

On May 29, 1453, the Turkish armies, led by Mehmed II, over-

*Vlad Tepes*

ran Constantinople, ending the Byzantine dynasty whose last ruler, Emperor Constantine XI, died in the battle for the city. Three years later, when Vladislav II allied himself with the Turks and attacked Hunyadi's territory, Hunyadi attacked and captured him with Dracula's help. Vladislav II was beheaded, and on July 3, 1456, Dracula, twenty-five years old, was made Prince of Wallachia for a second time.[7]

Dracula's second reign over Wallachia lasted until 1462, when, after a long and brilliant campaign against the Turkish armies, Dracula was driven from the throne and arrested by Matthias Corvinus, the son of John Hunyadi. The arrest appears to have been based on forged treacherous letters by Dracula addressed to the Turkish Grand Vizier. Dracula spent the next nine years in prison in Visegrad, after which he was sent to Pest for four more years.

While a privileged captive in Matthias's jail, Dracula

could not cure himself of the evil habit of catching mice and having birds bought at the marketplace so that he could punish them by impalement. He cut off the heads of some of the birds; others he had stripped of their feathers and then let loose.[8]

Dracula's imprisonment ended in 1475, when, at the intercession of his cousin, Stefan cel Mare, he was set free. For a while, he was back in action on the battlefield in Serbia. Then, on November 26, 1476, he was made Prince of Wallachia for the third time.

Once more it was a very brief reign. The trouble was there was another contender for the throne of Wallachia, Basarab Laiota, who had the support of both the Turks and the boyars, the local nobility. In late December or early January,

Supported by the Turks, Basarab Laiota returned, and during the battle that took place, the boyars killed Vlad with their lances but not before he butchered five of his assailants. . . . Tepes did not even have time to call his army.[9]

Other accounts say that Dracula was killed by the Turks. In any event, his head was sent to the sultan.

It is said that the headless body was found by monks from the nearby Snagov monastery who took it up and buried it in a crypt in their church. Just where in the church the body lies — or even if it is there — remains a mystery.

Before turning to a brief account of Dracula's crimes against humanity, I want to say something about the difference between our response to scary stories, novels, films, or plays compared with those we make when we read about actual atrocities.

I have to say here that I love the scary arts. Almost at the top of my voice, I have praised the juicy accounts of depravity in novels like Matthew Lewis's *The Monk*. I admire as a work of genius a film like *The Bride of Frankenstein*, whose mix of poignancy and horror brings tears to my eyes even as my hair stands on end. But descriptions of Auschwitz or A-bombed Hiroshima or the stories of mothers or fathers torturing their children produce an altogether different kind of reaction.

I account for the differences by noting that our eyes focus differently on the fictive world than on the real one. The terrors in a work of fiction are seen as through a lens of unlikelihood. It is what Aristotle had in mind when he spoke of tragedies as "imitations." Oedipus putting his eyes out is an *imitation* of a man putting his eyes out. The partying teenagers in the movie *Halloween* are similarly disembodied imitations. The awfulness we find in a work of literature, whether print or film, is always in the "what if or as if" mode. "What if this *could* happen?" Horror may well be piled on horror, but the reassuring truth is that we know that what we are seeing is artifice. Imaginary things are happening to imaginary people. Those tortured or murdered folk in the pages of a book or on screen are insubstantial. If their bones break, I do not need to find them crutches; if they die, I need not worry about their funerals.

Let me emphasize the point. Everything that happens in the print and film arts takes place on the other side of a line drawn in our minds that divides the imagined from the real. There, on the imagined side, Hamlet, Ophelia, King Kong, Claudius, Gertrude, the imperiled Pauline, Macbeth, Lady Macbeth, Othello, the Frankenstein creature, and Dracula can be tormented or die to their hearts' content. They leave behind no visitable grave. As for Hamlet or Othello, poor souls, nothing will change their destiny.

One thing more should be said about fiction of any kind, but especially about scary fiction. The consumer (read reader, film watcher, opera goer) willingly suspends not only disbelief, but his or her responses to the text are, from a social point of view, entirely personal, value free, unfettered by morality. In the pages of the Marquis de Sade, I am allowed to indulge the part of me that is a sadist. In horror fiction or film, I can choose to be a voyeur: I can view bestiality, torture, rape, death, emasculation, the entire gamut of incest possibilities; while my hands, my conscience, and my reputation as a solid citizen remain pure as the driven snow. Elsewhere I have asked, "Is it perverse to like such awful stuff?" and have answered, "Probably." But the mind is so multifaceted, why should it not accommodate a few surfaces that respond to lurid light? The point is that even in the most horrendous interplay of shadows, which is what the exchange between authors and readers of terror fiction is, there are no actual bodies taken to the morgue.

One's response to real-life terror is altogether a different matter. In the presence of stories of real suffering, of real torture, we become—we should become—responsible citizens of the world. Then our value system is involved. Newspaper accounts of children murdered or molested by their parents, stories of serial rapists, of "ethnic cleansing," of tribal massacres set off social feelings; then all talk of aesthetic distance and value-free enjoyment becomes irrelevant.

All of this is prefatory to saying that the historical Dracula, Vlad the Impaler, was a monumentally wicked man and that reading about him can make one very uncomfortable.

In the accounts of his atrocities, there is no saving "as if" line. They tell us what happened, not what might have happened. The men, women, and children Vlad Tepes tormented or slew were real. They lived in towns named Tirgoviste, Brasov, Sibiu. Their suffering and death are linked to statistics which tell us that, within a six-year period, anywhere between 40,000 and 100,000 men, women, and children were tortured or slain by him. This, in a comparatively thinly populated Europe (England 2.5 million and France 13.5 million), already ravaged by the Black Death and the Hundred Years' War.[10] The historians write:

> These victims included people of all nationalities (Romanians—from Moldavia, Wallachia, and Transylvania—plus Bulgarians, Germans, Hungarians, and Gypsies) all classes (boyars [nobility] as well as peasants), all religions (Catholic, Muslim, Orthodox, Jewish) and men, women and children.[11]

Dracula's specialty—since even cruelty is subject to classification—was live impalement, usually with the stake being thrust upward from anus to glottis, after which it was set into the ground while the victims writhed, sometimes for a very long time, before they died.

Some of the stories of Dracula's cruelties are laced with macabre humor:

> When some guest [at a banquet] expressed surprise that he could bear the odor emanating from the [impaled] victims . . . the prince directed the immediate execution of his guest on a higher pale than the others, so that he might not be incommoded by the odor he complained of.[12]

A delegation of Italians came to Vlad on a state visit. Though they took off their hats and caps, they left the skullcaps they wore beneath them on their heads. When Dracula asked for an explanation, he was told that keeping the skullcaps on was an Italian custom which they would not abrogate. Dracula then had every skullcap nailed down by large nails into the skull of each member of the delegation,

The accounts go on and on. We are told:

> he ordered that many people should be impaled; all kinds of people, whether Christians, Jews, or Pagans, struggled and came whirling down like frogs. Then he had their hands and legs pinned down. And he would often say in his own language, "What a nuisance they are!" This was his way of having a good time.[13]

In a piece of social engineering whose simplicity must take our breath away, Dracula decided to make his principality a clean, well-lighted place. To that end, he invited the halt, the blind, the unemployed, the beggars, and the other poor of Tirgoviste to a banquet at which the amazed guests could eat and drink to their hearts' content. Then, at the height of the festivities, the doors of the banquet hall were locked and the entire building was set on fire and reduced to ashes. The problem of poverty in Wallachia was solved.

We are told that one day Dracula observed a workman who was wearing a shirt whose sleeves were too short. He sent for the man's wife and had her impaled as a punishment for being insufficiently dutiful.

His punishment of unfaithful wives or unchaste girls was even more extreme:

*Vlad Tepeș (Vlad, the Impaler), 15th-century tyrant. The historical Drac-
ula at lunch.*

If any wife had an affair outside of marriage. Dracula ordered her
sexual organs cut out. She was then skinned alive and exposed in
her skinless flesh in a public square, her skin hanging separately
from a pole.[14]

On this theme, there is more and worse. More than enough to jus-
tify our including Vlad Tepeș's name in a list of the great monsters
of history, which would include Nero, Gilles de Rais, and Hitler.

I have devoted a considerable amount of time searching for an
explanation of how such people come to be. I have spent a couple of
years researching and writing a book about Gilles de Rais, the historical Bluebeard; and at intervals, over a three-year period I tape-
recorded conversations with Edmund Emil Kemper III, a
contemporary mass murderer.

I have learned something, but what I have learned is very old wisdom and, in a psychotherapeutic age, not very comforting. After all my labors were done, I found myself coming out the very same door wherein I went. I started, and I was left with the conviction that the capacity for evil is as built into human beings as the capacity for good. That they share the same DNA strand in the human chromosome.

I studied Gilles de Rais because I wanted to deal with someone whose crimes could not possibly be explained away or mitigated by reference to cultural relativism. There was, however, more to it than that. Gilles's life precisely illustrated the paradox about humanity that fascinates me and that fascinated Stevenson when he wrote *The Strange Case of Dr. Jekyll and Mr. Hyde:* the divided self. Gilles was

> . . . proud, young, pious, handsome, brave, skillful in arms, and had a fine ear for music. [He was] The young Marshal of France, companion on the battlefield of holy Saint Joan of Arc. He was also the courtier, soldier, scholar, the glass of fashion and the mold of form, the observed of all observers whom Ophelia mourns.[15]

But it was for none of those virtues that his name has come down to us, but rather for his avocation: the sexual-torture murder of a great many children. How many will never be precisely known, though chroniclers have cited numbers in the hundreds.

My own view of Gilles, whose sanity, like that of most mass murderers, has been questioned in our day, is that he was sane. Gilles, was a moral monster, not a case history. At his trial, "the swarm of his dreadful achievements pullulated into the courtroom until the particulars became so achingly rude that one of his judges left his place to draw a curtain over a portrait of Christ that hung there. . . ."[16] When he was asked why he committed his crimes, he replied:

> I did and perpetrated them following [the dictates] of my imagination and my thought, without the advice of anyone, and according to my own judgment and entirely for my own pleasure and physical delight and for no other intention or end.[17]

With Edmund Emil Kemper III, known as the Santa Cruz Killer, we are not dealing with knights and heraldic pennons flying. Kemper is part of our own world of superhighways, TV stars, and coeds, six of whom he murdered, along with both of his grandparents, his mother, and his mother's friend.

Like Gilles, Kemper was straightforward about why he killed his victims. "It's what I wanted to do," he said. When I asked him whether he did not sometimes feel sorry for them, he answered, "If I had let myself feel sorry for them, I could not have done what I did." Neither Gilles, facing his judges, nor Kemper, talking with me, ever claimed to be insane.

Acknowledging that there are and have been insane mass killers, I am impatient with the view that all such murderers are insane. For one thing, it begs the question of responsibility and it makes impossible the use of the word "evil" by substituting the word "sick"; and second, because it distances the sick killer from the decent rest of us who are well. By a trick of language, we shunt our mass murderers into a category so different from us that we can deny all kinship with them.

We *are* kith and kin. Sane people possess the capacity to commit such crimes. What separates us from our monsters is not our sanity, but the way we have chosen to exercise our will.

All of which leads me back to Vlad the Impaler.

By way of putting his behavior in context, some of his biographers remind us that he lived in a very violent age; that his father was assassinated; that he spent his formative years as a prisoner; that one of his brothers was blinded with hot irons and then buried alive; that his younger brother sided with his enemies against him. They have suggested, rather halfheartedly, that the frequent sexual focus of his crimes, and especially the phallicism they see manifested in his habit of staking his victims, may be a sign that Vlad was impotent.

Almost as irritating as the contextual and psychosexual explanations for Vlad's behavior are those that suggest that his crimes were exercises in statecraft or public policy. In Colonel Jean Lamouche's *Histoire de la Turquie,* we are told:

> Vlad was, nevertheless, an energetic, skillful prince, and his cruelty, which certainly was not always understandable, had at least the result that it made order reign in Wallachia as it completely suppressed brigandage, which before him was commonplace.[18]

And, commenting on the destruction of the Tirgoviste poor, described above, Vlad's biographers, Florescu and McNally write:

> In Dracula's defense one might allege that these vagabonds, infirm and destitute people who roamed the countryside, occasionally invading cities and preying upon the rich instead of working, constituted a social plague. These people were a threat to the prosperity of the land and gave his country a poor reputation. . . . In addition he may have been trying to liquidate the problem of the gypsies, the vagabond people, notorious for their thievery and wrongdoing.[19]

In 1994, in another book on Dracula by the same authors, there is a good deal more of the same:

> . . . one must bear in mind that there were two sides to Dracula's personality. One was the torturer and inquisitor who used terror deliberately as an instrument of policy while turning to piety to liberate his conscience. The other reveals a precursor of Machiavelli, an early nationalist and an amazingly modern statesman who justified his actions in accordance with *raisons d'état*. The citizens of Brasov and Sibiu were after all foreigners who attempted to perpetuate their monopoly of trade in the Romanian principalities. They were intriguers as well. The Saxons, conscious of Dracula's authoritarianism, were eager to subvert his authority in Transylvania and grant asylum to would-be contenders to the Wallachian throne. It is far too easy to explain Dracula's personality, as some have done, on the basis of cruelty alone. There was a method to his apparent madness.[20]

They add:

> Perhaps because of the exigencies of war Dracula could ill afford to feed useless mouths. Regarding the poor, Dracula may have imagined he was sending them to Paradise where they would suffer less, in accordance with Scripture. In the case of the sick, one might argue it was a form of mercy killing or perhaps an attempt to rid the country of the plague or other disease.[21]

It is a shaky line of reasoning made feebler by our still-vivid memories of a couple of other "amazingly modern" statesmen like Hitler and Goering who justified their acts as "in accordance with *raisons d'état*."

To bring order to the state at no matter what cost in human life and agony is not an imperative from on high. A man who would boil, dismember, stake, and mutilate men, women, children, and babies in order to achieve a crime-free reign needs to be seen for what he was: a monster criminal who arrogated to himself the right to commit all of his country's crimes.

No. Having made a desert, Vlad the Impaler could look down on it and call it peace.

# In Which the Reader Is Given a Raven's-Eye View of the Gothic Tradition in Literature

*"She's a Russian, by the look of her; but she's knocking about in the queerest way."*

[POE] REMAINS WHAT THE TRUE POET ALWAYS WILL BE—A TRUTH CLOTHED IN A STRANGE MANNER, AN APPARENT PARADOX . . . [HE] HAS CLEARLY SEEN, HAS IMPERTURBABLY AFFIRMED THE NATURAL WICKEDNESS OF MAN. THERE IS IN MAN, HE SAYS, A MYSTERIOUS FORCE WHICH MODERN PHILOSOPHY DOES NOT WISH TO TAKE INTO CONSIDERATION; NEVERTHELESS, WITHOUT THIS NAMELESS FORCE, WITHOUT THIS PRIMORDIAL FORCE, A HOST OF HUMAN ACTIONS WILL REMAIN UNEXPLAINED, INEXPLICABLE. THESE ACTIONS ARE ATTRACTIVE ONLY *BECAUSE* THEY ARE BAD OR DANGEROUS; THEY POSSESS THE FASCINATION OF THE ABYSS.

———CHARLES BAUDELAIRE (HYSLOP AND HYSLOP, BAUDELAIRE AS A LITERARY CRITIC)

One of the earliest scary tales that I know is to be found in the pages of the Bible. In the fourth chapter of Judges, we get the story of Jael, the wife of Heber, the Kenite, in whose tent the defeated Captain Sisera sought refuge. Jael soothed the frightened man and covered him with a mantle. When he asked for water to drink, she gave him milk. Then, when he went to sleep, "Jael, Heber's wife, took a nail of the tent, and took an hammer in her hand, and went softly unto him, and smote the nail into his temples, . . . So he died."

What makes literature of this little story is the author's lyric retelling of the events as he puts into the mouth of the prophetess Deborah the following song:

Blessed above women shall Jael the wife of Heber the Kenite be, blessed shall she be above women in the tent.

He asked water, and she gave him milk; she brought forth butter in a lordly dish.

She put her hand to the nail, and her right hand to the workman's hammer; and with the hammer she smote Sisera, she smote off his head, when she had pierced and stricken through his temples.

At her feet he bowed, he fell, he lay down: at her feet he bowed, he fell: where he bowed, there he fell down dead.[1]

It is just superb. The breathless delight in revenge that informs the passages makes the voice uttering them ring to the highest heavens:

So let all thine enemies perish, o Lord. . . .

There is plenty of aesthetic horror put before us in the tragic
Greek plays, but usually, the Greeks give us the frightful details filtered through the report of a messenger rather than by displaying
them onstage. We are spared the sight of Oedipus poking out his
eyes on stage, but the messenger is graphic enough:

> *He tore the brooches — [Jocasta's]*
> *. . . away from her and lifting them up high*
> *dashed them on his own eyeballs . . .*
> *and the bleeding eyeballs gushed*
> *and stained his beard. . . .[2]*

Roman tragedy uses messengers similarly, but their accounts of
violence are more lurid. In Seneca's play, *Thyestes*, a messenger tells
us how Atreus slew and then cooked his brother Thyestes's sons:

> Atreus sliced them open, tore out their quivering vitals, the little
> hearts twitching with life's last spark. Then, like a butcher, he
> hacked the limbs from the trunks, cracked their bones, and stripped
> off the flesh he fixed on cooking spits and set on the fire to turn and
> drip. Their organs he tossed into kettles to stew over fires that
> gagged at what they were made to do. The livers sizzled . . .[3]

That much and more, the messenger tells us, as well as the details of
how the father, eating his own children's bodies,

> *wipes his lips*
> *with a napkin and takes a sip of wine to wash down*
> *meat that has stuck in his throat.[4]*

There *is* a scene onstage in which Thyestes is informed of the contents of his meal and we see him being shown his sons' severed
heads. The theme of the play, as we may have guessed, is that "the
world is sick, mad and sick that such vile things can happen."[5]

The fresco on the wall of the Temple of Mars in Chaucer's
"Knight's Tale" is as "ghastly for to see" as Picasso's *Guernica*.

> *There I first saw the dark image*
> *Of all encompassing crime:*
> *The cruel rage, red as a glowing coal;*

*The pickpocket and also pallid fear;*
*The smiler with his knife under his cloak,*
*The slaughtered sheep burning with black smoke;*
*The treasonable murder done in bed;*
*Full scale war besplattered all with wounds*
*Knife-wielding strife, and menace just as sharp*

. . .

*And there I saw the slayer of himself,*
*His heart's blood clotting in his hair;*
*The spike driven into the skull at night;*
*And cold death, stiff and open-mouthed*
*The carcass in the grass, his throat all cut . . .*
*A thousand slain, but not by any plague*

. . . .

*The town destroyed — with nothing left at all*

. . .

*The sow devouring the baby in its cradle,*
*And the cook scalded in spite of his long ladle.*[6]

Particularly in the Revenge Tragedies, the English stage of the seventeenth century saw its share of ghosts and ghastly scenes. I can remember when my own children, whom I unwarily took to see *King Lear* when they were too young, turned from the stage with revulsion as Lear's daughter, Regan, plucked out Gloucester's eyes as she cried "Out, vile jelly!"[7] I did not take my children to Shakespeare's *Titus Andronicus*, so they have never seen: "Enter the empress's sons, with Lavinia, her hands cut off, and her tongue cut out, and ravished."[8] Nor, later, Lavinia carrying her father's severed hand between her teeth.

There is no need to belabor the point that there has always been plenty of violence in literature. The paragraphs above are meant only to emphasize that the aesthetic treatment of fear did not begin with the genre of fiction called Gothic that appeared in eighteenth-century England and about which I want now to say something because it is the genre to which Stoker's *Dracula* belongs.

Gothic fiction, an early manifestation of the Romantic Movement, appeared in England after nearly 150 years of the Neoclassical Age, when decorum and Right Reason, formality, balance, and the heroic couplet held sway, and when the word "enthusiasm" had the force of an accusation. The novels were called Gothic because they had scenes set in ruined castles, monasteries, and convents. Characteristically, they featured tall, dark, Italian villains who pursued beautiful young women of refined sensibilities, with intent to do them harm. Often the young women were saved from a fate worse than death by the providential arrival of a handsome—but sexually unthreatening—young man with whom they lived happily ever after.

What distinguishes Gothic fiction from mainstream literature is that its goal is to delight the reader by creating fear. If Aristotelian tragedy had as its goals the arousal—and then the purgation—of pity and terror, the aim of Gothic fiction is limited to the arousal of terror. That is why, from its beginning to the present day, fear literature has been regarded as a second-rank genre.

Because of its narrower scope, the Gothic novel became the fictive rug under which every unspeakable human act or fantasy could be swept. Atrocities of every kind—incest, murder, torture, rape— found their way into Gothic fiction.

Another characteristic of the genre was that, while mainstream novels were focusing more and more closely on life as it is really lived, the Gothic novelists made cheerful use of the supernatural. In their work, ghosts could walk, black magic could be practiced, pictures could step down from the wall, skulls could talk, and Satan or his minions could appear and make contracts with greedy humans.

There was an additional bonus. Readers were quick to feel pulsating beneath the surface of these fictions the folklore and fairy tale elements with which they had been familiar since childhood. In a Gothic romance, beautiful young women could be endangered by ogres and expect to be saved by knights in shining armor, as they had been for millennia.

A curious fact about the Gothic genre should be mentioned: The primary audience for these stories was women. Perhaps even more curious is that a great many of the authors, too, were women: Charlotte Dacre, Ann Doherty, Ann Fuller, Sarah Greene, Mary Ann Hanway, Isabella Kelly, Sophia Lee, Anna Maria Mackenzie, Eliza Parsons, and Mary Eleanor Sleath. And, of course, there is the towering past-mistress of horror, Ann Radcliffe. I have suggested elsewhere that

despite the triumphs of Lewis and Maturin, the Gothic novel was something of a cottage industry of middle-class women—as if women, oppressed by needlepoint whalebone stays, psychic frustrations, shame and babies, found in the making and consuming of these fictions a way to signal each other (and perhaps the world of men) the shadowy outlines of their own pain.[9]

Finally, one has to note another element of early Gothic fiction that is peculiarly British: the creepy settings in which the action of the novels took place. There is a cheerful British anti-Catholicism pervading Gothic fiction that is linked to the religious wars of the 1640s to the 1660s and the Glorious Revolution of 1688, which restored Protestant rule to England. It finds its expression in places where the heroines were oppressed—convents and monasteries—and in the frequency with which priests, monks, and sometimes nuns are villains. Sometimes the women victims were pursued by wicked priests or by the Inquisition. For eighteenth-century readers who had realistic villains like Lovelace in Samuel Richardson's novel *Clarissa* to deal with, it must have been soothing to British self-esteem to read about villains, all of whom were tall, dark, handsome, and Italian. As for the persecuting priests, there is nothing that will put a better aura of eroticism around a villain than to make him be a priest who has taken a vow of chastity.

The prose of Horace Walpole, the author of *The Castle of Otranto* (1764), which is credited with being the first English Gothic novel is not likely to find many admirers today. *The Castle* is a cumbersome, stiff, and occasionally quaint story with almost no relevance to human experience. Its author, Horace Walpole (1717–1797), a wealthy, cranky aesthete, believed that his novel marked a new fusion of two kinds of romance: the ancient and the modern, the imaginative with the realistic.

Like most of the great practitioners of scary literature, Walpole's novel had its origins in a dream in which he saw a giant armored hand. The fiction that grew out of this unremarkable experience has, as its protagonist, the tyrant Manfred, prince of Otranto, who sits uneasily upon his throne because of a prophecy that *"the Castle and Lordship of Otranto should pass from the present family whenever the real owners should be grown too large to inhabit it."* To avert this evil doom, the Machiavellian Manfred contrives a marriage between his sickly son, Conrad, and the Princess Isabella of Vicenza, a descendant of Alfonso the Good, a past ruler of Otranto, but Conrad does not live to be married. He is found smashed to death lying beneath an enormous helmet that has fallen from the statue of Alfonso. His plans for Conrad foiled, Manfred shifts his ground quickly. He decides to divorce his faithful wife, Hippolita, and undertakes to marry Isabella himself. Isabella, in turn, offended by Manfred's disloyalty to his wife, and already taken by the charms of a young peasant named Theodore, who, in turn, is in love with Manfred's daughter Matilda, flies from the tyrant's clutches. We get some whiff of Gothic ambience in the description of her flight:

> The lower part of the castle was hollowed into several intricate cloisters. . . . An awful silence reigned throughout those subterranean regions, except now and then some blasts of wind . . . shook the doors she had passed . . . which, grating on the rusty hinges . . . reechoed through that long labyrinth of darkness. Every murmur struck her with new terror. . . . In one of those moments she thought she heard a sigh. She shuddered, and recoiled a few paces. In a moment she thought she heard the step of some person. Her blood curdled. . . . Every suggestion that horror could inspire rushed into her mind.[10]

Other Gothic elements include a portrait that heaves a great sigh, steps out of its frame and walks, and a statue with a nosebleed. Finally, the castle itself comes tumbling down.

As the novel ends, Manfred, in a fit of rage, tries to stab Isabella and manages to kill his daughter, Matilda. Overwhelmed by guilt, Manfred retires to a monastery, his wife Hippolita to a convent. Isabella marries Theodore after a suitable time has passed so that he can overcome his grief for Matilda. Theodore, who we thought all along was a peasant, turns out to be the rightful heir to the throne of Otranto.

Ann Radcliffe (1764–1823), to whose work we now turn, was a writer of superior achievement. The two most important of her Gothic romances, *The Mysteries of Udolpho* (1794) and *The Italian* (1797), were written before she was thirty-three years old. Then she stopped writing.

*The Mysteries of Udolpho* has all the earmarks of a Gothic romance. Its heroine is Emily St. Aubert, a beautiful, sensitive young woman, who is pursued by a tall, dark, sinister Italian, whose intentions are strictly dishonorable. He is the nobleman Montoni, who has married her aunt. In Montoni's gloomy castle, to which he takes her, Emily is exposed to fearful sights and sounds: there are drunken brawls, mysterious groans, walls that seem to sigh, and sourceless music floating through the air. And always, of course, there hovers over the fiction the dreadful and enticing question that titillated English readers from the time of Richardson's *Pamela,* and even more profoundly, his *Clarissa:* Will he or won't he catch her, and if he does, what *will* he do?

*The Italian* is a novel of considerably greater stature and certainly more power than *The Mysteries of Udolpho.* Here the villain is the monk, Schedoni. His victim is Ellena Rosalba who is loved by a young nobleman, Vicentio di Vivaldi. Vicentio's mother, however, does not think that Ellena's antecedents are sufficiently worthy to make her a fit mate for her son. To prevent their marriage, Vicentio's mother engages the help of Schedoni, who has Ellena kidnaped and locked away in the convent of San Stephano, where Ellena is subjected to a variety of mistreatment.

Though Ellena escapes from the convent with Vivaldi's help, their happiness is short-lived. Schedoni manages to get Vivaldi imprisoned by the Inquisition while Ellena is shipped off to a seaside villa. There the impatient Schedoni, whose hired assassin, Spalatro, has balked at his task, decides to kill Ellena himself. There is an appalling moment when, as he is about to do the deed, he discovers that Ellena is his daughter.

As it turns out, she is *not* his daughter, but Ann Radcliffe and the reader have enjoyed the shuddering possibility of incest.

Eventually, Schedoni's schemes fail, and the novel comes to its requisite happy ending.

Schedoni is unforgettable. He belongs in the long gallery of fictional villains that seem descended from Milton's Satan: The line includes Richardson's Lovelace in *Clarissa* (1748), Choderlos de Laclos's Valmont in *Les Liaisons Dangereuses* (1782), Byron's *Manfred* (1817), Ambrosio in Lewis's *The Monk* (1796), Goethe's *Faust* (1808), and Stoker's Dracula (1897). These "heroes of iniquity" are invariably fascinating. They have the vitality of rebels, the attraction of exiles, and the sexual aura of the classic "handsome stranger" like Perseus, or the photographer in Robert Waller's novel, *The Bridges of Madison County,* or the nearest cowboy who has spurs that jingle-jangle as he rides away from the last woman whose heart he has broken but whose erotic vistas he has enlarged. In Schedoni's case (as with the various monastic villains that populate Gothic fiction), he has the added cachet of the priesthood and is therefore presumed to be a volcano of seething lust on the verge of eruption.

Reading Radcliffe can easily turn into a private vice if one enjoys hearing the murmur of educated speech. But she has irritating habits. Among them are her long passages of scenic description, which are doubtless intended to create a complementary background to her character's feelings, but which, to my taste, read like long excerpts from travel diaries. Her second, nearly unforgivable sin is that, having engrossed us by elaborating scenes in which wondrous or miraculous events take place, Radcliffe, at the end of her novels, pulls the rug out from under us by providing rational explanations of how the wonders came to be.

This is a sin which Matthew G. Lewis (1775–1818) magnificently, exuberantly does not commit. Like *The Castle of Otranto*, Lewis's *The Monk* which influenced Radcliffe's *The Italian*, was written in a great hurry. Lewis tell us that it took him only ten weeks to write the book. Ambrosio, Lewis's monk, starts his career of villainy by being a pure, unspotted, virtuous, chaste, and pious figure. Thirty years old at the time the novel begins, he is famous in Madrid as a paradigm of all that is good, beautiful, and true. When we meet him, he has just been made the abbot of his monastery, which requires him to give a public discourse on religion at certain times of the week. We learn that all Madrid is enamored of his sermons and his saintliness.

That Ivory soap purity, of course makes him a wonderful target for our ill wishes. John Berryman writes:

> . . . the point [of *The Monk*] is to conduct a remarkable man utterly to damnation. It is surprising, after all, how *long* it takes — how *difficult* it is — to be certain of damnation.[11]

Byron, sneering at *The Monk*, complained it was often forced and contained "the filtered ideas of a jaded voluptuary."[12] Byron is wrong on two counts. First, Lewis was twenty-one years old when he wrote *The Monk*. He had hardly had enough time to become a jaded voluptuary. Byron's second error is that there is nothing forced about Lewis's prose. If *Dracula* is the novel of sexual sublimation, Lewis's is almost all sexual exclamation. There are no hints or delicate euphemisms in Lewis's prose. Though there is never an instance of the kind of gross language about sexuality that is fairly commonplace in late twentieth-century American fiction, one is never in doubt that tumescence and the tidal forces of repressed and forbidden desire are what drive his fiction.

His Ambrosio is served in his monastery by the young novice, Rosario, who is so shy that even Ambrosio has not seen his features.

Ambrosio, for his part, is a perfect model of a chaste cleric. We learn, however, that he dotes on a portrait of the Virgin Mary, whose beauty he admires in the following terms:

> ... how graceful is the turn of that head! what sweetness, yet what majesty in her divine eyes! how softly her cheek reclines upon her hand! Can the rose vie with the blush of that cheek? can the lily rival the whiteness of that hand? Oh! if such a creature existed, and existed but for me! were I permitted to twine round my fingers those golden ringlets, and press with my lips the treasures of that snowy bosom! gracious God, should I then resist the temptation?[13]

As we will learn later, the portrait is not a detail of simply passing interest. Meanwhile, it is made clear to us that Ambrosio has a paternal affection for young Rosario. However, it is not long before the situation changes. One fateful day, Rosario says:

> "Listen to me with pity, revered Ambrosio! Call up every latent spark of human weakness that may teach you compassion for mine! Father!" continued he, throwing himself at the friar's feet, and pressing his hand to his lips with eagerness, while agitation for a moment choked his voice; "Father!" continued he in faltering accents, "I am a woman!"[14]

But, lest we think Rosario/Matilda has hanky-panky on her mind, she assures Ambrosio that her love for him is pure:

> "No, Ambrosio! learn to know me better; I love you for your virtues; lose them, and with them you lose my affections. I look upon you as a saint; prove to me that you are no more than a man, and I quit you with disgust."[15]

Eventually, the inevitable happens.

> The hour was night. All was silence around. The faint beams of a solitary lamp darted upon Matilda's figure, and shed through the chamber a dim, mysterious light. No prying eye or curious ear was near the lovers: nothing was heard but Matilda's melodious accents. Ambrosio was in the full vigor of manhood; he saw before him a young and beautiful woman, the preserver of his life, the adorer of his person; and whom affection for him had reduced to the brink of the grave. He sat upon her bed; his hand rested upon her bosom; her

head reclined voluptuously upon his breast. Who then can wonder if he yielded to temptation? Drunk with desire, he pressed his lips to those which sought them; his kisses vied with Matilda's in warmth and passion: he clasped her rapturously in his arms; he forgot his vows, his sanctity, and his fame; he remembered nothing but the pleasure and opportunity.

"Ambrosio! Oh, my Ambrosio!" sighed Matilda.

"Thine, ever thine," murmured the friar, and sunk upon her bosom.[16]

Following on that ecstatic moment, as the paragon of virtue discovers the lusts of the flesh, the novel takes a sudden turn toward the banal as, for nearly 117 pages, we read a couple of love stories over which we need not linger beyond noticing that there are some details in the digression that Stoker may have borrowed for his novel. For instance, the mark of the cross that is burned into the Wandering Jew's forehead and the burning circle within which the Jew encloses the Marquis de las Cisternas to protect him from the ghost of the Bleeding Nun. The Wandering Jew's description of his life, too, sounds like something Dracula might have said:

> ". . . Fate obliges me to be constantly in movement; . . . I have no friend in the world, and, from the restlessness of my destiny, I never can acquire one. Fain would I lay down my miserable life, for I envy those who enjoy the quiet of the grave: but death eludes me, and flies from my embrace. . . . God has set his seal upon me, and all his creatures respect this fatal mark."
>
> . . .
>
> "Such is the curse imposed on me . . ." he continued: "I am doomed to inspire all who look on me with terror and detestation."[17]

As I have said, the digressions does not compare in intensity with the main story, to which we now return. In it, we learn that not long after he has sated his lust with Matilda, Ambrosio is filled with revulsion: ". . . the delirium of passion being past, he had leisure to observe every trifling defect; where none were to be found, satiety made him fancy them." Finally: "In spite of her beauty, he gazed upon every other female with more desire. . . ." However, Matilda takes no umbrage. Instead, she encourages Ambrosio "to indulge in those pleasures freely, without which life is a worthless gift. . . ."[18] His appetite for sin fully whetted, he is eager to take her advice.

Then his eye falls on the fifteen-year-old Antonia, whose gentle beauty has already stirred the heart of Don Lorenzo. Ambrosio, in turn, is immediately smitten by her. In his guise as the purest and saintliest man in Madrid, he easily gains access to the house where she lives with her mother, Elvira, and her foolish, if good-hearted aunt, Leonella.

Misled by Antonia's artless confession that he is the man who makes her heart glow, Ambrosio makes a clumsy pass at her, but she is saved by the providential appearance of her mother, who is suspicious of the monk.

Though Ambrosio is foiled, he is by no means deterred. Matilda, who has been his minion, now offers herself as his panderer. In a scene whose lubricity matches the one in Dracula's castle where Jonathan Harker is surrounded by the three luscious vampire women, Matilda gives Ambrosio a magic mirror, in which he sees Antonia getting ready for her bath:

> [Antonia] threw off her last garment, and advancing to the bath, put her foot into the water. It struck cold, and she drew it back again. Though unconscious of being observed, an in-bred sense of modesty induced her to veil her charms; and she stood hesitating upon the brink, in the attitude of the Venus de Medicis. At this moment a tame linnet flew toward her, nestled its head between her breasts and nibbled them in wanton play. The smiling Antonia strove in vain to shake off the bird, and at length raised her hands to drive it from its delightful harbor. Ambrosio could bear no more. His desires were worked up to frenzy.
>
> "I yield!" he cried, dashing the mirror upon the ground: "Matilda, I follow you! Do with me what you will!"[19]

I submit that this is literary pornography of the highest order. Delicate, delicious, tasteful, significant, and calculated to drive not only Ambrosio but the panting reader up the wall.

By now it should be clear that Matilda is something more than Rosario, more even than Matilda. She is—and always has been—the devil's minion. She now arms Ambrosio with a magic silver myrtle twig which he takes with him to Antonia's house. At a touch from this talisman, the first door flies open, as does the next. Now he is in the sleeping girl's bedroom.

The magic myrtle placed on Antonia's pillow casts her into a deep sleep; she is absolutely in Ambrosio's power. Then he begins to caress her inert form. He kisses her, breathes in her breath until "His desires were raised to that frantic height by which brutes are agitated."[20] Unwilling to wait another moment, he tears off what little clothing still covers her.

" 'Gracious God!" exclaimed a voice behind him: 'Am I not deceived? Is not this an illusion?' "[21]

It is Elvira, Antonia's mother. Again! Ambrosio, in a situation from which no speech can extricate him, does the only thing he can under the circumstances. He kills Elvira.

There follows a series of complicated maneuvers that ends with Ambrosio taking Antonia's drugged body into the charnel vaults of the convent. There,

> By the side of three putrid half-corrupted bodies lay the sleeping beauty. A lively red, the forerunner of returning animation spread itself over her cheeks . . . she seemed to smile at the images of death around her . . . [Ambrosio] longed for the possession of her person; and even the gloom of the vault, the surrounding silence, and the resistance which he expected from her, seemed to give a fresh edge to his fierce and unbridled desires. . . .[22]

Like Juliet awakening in *her* tomb, Antonia opens her eyes. " 'Where am I?' she said abruptly." Ambrosio's blazing eyes inform her of his intent, and she begs him to spare her. " 'What matters it where you are? This sepulcher seems to me Love's bower. . . . Your veins shall glow with the fire which circles in mine, and my transports shall be doubled by your sharing them.' "[23]

Surely that is the magic thought lodged in every rapist's brain, that the violence gathered in his loins will rouse his victim to passion. Ambrosio is explicit:

> ". . . You are absolutely in my power, and I burn with desires which I must either gratify or die: . . . My lovely girl! my adorable Antonia! let me instruct you in the joys to which you are still a stranger. . . . Can I relinquish these limbs so white, so soft, so delicate! these swelling breasts, round, full, and elastic! these lips fraught with such inexhaustible sweetness? . . . No, Antonia; never, never! I swear by this kiss! and this! and this!"[24]

Do we remember where he is? In an underground charnel house, sitting on a tomb, with three rotting corpses nearby. Long before Krafft-Ebing, *Psychopathia Sexualis* is being written before our eyes. Rape and necrophilia—and murder. Because, as he tells Antonia, " 'You shall not from hence to tell Madrid that I am a villain. . . . Wretched girl, you must stay here with me. . . .' "[25]

And whom does he blame for the disaster, do you suppose?

> "Fatal witch!! was it not thy beauty! Have you not plunged my soul into infamy? Have you not made me a perjured hypocrite, a ravisher, an assassin?"[26]

It's all Antonia's fault. The poor rapist, driven to violence by the unforgivable beauty of a fifteen-year-old's body.

Properly, the rest of the book should be only anticlimax. But, as with Stoker's amazing rising action at the end of *Dracula*, Lewis gives us a denouement that is almost as terrifying as all that preceded it.

Ambrosio is arrested by the Inquisition and condemned to die in an auto-da-fé. At the penultimate moment, Matilda comes to his aid with an offer of escape if he will invoke the devil's help by signing a contract in blood with him. " 'Dare you spring, without fear over the bounds which separate men from angels?' "[27] she asks. For a considerable while, he vacillates. Then when he hears the tramp of his executioners' feet, Ambrosio signs hastily.

Then all the ironies rain down. Ambrosio does indeed escape from the Inquisition, only to find himself gripped in the devil's claw, while the fiend tells him:

> "Hark, Ambrosio, while I unveil your crimes. . . . That Antonia whom you violated, was your sister! that Elvira whom you murdered, gave you birth! Tremble, abandoned hypocrite! inhuman parricide! incestuous ravisher! . . ."[28]

I do not know what psychodynamic in us makes us hunger for poetic justice at the end of our novels, but we dearly want our villains punished and our good guys (male and female) rewarded. Perhaps it is because we know that the endings of real-world dramas are not quite so satisfactory. Lewis's *Monk* achieves two things brilliantly: a superbly villainous villain; and then, a punishment *in this world* that fits his crimes perfectly:

> The caves and mountains rang with Ambrosio's shrieks. The daemon continued to soar aloft, till reaching a dreadful height, he released

the sufferer. Headlong fell the monk through the airy waste; . . . and he rolled from precipice to precipice, till, bruised and mangled he rested on the river's banks . . . his broken and dislocated limbs refused to perform their office. . . . Myriads of insects were called forth by the [sun's] warmth; they drank the blood which trickled from Ambrosio's wounds. . . . The eagles of the rock tore his flesh piecemeal, and dug out his eyeballs with their crooked beaks . . . six memorable days did the villain languish. On the seventh a violent storm arose: the winds in fury rent up rocks and forests: . . . the rain fell in torrents . . . the waves overflowed their banks; they reached the spot where Ambrosio lay, and, when they abated, carried with them into the river the corpse of the despairing monk.[29]

If, in *The Monk*, the nightmare is tenaciously sexual, the one into which we are drawn in Charles Robert Maturin's *Melmoth the Wanderer* (1820) leaves us, when we wake from it, with a sense of horror about the nature of humanity itself. Maturin (1782–1824), an Irish cleric who augmented his insufficient salary as curate of St. Peter's Church in Dublin by writing fiction and then, later, plays, was, like Sheridan Le Fanu, to whom he was distantly related, descended from a French Huguenot family that had taken refuge in Ireland after the Revocation of the Edict of Nantes in 1685.

*Melmoth the Wanderer*, Maturin's most important work and, in my view, the finest Gothic novel (excepting *Dracula*) ever written, has epic themes bolstered by the sort of specificity of incident that we admire in tapestries: exquisite close detail forming part of an equally exquisite larger design. The two intertwining themes of the novel are the human uses of time and the pervasive presence and disastrous effects of religious hypocrisy.

As a Gothic fiction, *Melmoth,* more than the others discussed here, has left its mark on Bram Stoker's *Dracula*. Maturin's Melmoth is tall, dark, and dynamic. Like Dracula, he is a man whom we meet rarely; but when he does appear, he is a cold, sardonic, aloof, and profoundly lonely figure with blazing eyes whose avidity for life pushes him to make the Faustian bargain. The critical difference between him and Dracula is that Dracula never excites our pity.

As in Stoker's novel, we hear about the events that make up the plot in *Melmoth* from several voices and points of view. As the novel begins, a third-person narrator introduces us to John Melmoth, a young Irishman who is on his way to the bedside of a dying skinflint uncle. We ought to cherish the pages of these opening two chapters because whatever there is of whimsy or humor in the entire 412-page work happens here. Then all smiling stops. From Chapter 3 on, the shades of emotion we move through range from earnest to bleak to desperate to appalling. Long before Kafka, long before Sartre or Beckett, Maturin held up his mirror to the world and saw nothing but tarnish reflected in it.

In any case, the skinflint uncle dies and leaves his property to young Melmoth, his needy nephew. In a corner of the old man's will is scrawled an injunction that his heir burn a portrait of an ancestor that will be found in a storeroom and to read (and destroy) a manuscript reposing in a mahogany cabinet. The portrait is dated 1646, some 170 years before 1816, the present time of the novel. The local Irish peasant gossip says that the devil has helped this ancestor remain alive, and that when any family member sees him, the sight is a presage of death.

Young John reads the manuscript within which, as in a nest of boxes, six stories are found. The longest of these, and the one that is thematically most dense is narrated by a Spaniard named Moncada who recounts the torments he endured in a monastery where he was forced to become a monk by family pressures and those exerted by the Church. This central section of the novel is something of a tour de force as a catalog of all that human beings can contrive in the way of torments for each other. Maturin is as inventive as the torturers he describes as inflicting pain on Moncada and on other hapless victims of the Inquisition and the Catholic monastic system. One such torturer, a confessed parricide, describes the pleasure he takes in other people's pain:

> "It is actually possible to become *amateurs of suffering.* I have heard of men who have traveled into countries where horrible executions were to be daily witnessed, for the sake of that excitement which the sight of suffering never fails to give, from the spectacle of a tragedy, or an *auto da fé,* down to the writhings of the meanest reptile on whom you can inflict torture, and feel that torture is the result of your own power. . . ."[30]

Though *Melmoth* abounds in them, there is no need to cite one episode of horror after another. The main point is that Maturin is not content merely to raise the hackles on our necks. He is aware that there are people in the world for whom evil is a complex attraction. In *Melmoth*, he comes close to enunciating a truly forbidden idea: that there may be both an ethos and an aesthetics of evil. Maturin's parricide says:

> "... some kind of creed is necessary, and the falser perhaps the better for falsehood at least flatters. . . . If I persecute and torment the enemies of God, must I not be the friend of God? Must not every pang I inflict on another, be recorded in the book of the All-remembering. . . . I have no religion, I believe in no God, I repeat no creed, but I have that superstition of fear and of futurity, that seeks its wild and hopeless mitigation in the sufferings of others when our own are exhausted. . . . I am convinced that my own crimes will be obliterated, by whatever crimes of others I can promote or punish. . . . I need not repent, I need not believe; if you suffer, I am saved — that is enough — that is enough for me. . . . I have literally worked out *my* salvation by *your* fear and trembling."[31]

The point is not that this parricide's self-justification is correct, but that it is systematic and thorough, and that Maturin does not offer the easy [and very modern] explanation that this vile monk is mad.

After several scenes of battering violence in Madrid, we are transported, geographically and lyrically, to a distant island in the Indian Ocean, where we meet a white goddess named Immalee. She is, of course, beautiful beyond compare. She has auburn hair and seems to be wearing only flowers entwined with peacock feathers. A finch perches on her shoulder, and on her neck

> a string of pearl-like eggs, so pure and pellucid, that the first sovereign in Europe might have exchanged her richest necklace of pearls for them. Her arms and feet were perfectly bare.[32]

The entire island episode is a gorgeous figment of the romantic imagination and a welcome change from the series of dangers and torments we have read so far. We need not be so callow as to ask whether the Edenic island episode is believable.

Into that paradise where Immalee has lived alone feeding on figs and drinking water from her cupped palms, there comes a stranger, Melmoth the Wanderer. She falls hopelessly in love with him, and he urges her one stormy night to "Hate me — curse me! . . . hate me,

for I hate you — I hate all things that live — all things that are dead —
I am myself hated and hateful!"[33]

"Doom" says W. H. Auden, "is dark and deeper than any sea-dingle," and by the word "dingle" he means an abyss.[34] Three years pass and we see Immalee, now Isadora, in Madrid and restored to her lost parents. Then, because this is after all a tragic tale, she comes upon Melmoth. "She saw him, too, recognized him, and, uttering a wild shriek, fell on the earth, senseless."[35] It does not take long for her dark doom to be accomplished. It hastens her to a chill marriage to her demonic bridegroom in a ruined monastery:

> The place, the hour, the objects, all were hid in darkness. She heard a faint rustling as of the approach of another person — she tried to catch certain words, but she knew not what they were, — she attempted also to speak, but she knew not what she said. All was mist and darkness with her, — she knew not what she muttered — she felt not that the hand of Melmoth grasped hers, — but she felt that the hand that united them, and clasped their palms within his own, was as *cold as that of death.*[36]

As the book ends, we get a final glimpse of Melmoth the Wanderer: this time we enter his dream and see with him the lashing waves of an ocean of fire.

> Every billow of fire was thus instinct with immortal and agonizing existence, — each was freighted with a soul, that rose on the burning wave in torturing hope, burst on the rock in despair, added its eternal shriek to the roar of that fiery ocean, and sunk to rise again — in vain, and — forever![37]

Looking up, Melmoth the Wanderer sees the face of a clock fixed to the top of a precipice. "He saw the mysterious single hand revolve — he saw it reach the appointed period of one hundred and fifty years. . . ." Then, like Ambrosio the monk, he falls.

> His last despairing reverted glance was fixed on the clock of eternity — the upraised black arm seemed to push forward the hand — it arrived at its period — he fell — he sunk — he blazed — he shrieked! The burning waves bloomed over his sinking head, and the clock of eternity rung out its awful chime — "Room for the soul of the Wan-

derer!"—and the waves of the burning ocean answered, as they lashed the adamantine rock—"There is room for more!"—The Wanderer awoke.[38]

The dream is an accurate presage of Melmoth's end, though we do not witness his death. Instead, the last material evidence that Melmoth the Wanderer had existed is the handkerchief that young Melmoth removes from the cliffside furze to which it has clung.

*Melmoth the Wanderer* is a somber work which demands an unusual amount of attention and patience from its readers. But it leaves them with the sense that they have heard, as a counterpoint to Wordsworth's "still, sad, music of humanity,"[39] the equally present pulsations of despair.

In America, Gothic fiction found its expression in the novel *Wieland* (1798) by Charles Brockden Brown (1771–1810), who is sometimes called "the father of American literature." It's a slapdash piece of work in which characters are occasionally mislaid or forgotten. What is memorable about Carwin, the novel's villain, is that his face shows simultaneously marks of bestialism as well as a "radiance inexpressibly serene and potent . . . betoken[ing] a mind of the highest order. . . ."[40] In addition to all that, he has a very beautiful voice.

Mary Shelley's *Frankenstein* (1818) marks an early departure from the usual plotting of Gothic fiction. Though it retains the endangered beautiful woman who becomes the victim of the Creature, the Creature itself ends by representing suffering humankind. In a miraculous leap forward to the twentieth century, with its alertness to psychological nuances, Mary Shelley is astute enough to see that Victor, her protagonist, is the villain of her piece.

With *The Private Memoirs and Confessions of a Justified Sinner* (Thomas Jefferson Hogg, 1824), we have one more scary novel that departs from the Gothic formula. This story, which was to have an impact on Robert Louis Stevenson's *The Strange Case of Dr. Jekyll and Mr. Hyde,* has a doppelganger theme. Robert Wringhim has a demonic familiar named Gil Martin, who provokes him to commit crimes. Today the novel seems more successful as a satire against religious fanaticism than as a psychological study.

William Child Green's *The Abbot of Montserrat* (1826) retains the apparatus of Gothic fiction: lustful monks, dashing robbers, and a demon named Zatanai. Readers who find Stoker's novel, *The Lair of the White Worm,* as fascinating as it is repulsive may enjoy comparing Green's description of his reptilian demon with Stoker's Lamia-figure, Lady Arabella.

In some sense, *The Strange Case of Dr. Jekyll and Mr. Hyde* (1886), the work for which Stevenson is best known, cannot properly be included in a discussion of Gothic fiction for the reason that there is no female character of any consequence in it, but that ambiguity, I suggest, adds considerable spice to the fiction. It does not take us long to recognize that the requisite missing endangered young woman is represented here by Dr. Henry Jekyll and that the sinister, dark pursuer with evil intentions is Edward Hyde. And the Gothic ruin in which the critical action takes place is Jekyll's laboratory.

By the time we get to Oscar Wilde's *The Picture of Dorian Gray* (1891), which appeared only six years before *Dracula*, the original formula for Gothic fiction had been much modified. In *The Picture of Dorian Gray*, though there is a villain, Lord Henry Wotton, whose decadent philosophy—"nothing can cure the soul but the senses, just as nothing can cure the senses but the soul"[41]—pushes Dorian Gray to make his deal with whatever force in the universe fulfills people's evil wishes. By Wilde's time, fear literature had accommodated to the notion that would haunt twentieth-century Gothic fiction: the primary villain of one's life can be the self.

This, then, is the stream of fictive fear in which Bram Stoker went fishing and in which he caught the leviathan we call *Dracula*.

## CHAPTER 6

# In Which We Meet the Fictional Precursors of the Vampire Brood

*"There was Bersicker a-tearin' like a mad thing at the bars as if he wanted to get out."*

ONLY LE FANU SEEMS TO HAVE EQUATED THE HAUNTED SWAMPS AND
STRANGE FLUTTERING BIRDS AND FIERCE ANCESTRAL PORTRAITS
WITH THE GUILT LAYERS OF A MAN'S MIND.

—E. F. BLEILER IN THE INTRODUCTION TO
BEST GHOST STORIES OF J. S. LE FANU

In the grab bag of possible nineteenth-century influences on Stoker's *Dracula*, there are several bright and shiny surprises to be found. When I was in junior high school the entire English Romantic Movement was jammed into our memories, encapsulated in the little mantra: "Byron and Shelley and Keats, Byron and Shelley and Keats." The mantra for the Romantic poets who most influenced Stoker's *Dracula* is "Byron and Coleridge and Keats, Byron and Coleridge and Keats."[1]

I can't shake the conviction that Byron, Coleridge, and Keats met one night on a darkling heath around a caldron into which they tossed morsels of vampiric reference and implication from their works then stirred the pot. The steam that rose from the caldron went drifting toward the Victorian age, where it sifted down through the poisonous London fog to settle softly in Bram Stoker's brain. What is striking about their contribution to what we may think of as Stoker's mine of imagery is the enthusiasm with which they embraced the macabre in their own poems.

What did Stoker borrow from "The Rime of the Ancient Mariner"? I suspect that he remembered the living dead men who work the sails of the Mariner's stricken ship and the Mariner's desperate drinking of his own blood. The most influential image from this poem is the one of the grisly pair in the small ship through whose ribs the sun's rays "shine as through a dungeon grate." The occupants of that ship are Death and "the Nightmare Life-in-Death." What a perfect name for a vampire! Nor is that all; except for the slight uncertainty about the color of her hair, she looks perilously like Stoker's Lucy after she has been vampirized:

> *Her lips were red, her looks were free,*
> *Her locks were yellow as gold:*
> *Her skin was as white as leprosy,*

*The nightmare LIFE-IN-DEATH was she,*
*Who thicks man's blood with cold.*[2]

Byron's 1813 poem, "The Giaour" (pronounced "Djour," to rhyme with "your"), and his verse play *Manfred* also have vampire imagery that is frequently cited as affecting Stoker's imagination. And Keats's *Lamia*, which is a truly exquisite verse tale of the love of a serpent woman for a mortal, surely influenced Stoker's novel *The Lair of the White Worm.*

---

The vampire novel entered English literature in a most unlikely way. It was introduced to English readers by John Polidori (1795–1821), who was Lord Byron's personal physician and traveling companion for a time. Polidori and Byron shared a relationship that was profoundly ambivalent. Byron referred to Polidori condescendingly as "poor Polly." Just the same, Polidori was present on the famous rainy summer evening in Geneva in 1816, when Byron asked his guests to write a scary tale. Mary Shelley describes what happened:

> Some volumes of ghost stories, translated from the German into French fell into our hands. There was the "History of the Inconstant Lover," who, when he thought to clasp the bride to whom he had pledged his vows, found himself in the arms of the pale ghost of her whom he had deserted. There was the tale of the sinful founder of his race, whose miserable doom it was to bestow the kiss of death on all the younger sons of his fated house, just when they reached the age of promise. His gigantic, shadowy form, clothed like the ghost in *Hamlet* in full armour, but with the beaver up, was seen at midnight. . . . "We will each write a ghost story," said Lord Byron; and his proposition was acceded to. There were four of us. The noble author began a tale, a fragment which he printed at the end of his poem of Mazeppa. Shelley, more apt to embody ideas and sentiments in the radiance of brilliant imagery, and in the music of the most melodious verse that adorns our language, than to invent the machinery of a story, commenced one founded on the experiences of his early life. Poor Polidori had some terrible idea about a skull-headed lady, who was so punished for peeping through a keyhole—what to see I forget—something very shocking and wrong, of course; but when she was reduced to a worse condition than the renowned Tom of Coven-

try, he did not know what to do with her, and was obliged to dispatch her to the tomb of the Capulets, the only place for which she was fitted. The illustrious poets, also, annoyed by the platitude of prose, speedily relinquished their uncongenial task.[3]

Written in 1831, Mary Shelley's description of the occasion gives us the impression that the evening in Byron's house was a congenial event, during which Byron invited his guests to write a scary tale. According to her, the five people present included Byron, Percy Shelley, John Polidori, Claire Clairmont, and herself. The roomful of people shared a cluster of tangled and barbed relationships. At eighteen, Mary Shelley was in Geneva as the mistress of Percy Shelley, who had abandoned a wife and two small children. Claire Clairmont, her foster sister, had attached herself to the Shelley ménage and had managed to have an affair with Byron, whose baby she was carrying. Byron wished her elsewhere passionately. I have already spoken of the bared-knives relationship between Byron and Polidori.

> The other lines of feeling drawn between the people in the Villa Diodati on that famous night are almost too intricate to be drawn in detail. Polidori was jealous of Shelley's growing friendship with Byron. Byron treated Polidori like a plaything. Mary Shelley was jealous of Byron, who took Shelley away from her for whole days at a time to go sailing. Claire was yearning for Byron, but at the same time managed a strangely erotic relationship with Shelley, with whom she often stayed up late at night when Mary was not feeling well. Shelley, in turn, comforted Claire by telling her tales of blood and gore until he rendered her hysterical, after which he put her tenderly to bed.[4]

It is a room full of emotional land mines, a fact that Ken Russell both appreciated and exploited in his 1987 film *Gothic,* in which all the people present at the Villa Diodati in Geneva are transformed into sexual perverts of one nasty sort or another and in which John Polidori is shown drinking a beaker full of leeches and Claire Clairmont as a naked madwoman carrying a dead rat between her teeth.

The point is that Polidori and Mary Shelley were the only two who produced substantive fictions in response to Byron's challenge. Mary Shelley gave us *Frankenstein* while John Polidori left his mark on literature with his novel, *The Vampyre* (1821). The novel was widely believed to have been written by Lord Byron. Byron had in fact referred to a vampire in his poem "The Giaour," a poem that early links vampirism with incest. Stoker quotes Byron's poem in Chapter 13, where he has Seward say that instead of "decay's effacing fingers" leaving traces on the newly dead Lucy, she looked amazingly alive. The relevant lines in "The Giaour" are:

> "He who hath bent him o'er the dead
> Ere the first trace of death is fled
> The first dark day of nothingness,
> The last of danger and distress,
> (Before Decay's effacing fingers
> Have swept the lines where beauty lingers,)
> And mark'd the mild angelic air,
> The rapture of repose that's there . . ."⁵

Some readers find *The Vampyre* more admirable than I do. The book's major contribution to vampire/Dracula lore is the nobleman vampire. Lord Ruthven, Polidori's protagonist, is a suave, chilling, brilliant figure, said to be fascinating to women. Because Ruthven was the name Caroline Lamb had given to a character in her novel, *Glenarvon,* a character widely perceived to be a satire of Byron, one has to assume that Polidori, too, was unsheathing his claws against his former friend and lover.

E. F. Bleiler has observed perceptively that "in the history of the English novel, Polidori's *The Vampyre* has interest beyond its literary merit."⁶ Polidori's prose is pretentious and affects a weary sophistication. Nonetheless, his Ruthven seems to have struck a chord in his early readers. For a couple of decades after the appearance of the book, versions, rip-offs, or parodies of Ruthven made popular appearances on English and French stages in plays written by Eugène Scribe, Charles Nodier, and Alexandre Dumas père (France); James Robinson Planché and Dion Boucicault (England).

The Lord Ruthven we meet in London is described as having a dead gray eye and a complexion that has a deadly hue. Nevertheless, he is said to be appealing to women and is invited to the fashionable homes of London. But Lord Ruthven is not the protagonist of Polidori's novel. That honor belongs to Aubrey who, we should note, has a marriageable sister. Intrigued by Ruthven, Aubrey accepts his invitation to travel with him on the Continent. Aubrey begins to suspect that Ruthven is an evil man and leaves him to go to Greece. There he falls in love with the beautiful Ianthe, from whom he learns about the existence of vampires. He is skeptical of her stories until, one day, on one of his excursions, he hears a woman shrieking and the sound of a mocking laugh. Rushing to save the woman, he comes upon her — too late. "Upon her neck and breasts was blood, and upon her throat were the marks of teeth. . . ."[7]

The sight of the murdered Ianthe puts Aubrey into shock. When he returns to consciousness, he finds himself being cared for by Ruthven, and their old relationship is reestablished.

The complication on which the plot now turns makes almost no sense to a modern reader. Ruthven is killed in an encounter with bandits; but as he lies dying, he makes Aubrey swear not to reveal his crimes for the space of one year. Aubrey takes the oath.

On his return to England, Aubrey finds Ruthven, revitalized by the rays of the full moon. Worse, Ruthven is paying court to Aubrey's sister. Bound by his oath, Aubrey cannot warn her. The story winds down to its inevitable tragic end.

"Wake Not the Dead" is a story by Johann Ludwig Tieck, the German playwright, fairy-tale collector, novelist, and short-story writer, who was one of the creators of German Romanticism. It is a stark, somber story, that can easily be mistaken for a Poe tale. At the center of the story is Walter, a Burgundian lord, whose exquisite, dark wife, Brunhilda, is a source of sensual splendors for him. Walter's happiness with Brunhilda is cut short when Brunhilda dies suddenly. Though he believes himself at first to be inconsolable, Walter is drawn very soon to the blonde Swanhilda — Hilda is the constant in both names. Swanhilda's "golden locks wave bright as the beams of morn. . . . Her limbs were proportioned in the nicest symmetry, yet did they not possess the luxuriant fullness of animal life."[8] The Romantic dichotomy between the passionate dark woman, wildly attractive to men, and the pale blonde, attractive to the eye but erotically cold, is at work here. It is not long before Walter, deprived of the wild nights Brunhilda and he had shared, takes to lying on Brunhilda's grave in painful yearning.

Finally, Walter's yearning produces a miracle. A puissant sorcerer is persuaded by Walter to bring Brunhilda back to life. And here, in the description of the reanimated Brunhilda, Tieck early creates the distinction that will permeate vampire fiction forever: between life that is in motion and life that has emotion. Tieck writes that Brunhilda had "an artificial life . . . yet, this body was not able of itself to keep up the genial flow of vitality, and to nourish the flame whence springs all affections and passions . . . all that Brunhilda had was a chilled existence, colder than that of the snake."[9] For her to be able to create a semblance of feeling, she needs to drink human blood. Blinded by his revived transports of delight, at first Walter pays no attention to the deaths of his vassals' children. Finally, however, Walter discovers her supping sustenance from his own breast. When he accuses her, she reminds him with icy logic that *he* is the true murderer because "I was obliged to pamper myself with warm youthful blood in order that I might satisfy thy furious desires."[10] He rids himself of Brunhilda, but he does not escape the consequences of his many vile acts. As he is about to unite himself to a new and mysterious bride, she turns into a snake, which, "entwining him in his horrid folds crushed him to death."[11]

"Wake Not the Dead," published in English in 1823, clearly influenced Poe's "Ligeia," in which a dynamic dark woman is also replaced by a vapid blonde. As with Brunhilda, Ligeia returns from the dead, inhabiting the body of the dead Rowena. Some readers have found vampirism in the Poe story, though it seems to me that Poe's story works best as exemplifying what Poe tells us is his theme:

> And the will therein lieth, which dieth not. Who knoweth the mysteries of the will, with its vigor? For God is but a great will pervading all things by nature of its intentness. Man doth not yield him to the angels nor unto death utterly, save only through the weakness of his feeble will.[12]

As an aside, I should note that Ligeia's husband regrets her passing because of her intellectual prowess and not because of her capacity to give him wild nights.

A story that very likely influenced Stoker is Théophile Gautier's *La Morte Amoureuse*, "Amorous Death" (1836) in which Gautier, in a lyric, passionate prose, establishes the link between vampirism and eroticism. Following in the footsteps of Matthew Lewis, Gautier pretends that his story is an exemplum: a tale exemplifying a moral truth. As such, *La Morte Amoureuse* is absurdly unsuccessful; but as an account of the sumptuous, lascivious, and ecstatic physical delights that await a man who is victimized by a vampire, it is supremely successful fiction.

*Edgar Allan Poe*

Like Matthew Lewis's monk, Gautier's protagonist is a priest, which means, of course, that the sexual tension built into the story is heightened because, as we know, the priest Romuald has taken a vow of chastity.

The story comes to us as a first-person narrative in the form of a letter from Romuald, now an old man, who is answering a fellow priest's question: "Have I ever loved? The answer is 'yes.'" The rest of the letter gives his correspondent—and us—the details of that love.

Romuald, tells us that, for three years, he

was the plaything of a singular and diabolical illusion. I, a poor country priest, I lived a dream life at night (God grant that it was a dream), a life of the damned, a worldly life worthy of Sardanapalus [a king, of Nineveh, famous for his dissipated and luxurious life], . . . By day I was a priest of the Lord, chaste, and busy with prayer and

holy things . . . at night, the moment my eyes closed, I became a
young lord, a connoisseur of women, dogs and horses, playing dice,
drinking and blaspheming . . .[13]

Romuald was twenty-four when, on the very day of his ordina-
tion as a priest, his eye fell on a young woman of rare beauty:

It was as if scales had fallen from my eyes. I felt like a blind man who
could suddenly see.[14]

Like Jonathan Harker, he sees this beauty through closed eyelashes, "through eyelashes sparkling with the colors of a prism."[15]
She is as beautiful as a goddess: blonde, with eyes whose pupils
were as green as the sea. Those eyes

had a life, a clarity, an ardor, a brilliant liquidity I had never seen in a
human eye . . . I was born into a new life . . . Oh! How beautiful she
was! The greatest painters searching the heavens in order to bring
down to earth ideal beauty, the divine portrait of the Madonna,
could not approach the fabulous reality [of Clarimonde].[16]

This vision of loveliness is named Clarimonde (meaning illuminated world, or clear world), a name that we will recall when we
meet Stoker's Lucy Westenra, whose first name means "light."
Romuald cries, "Oh! How right Job is when he says that that
man is prudent who does not conclude a pact with his eyes."[17] Dazzled by Clarimonde's beauty, and all his other senses now awakened
by the sight of her, Romuald is easy prey to her blandishments. She
seeks him out and tells him that she loves him:

"If you will belong to me, I will make you happier than God himself
in paradise. The angels will envy you . . . I am beauty, youth, life . . .
I will transport you to unknown islands; you will sleep on my breast,
on a bed of massive gold in a silver tent."[18]

However, it takes Clarimonde's death to bring her together with
Romuald. As priest, one night he is brought to the home of a woman
said to be dying. It is Clarimonde, and by the time he arrives, she is
dead. The scene that follows is profoundly reminiscent of the scene
in Lucy's tomb that Stoker gives us. Romuald gazes at the dead body
and is amazed at how alive Clarimonde looks:

Strange thoughts crossed my mind. It struck me that she was not really dead and that her death was a trick that she had used to bring me to her chateau so that she could show me her love. . . . Shall I confess it? The perfection of her shape, though purified and sanctified by the shadow of death, roused in me impermissible voluptuous thought. . . . I forgot that I had come here to perform a rite and imagined myself to be a young bridegroom, entering his fiancée's chamber. . . .[19]

Finally:

I could not refuse myself the supreme and sad sweetness . . . to kiss the dead lips of her who had all my love.[20]

Like the kiss in "Sleeping Beauty," Romuald's kiss rouses the dead Clarimonde. And from here on, they lead an exquisitely voluptuous life.

Starting with that night, my nature in some sense became doubled. There were in me two men, neither of whom knew the other. . . . Two spirals, entangled in each other, though never touching.[21]

The story of this obsession is complicated by Gautier's understanding that even the most compelled physical desire can rouse hungers in the soul; and, though on the face of it, Romuald is in the grip of a succubus, his frequent and delicious fulfillment in her arms rouses in him all the joys of love.

However, the couple's transports are threatened by the perceptible decline in Clarimonde's health. It becomes clear that she is once more facing death. Another scene reminds us of Harker in Dracula's castle: Romuald cuts his finger as he is peeling fruit. The sight of the blood makes Clarimonde's eyes sparkle, and ". . . with the agility of a monkey or a cat, she leaped toward my wound, which she began to suck with an air of unspeakable delight."[22]

From here on, it is clear to Romuald that the tie between them, in addition to pleasure and love, includes the bond of blood. I cannot resist quoting the ebullient passage in which Clarimonde, speaking to the apparently sleeping Romuald, apostrophizes him:

"One drop, no more than one red drop, a ruby at the tip of my needle . . . since you still love me, you must not die . . . Ah! Poor love! His beautiful blood, the color of purple and so bright . . . I'm going to drink it. Sleep, my sole comfort; sleep my God, my child; I'll do you no harm. . . . If I did not love you so much, I might have chosen to have other lovers, whose veins I might have sucked dry."[23]

That passage goes on at some length, and it imposes a complexity over their relationship. Succubus though she is, Clarimonde is well and truly in love.

Since we are, after all, inside a story intended to be an exemplum, we know that this must all end badly. Depending as it does on measured extractions of Romuald's blood, Clarimonde's life is not a true one. Though Romuald is quite willing to keep her alive with his blood, reality intrudes into this macabre—if happy— arrangement. Throughout the story, we have been aware of Father Serapion, a priest who has been Romuald's mentor. Serapion, an early version of Dr. Van Helsing, is aware of the moral pit of degradation into which Romuald has fallen. "Serapion's zeal," Romuald says, "had something harsh and savage in it, which made him resemble a demon more than an apostle or an angel."[24] It is Serapion who leads Romuald to Clarimonde's tomb. There they find her

pale as marble, her hands folded, her white shroud making a single fold from head to foot, a tiny drop, like a rose, glistened at the corner of her pale mouth.[25]

The implacable Serapion sprinkles holy water over her.

Poor Clarimonde. No sooner had she been touched by the holy dew, than her beautiful body crumbled to dust; it was no more than a frightful and shapeless mixture of cinders and half-burned bones.[26]

Serapion exults in his holy work, but Romuald tells us:

I lowered my head; within myself I felt the creation of great ruin.[27]

As the story ends, Clarimonde makes one last appearance as a spirit who chastises Romuald sadly:

"Why did you listen to that imbecile preacher? Weren't you happy? What had I done to you that you should violate my poor tomb to expose once again the miseries of my non-being? . . . Adieu, you will regret me."[28]

And regret her Romuald does, though he ends his letter with the pious advice:

> Never look at a woman and walk with your eyes fixed on the ground because however chaste and calm you may be, it only takes a moment for you to lose eternity.[29]

What the reader will remember beyond this trivial piety is the phrase that precedes it and in which is distilled all of Romuald's regret: "The peace of my soul has been dearly purchased. God's love has not been enough to replace hers."[30]

In an important sense, Gautier's *Amorous Death* is not properly a tale of terror. It is instead, an intensely romantic short novel in which the delights as well as the torments of love are described magnificently. The emotional thrust of the story is delight, rather than fear. Vampire fiction should fill us with revulsion. Instead, despite the pious self-denunciation at the story's end, we cannot help feeling that Romuald made the worse of his two choices. Between a desiccated salvation and an ecstatic damnation, he was a deluded fool to have chosen the first.

From that tale of rosy, if macabre sensuality, we turn now to "The Vourdalak Family," a Russian story published in 1847 by Aleksei Tolstoi. The subtitle of the story is "The Unpublished Fragment of the Memoirs of Someone Unknown." The narrator is the Marquis d'Urfé, who tells the story in Vienna of 1815. D'Urfé describes a voyage he took into Moldavia, where he went to escape the inconveniences of an unhappy love affair with the Duchess Gramont. In Moldavia he comes to a village whose inhabitants seem to be very disturbed, though they treat him cordially; Gorcha, the father of the family, is about to leave home in pursuit of an outlaw named Alibek, who has been ravaging the countryside. Gorcha warns his family:

> "If I come back at the end of ten days, as you value your souls, do not let me in. In that case, I command you that you forget that I am your father and that you drive an aspen stake through my heart, no matter what I may say because then I will be a cursed Vourdalak, who has come to suck your blood."[31]

In an aside, d'Urfé tells us that vourdalaks, or vampires, prefer members of their own family or their closest friends for their victims. Once dead, the relatives become vampires, too.

In the ten-day interval during which Gorcha is gone, d'Urfé falls in love with Sdenka, sister to Gorcha's two sons, Georges and Pierre. When the waiting period is over, Gorcha is seen approaching the house, but his dog, his fur bristling, sets up a furious barking. It is the first clue we have that Gorcha has passed the time limit he has set himself. Meanwhile, despite the warning Gorcha gave his family, he is welcomed into the home, but Gorcha neither eats nor drinks what is offered him. However, he reports that he has caught up with Alibek, and with that, he displays the brigand's head.

By now, his two sons suspect the truth about their father.

The rest of the story, with various shifts and turns, is taken up with the manner in which Gorcha vampirizes the members of his family one by one, and with what happens to d'Urfé who first manages to escape from the nest of vampires but then returns to the village six months later. Unable to find lodging in the village, he decides to visit the home of his former hosts, the Gorcha family. In their home, he finds an empty bedroom, where he falls asleep.

> I opened my eyes and I saw Sdenka beside my bed. The moon shown so brightly that I could distinguish the smallest details of her adorable features which had been so dear to me before . . . she seemed more beautiful and more developed.[32]

For a little while, the conversation between the two has the sad tone of lovers who have departed. Then Sdenka urges him fiercely to get away; but entranced by her beauty, he determines to stay. "Meanwhile, little by little, I noticed a great change in Sdenka. Her former shyness had given way to a strange indifference that had something crude in it. Finally, I saw with surprise that her manner of being with me was much different from the modesty that had formerly distinguished her."[33] D'Urfé thinks to himself: "What difference does it make? If Sdenka is no longer a Diana as I once thought she was, I can compare her to another Goddess, no less amiable and, God be praised, I prefer the role of Adonis to that of Acteon."[34]

He decides then to make the most of the moment, but, as he is playfully decking her out in jewels, he tries to place the enamel crucifix that the Duchess Gramont had given him on her neck. Sdenka recoils from it, then announces that he must go.

D'Urfé's flight from the vampirized Sdenka and her family is utterly bizarre. As he spurs his horse's flanks, he hears Sdenka calling, "Wait, wait, my dear! I love you more than my own soul. Wait, wait, your blood belongs to me."[35] Sdenka leaps up onto his galloping horse and endeavors to drink his blood. D'Urfé, a skilled horseman, manages to flings her from him.

But he is not out of the woods yet. He is pursued by Georges and his brother Pierre, whom he escapes, only to find Gorcha chasing him. Gorcha's daughter-in-law and her children are also part of the pack. The daughter-in-law, like Ajax hurling stones at Hector, catapults one after another of her children after him.

By now the story has taken on the sort of ludicrous and meaningless hilarity we associate with a Three Stooges comedy. And that, after all, may be what Tolstoi, who would never see the Three Stooges, may have had in mind: an absurdist satire on the politics of early nineteenth-century Europe whose moral may be "The family that slays together, stays together."

With Prosper Mérimée's novel *Lokis* (1869), we get a vampire tale that should be dear to the hearts of language buffs because of the way it fuses a passion for linguistic scholarship with a romantic tale of love and death. Mérimée, who among other things is the author of the novella *Carmen*, tells an unhurried tale of a linguistic scholar named Wittembach who travels to Lithuania in search of a rare volume, the *Catechismus Samogiticus*. There, in the home of the Count Szémioth, he finds the book — but he finds much else besides.

Count Szémioth is the son of a woman who, while pregnant with him, was attacked and mauled by a bear, a trauma so dreadful that it left her bereft of reason. As an adult, the count is also attacked by a female bear, but he plays dead and the bear, "being an animal that does not eat cadavers," left him alone.

The count, we learn, is in love with the Lady Iwinska, who is young, beautiful, irrepressible, whimsical, and given to practical jokes. She seems uninterested in the count's suit. She does however, keep him dangling, because "the Count Szémioth, is a young fisherman, very foolish, who exposes himself to my claws and I to attenuate my pleasure undertake to fascinate him by dancing around him for a while."[36] In short, she is a beautiful flibbertigibbet, a coquette, on whom, one suspects Lucy Westenra is modeled.

After a considerable number of pages dealing with folklore and language, a new theme is introduced into what thus far has been a friendly and detailed account of noble life in Lithuania in the course of which the narrator has told the story of his own adventures in Uruguay where he was once lost on the plains of that country and where, to survive, he imitated a local practice of the gauchos, and drank his horse's blood. That story sinks deeply into the count's mind.

Meanwhile, the narrator tells us, despite every indication that Iwinska is impervious to Szémioth's suit, two months after his departure from Lithuania, he receives an invitation to Count Szémioth's wedding with the mischievous Iwinska. Not only that, our linguist narrator who, it turns out, is also an ordained minister, is asked to perform the wedding. The narrator returns and performs the marriage, which is interrupted briefly by the appearance of the Count's insane mother. The festivities are described in considerable detail, and the happy couple retire to their bridal chamber. At this point, with only a page and a half of the story left to go, every terror that a vampire tale is capable of creating unfolds, as the Count Szémioth, long toyed with and teased by his bride, becomes a vampire on his wedding night.

———◦———

I do not know whether Stoker read any of the tales I have discussed here. It is enough to know that they were in the mainstream of the fiction written before his time.

The novel *Varney, the Vampyre* is a braying ass of a totally different color from those Continental vampire fictions.

The complete title of the Englishman Rymer's 1847 wild and wonderful book *Varney, the Vampyre or The Feast of Blood* gives us immediately some inkling of Rymer's marketplace agility with words. For a long time, the book's author was thought to be Thomas Preskett Prest, but more recent scholarship has established that it was written by James Malcolm Rymer (1814–1881). Writing in *The Penguin Encyclopedia of Horror and the Supernatural*, E. F. Bleiler warns us:

> *Varney, the Vampyre* is not recommended reading for most people; it is chaotic, badly written, padded and somewhat longer than *War and Peace* and *Gone with the Wind* combined.[37]

*Varney, the Vampyre* is everything that Bleiler says it is, but it is also a bumptiously enthusiastic horror fiction in which the author's delight in all that is loathsome, ghastly, lubricious, and macabre keeps pace with our willingness to be so entertained.

# VARNEY, THE VAMPYRE;

## OR,

# THE FEAST OF BLOOD

### A Romance,

## CHAPTER I.

----" How graves give up their dead,
And how the night air hideous grows
With shrieks !"

MIDNIGHT. — THE HAIL-STORM. — THE
DREADFUL VISITOR.—THE VAMPYRE.

THE solemn tones of an old cathedral clock have announced midnight—the air is thick and heavy—a strange, death-like stillness pervades all nature. Like the ominous calm which precedes some more than usually terrific outbreak of the elements, they seem to have paused even in their ordinary fluctuations, to gather a terrific strength for the great effort. A faint peal of thunder now comes from far off. Like a signal gun for the battle of the winds to begin, it appeared to awaken them from their lethargy, and one awful, warring hurricane swept over a whole city, producing more devastation in the four or five minutes it lasted, than would a half century of ordinary phenomena.

It was as if some giant had blown upon some toy town, and scattered many of the buildings before the hot blast of his terrific

*Opening page of* Varney, the Vampyre

In *A Dream of Dracula,* I commented:

The effect is splendid. Tinsel thunder; cellophane lightning. Death, blood, pistol shots, stabbings, caves, moonlight resurrections. Indeed, Varney is resurrected so frequently that the idea of dying takes on a thoroughly ludicrous aspect. . . . Varney is shot, hanged, staked, drowned. It doesn't matter. All he requires is a little moonlight to make his corpse twitch and jerk. Before long, he is among the living again, feeling the revival of an old thirst: "I was . . . ruminating what I should do, until a strange feeling crept over me that I should like—what? Blood!—raw blood, reeking and hot, bubbling and juicy, from the veins of some gasping victim."[38]

Rymer's prose neither requires—nor can bear—analysis. He was a penny-a-line writer who was worth every penny. But his plotting is so inventive, his voyeur's enthusiasm so irrepressible that, without supposing for a moment that he is a great writer, one can form an attachment to an author whose work is so tumultuously, so horridly busy.

Yes, the book is certainly too long, but no one is required to— perhaps no one can—read it at a single sitting. I suggest leaving it on a convenient table in the bedroom or the bathroom, so that one can, at intervals, read ten or twelve pages for the sheer fun of it.

Here, for example, is a typically breathless scene as Ringwood, fearful that his daughter Clara has been vampirized, hears a strange scraping sound in the church where she is in her coffin. It is midnight:

"She is my own, my beautiful Clara, as she ever was, and as, while life remains, to me she ever will be.

At the moment that he uttered these words a slight noise met his ears. . . .

"What was that?" he said. "What was that?"

All was still again, and he was upon the point of convincing himself, that the noise was either some accidental one, or the creation of his own fancy when it came again.

He had no doubt this time. It was a perceptible, scraping, strange sort of sound. . . .

Then slowly and solemnly there crossed his excited vision a figure all clothed in white . . . and he knew by their fashion that they were not worn by the living, and that it was some inhabitant of the tomb that he now looked upon . . . his heart told him who it was. Yes, it was his Clara.

It was no dream.[39]

From the squeaky-shrieky prose of Rymer's lightweight but amusing *Varney, the Vampyre,* we turn to Sheridan Le Fanu's somber masterpiece, *Carmilla.*

Le Fanu (1814–1873), the grandnephew of the playwright Richard Brinsley Sheridan, had a successful career as a writer of scary fiction. Though he was the author of fourteen novels, only one, *Uncle Silas* (1864), which is a fine fusion of the locked-room mystery with the horror tale, is still worth reading. His best work is to be found among his short stories and novellas. Though he shared with the writers of Gothic fiction who preceded him the desire to produce works that frightened their readers, Le Fanu enlarged the focus of the genre by his close and often subtle analysis of the psychology of his characters.

Le Fanu's interest in the processes of the mind opened the way for the scary psychological fiction that came after him: Stevenson's *The Strange Case of Dr. Jekyll and Mr. Hyde* (1886), Wilde's *The Picture of Dorian Gray* (1891), Stoker's *Dracula* (1897), and Henry James's *The Turn of the Screw* (1898).

In his short story "Green Tea," which would seem to be a straightforward account of how Mr. Jennings is haunted by a ghostly monkey, Le Fanu gives us the clear sense that the phantom creature that torments him has its origins in some twist in Jennings's mind related to his ambivalence about his duties as a Christian minister.

On the surface, "Mr. Justice Harbottle" is a dynamic ghost story in which the haunting should be of interest to us, but which, in addition, gives us a portrait of the lustful, swinish, and tyrannical Harbottle that is so vivid that we can hardly wait to see the very human monster destroyed.

*Carmilla,* Le Fanu's 1872 vampire novella, may be his finest work. The staking scene at the end, particularly, clearly influenced Stoker. A nineteen-year-old first-person narrator named Laura tells us that she is the only daughter of an Englishman who retired on a small pension from the Austrian army to a castle somewhere in Styria, a province in eastern Austria. Laura confides the homely detail that "A small income, in that part of the world, goes a great way . . . here in this lonely and primitive place . . . everything is so marvellously cheap."[40]

One of the sources of power of this novella is the way that its setting is so profoundly isolated from the rest of the world. The nearest village is seven miles away; the nearest castle, twenty miles away. Laura's extreme loneliness, coupled with the fact that she has just entered into womanhood, are important elements in her readiness to be victimized, as we will soon see.

*Joseph Sheridan Le Fanu. From an ink drawing by the novelist's son, Brinsley Le Fanu, 1916.*

We are told, too, that when Laura was only six years old, she had a nighttime visitor to her room. She says that she

> saw a solemn, but very pretty face looking at me from the side of the bed. It was that of a young lady who was kneeling, with her hands under the coverlet. . . . She caressed me with her hands, and lay down beside me on the bed, and drew me towards her, smilng. . . . I was wakened by a sensation as if two needles ran into my breast very deep at the same moment, and I cried loudly. The lady started back, with her eyes fixed on me, and then slipped down upon the floor, and, as I thought, hid herself under the bed.[41]

At the time that Laura's story begins, this episode is merely an old memory. But the serenity of her life is ended suddenly when a runaway coach breaks down on the road bordering the castle. Two people are rescued from the disabled coach: an older woman "tall, but not thin, and dressed in black velvet . . ." and a young lady who "appeared to be lifeless."

The older woman explains that she is on a mission of life and death and begs Laura's father to take her daughter into his charge for a while. Urged by the lonely Laura, who anticipates a friendship with the interesting young woman, he acquiesces. Suddenly, Carmilla, which is the young woman's name, is a guest in the house while her mother goes off on her mysterious journey.

At first, Carmilla is a welcome addition to the lonely inhabitants of the castle. Then, though she has learned to love Carmilla, it is borne in upon Laura that she had seen her twelve years ago on the night of the strange visitation. When she confides her conviction to Carmilla, Carmilla says, "At all events, it does seem as if we were destined, from our earliest childhood, to be friends. . . ."[42]

Very soon we perceive that more than friendship is at stake. Carmilla rouses strange feelings in Laura: "I did feel, as she said, 'drawn towards her', but there was also something of repulsion."[43]

Though their relationship becomes closer and closer, the ambiguity (and ambivalence) surrounding it intensifies and we get mysterious outbursts from Carmilla, like this one:

> "Dearest, your little heart is wounded; think me not cruel because I obey the irresistible law of my strength and weakness; if your dear heart is wounded, my wild heart bleeds with yours. In the rapture of

my humiliation I live in your warm life, and you shall die—sweetly die—into mine. I cannot help it; as I draw near to you, you, in your turn, will draw near to others, and learn the rapture of that cruelty, which yet is love; so, for a while, seek to know no more of me and mine, but trust me with all your loving spirit."[44]

With the passing days, Carmilla's caresses puzzle Laura:

. . . it was like the ardour of a lover; it embarrassed me; it was hateful and yet overpowering and with gloating eyes she drew me to her, and her hot lips travelled along my cheek in kisses.

    Was she [Carmilla] . . . subject to brief visitations of insanity; or was there here a disguise and a romance? . . . What if a boyish lover had found his way into the house, and sought to prosecute his suit in masquerade . . .[45]

We see that, early on, Le Fanu guesses at the way the vampire's blood-taking can seem to be a form of intimacy, and can stand for the androgynous nature of love.

    If *Carmilla* is a tour de force because, in the Victorian Age, Le Fanu could explore, albeit within the context of a vampire fiction, the power of a "love that dare not speak its name," it is nevertheless a mistake to think of it as a lesbian fiction. The theme of the entire story is encapsulated in the phrase, "[you will] learn the rapture of that cruelty, which yet is love," and the paragraph in which it appears is as close to being a fully expressed understanding of the complex nature of love as I have ever read. James L. Campbell Sr.'s observation, "Central to Le Fanu's conception in *Carmilla* is his metaphor equating vampirism with lesbianism . . ."[46] seems singularly wrongheaded because it trivializes Le Fanu's achievement. Le Fanu takes no unseemly interest in the fact that both the vampire and her victim are women. His concern is his discovery of "the rapture of that cruelty, which yet is love." Surely it is a mark of greatness to have been aware of that profundity and to have embodied it in believable—and anguished—fiction.

    The last of the precursor fictions we ought to look at is Stoker's own "Dracula's Guest," which, though it was not published until 1914 by Mrs. Stoker in the collection, *Dracula's Guest and Other Weird Stories*, was intended to be the second chapter of *Dracula* at one stage in Stoker's planning. The internal details of the story do not fit the plot of the novel as we now have it.

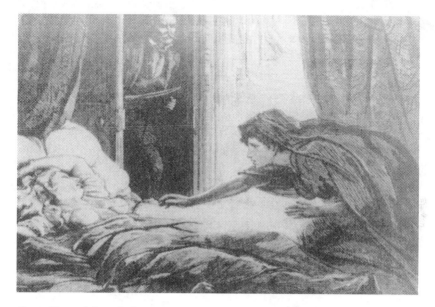

*Carmilla and her victim*

"Dracula's Guest" does not work very well as a short story because the meaning of the events it describes elude the reader who has not read *Dracula*. Without the novel as a reference point, all that we have is an unaccountable story of a young man caught in a storm on the outskirts of Munich in early summer. He takes refuge from a snowstorm (in early June!) in the mausoleum of a certain Countess Dolingen of Gratz who killed herself in 1801. When the mausoleum is illuminated by a flash of lightning, he sees

> a beautiful woman, with rounded cheeks and red lips . . . [who] rose for a moment of agony, while she was lapped in the flame, and her bitter scream of pain was drowned in the thunder crash.[47]

After a lapse of consciousness, the young man wakes to find an enormous wolf lying on top of him, whose body warmth has evidently kept him from freezing to death. Moments later, he is rescued by soldiers who, under instructions from Count Dracula, have come looking for him.

The story reads like a segment of a larger work and would not be worth our while if it did not cast some light on the evolution of *Dracula* in Stoker's mind. This young man, for instance, can evidently read Russian, a skill that Jonathan Harker does not claim for himself. As in the novel, we get a reference to Gottfried August Bürger's long poem "Lenore." And the mysterious appearance and then disappearance of "a man tall and thin," whose presence sets the coach horses screaming, reminds us of the coachman who drives Harker to Dracula's castle. The atmospherics of *Dracula* are prefigured here, too. Walpurgisnight stands in for St. George's Eve; there is the same howling "as of many dogs or wolves." In the glimpse of the red-lipped countess, we get a foreshadowing of the three loathly ladies whom Jonathan Harker meets in the novel. Here, too, the young man looks out at a scene through his eyelashes and smells the acrid breath of a powerful creature. There is, too, an ambiguity about whether the young man has actually been bitten by a vampire. One of the soldiers in the rescue party says of him, "He is all right; the skin [of his throat] is not pierced."[48] But moments later, we get the following exchange,

"Dog! That was no dog," cut in the man who had exhibited such fear. "I think I know a wolf when I see one."

The young officer answered calmly: "I said a dog."

"Dog," reiterated the other ironically. . . . "Look at his throat. Is that the work of a dog, master?"[49]

Finally, there is Dracula's courtly premonitory warning telegram to the maître d'hotel of the Quatre Saisons, in which we hear the first accents of the mysterious count who is waiting in Transylvania for his guest. A voice which, when we come to the next chapter will become ominously familiar.

# In Which Bram Stoker, the Mysterious Inventor of the King Vampire, Dracula, Steps Onstage

*"... the child that up to now she had clutched strenuously to her breast, growling over it as a dog growls over a bone."*

STOKER, DEFENDING HIMSELF AGAINST THE CHARGE THAT HE DID NOT KNOW THE LANDSCAPE OF TRANSYLVANIA, REPLIED, "TREES ARE TREES, MOUNTAINS ARE, GENERALLY SPEAKING, MOUNTAINS, NO MATTER IN WHAT COUNTRY YOU FIND THEM, AND ONE DESCRIPTION MAY BE MADE TO ANSWER FOR ALL."

——BARBARA BELFORD, BRAM STOKER, 220.

HOW SWEET A THING IT IS FOR A STRONG HEALTHY MAN WITH A WOMAN'S EYES AND A CHILD'S WISHES TO FEEL THAT HE CAN SPEAK SO TO A MAN WHO CAN BE IF HE WISHES FATHER, BROTHER AND WIFE TO HIS SOUL.

——BRAM STOKER, LETTER TO WALT WHITMAN (FEBRUARY 18, 1872)

**B**ram Stoker, the author of *Dracula*, is almost as ambiguous a figure as his King Vampire, and much of the ambiguity is by his own design. As we will see, Stoker cultivated the art of being a public man as a way of keeping the private one hidden.

Until recently, the two biographies of Bram Stoker that we had were, each in their own way, nearly useless at illuminating his character: Harry Ludlam's *A Biography of Dracula*[1] and Daniel Farson's *The Man Who Wrote Dracula*.[2] Neither author was courteous enough to name Stoker in the main title, and both books are not much better than gossipy anecdotal treatments of his life. Ludlam gave a barely useful summary of what was known publicly about Stoker but he shied away from anything like character analysis or judgment. On the other hand, Farson, Stoker's great-nephew, ventured a short distance in both directions, but his book, essentially undocumented, reads too frequently like a collection of ill-intentioned family anecdotes.

We now have Barbara Belford's *Bram Stoker: A Biography of the Author of Dracula*, which is a closely researched, scrupulous, and responsible account of Stoker's life. Belford's book is rich in the kind of detail that scholars can find in libraries and archives and it documents abundantly the world of the British nineteenth-century theater in which Stoker lived. But Belford, too, found Stoker

> not an obliging person to think about for five years. He frustrated intimate probing; his reticence was monumental . . . In response to the question, "Who are you?" I imagine him saying, "I am who you want me to be."[3]

And a bit later, he is described as passing through memoirs and "leaving a whiff of lofty manners and an aftertaste of no identity."[4]

And yet, a man who was capable of writing one of the world's most terrifying fictions, a man who could invent a figure of evil so overpowering that it has taken on mythic proportions, cannot have lived the life of a man with no identity. There is a real Bram Stoker, but who he is, may leave us grieving for the tragic figure that emerges when we have finally pieced together what he wanted us to know with what he tried to hide.

Stoker was born not far from Dublin in Clontarf, Ireland, into a Protestant family on November 8, 1847. He was the third of the seven children that his mother, Charlotte Stoker, then twenty-nine years old, would bring into the world.

For Ireland, the 1840s were a dreadful decade. It was the time of the Great Irish Potato Famine. Barbara Belford writes:

> Out of a population of eight million, five and a half million were dependent on agriculture. There were riots, looting, marches; landlords evicted tenants too weak to tend their crops; overcrowded poorhouses locked out the homeless, and starving families roamed the countryside. More than one and a half million people died from starvation and disease, and an equal number emigrated.[5]

It must be emphasized that the Stokers were Protestant Irish: members of the privileged class known as the Protestant Ascendancy, the minority rulers of Ireland's Catholic majority. Indeed, Abraham Stoker, Bram Stoker's father, was a civil servant working for that government in Dublin for nearly fifty years. Sheridan Le Fanu, that other Irish author of terror tales, whose vampire novella, *Carmilla* (1872), preceded Stoker's *Dracula* by twenty-five years, was also a member of that class, as were Oscar Wilde and George Bernard Shaw.

Abraham Stoker, was an inward, quiet, theater-loving man of little or no ambition. For several generations before him, the Stokers had been solidly middle or lower-middle class. Sometimes they were shoemakers, sometimes goldsmiths. Abraham's grandfather, William, was a tailor who began his career as a maker of stays for women's underwear. Abraham himself seems to have been the kind of man who, by temperament, does not make waves. He spent years as a minor bureaucrat, keeping his family's financial head above water, but only barely. He took on a mountain of debt to be able to give three of his sons a medical education and to send Bram to Trinity College. At the time of his retirement, at the age of sixty-five, the most that he could say of himself, after nearly fifty years of service, was, "I can with truth say that I am not conscious of ever having unduly neglected my duties."[6] When he was sixty-five, to save money, he took his wife and two daughters to live on the Continent, moving from from one inexpensive pension in France or Switzerland to another. Stoker's mother, on the other hand, though she, too, descended from a family that was solidly middle class—tailors, shoemakers, hatters—was a feisty woman, twenty-five years younger than her husband, who in the course of raising seven children, managed at the same time to create an aura of creativity in the home by telling her children stories about her own childhood. She was also something of an early feminist who defended the rights of the poor and made public speeches on their behalf.

Stoker made much of the fact that, until his seventh year, he was bedridden with a disease which, though he was the nephew of one doctor and the brother of three others, has never been identified. In any case, at the age of seven, he recovered miraculously, but the effect of the years of inaction made him bookish. And yet, unlike the usual experience of studious children who grow up to be inward and reserved, by the time he was enrolled in Trinity College, he had become the sort of young man who, on every known psychological test today, would score high as an extrovert.

While his father was drudging his way through the civil service, the seventeen-year-old Bram Stoker entered Trinity College in Dublin, where it was expected he would acquire the education that would enable him to follow in his father's footsteps. By now, he was anything but the invalid that his sickly childhood had promised. Harry Ludlam describes him as

> over six-feet two in his stockings [he] weighed over twelve stone [168 pounds]. A rich auburn beard, contrasting with his brown hair, added to his strong presence, and he was as quick, confident, and big in conversation as in build.[7]

At Trinity he was what nowadays we would call a jock. He was a long-distance walker, a rugby player, and a weight lifter. In addition to having a sound body he was in energetic pursuit of a sound mind.

He was particularly attracted to the debating society and was a member of the prestigious university organizations: the Hist and the Phil, the philosophical society, of which he became president in 1867. In the debating society, he discovered that he had two talents:

he was a ready speaker and he had a theatrical flair. He already had a taste for theater that he had acquired from his father. For a while Bram nursed the ambition to become an actor, and occasionally he tried out for and got parts in local plays.

Then, on August 28, 1867, there occurred an event that, at the time, seemed to have very little significance. The twenty-nine-year-old Henry Irving, destined to become the greatest actor on the Victorian stage, appeared in Dublin as Captain Absolute in Richard Brinsley Sheridan's classic comedy of manners, *The Rivals*. Stoker was impressed by the authenticity of Irving's performance; but more than that, he was offended when the local newspapers made no or scant mention of Irving's achievement.

Irving returned to Dublin in 1871. In the interval, he had become a star of the English stage, mostly because of his interpretation of the role of Mathias in *The Bells*, a play based on the French drama, *Le Juif Polonais*, "The Polish Jew" (1869), by the French duo Erckmann-Chatrian. On this second visit to Dublin, Irving appeared as Digby Grant in the comedy *Two Roses*. For a second time, no reviews of Irving's performance appeared in the press, which so irritated the young Stoker that he applied for and got the job of unpaid drama critic for the *Dublin Evening Mail*. By a curious coincidence, the paper was partly owned by Sheridan Le Fanu. It was a plucky thing for Stoker to do because it meant that he would now have to write his responses to the plays he saw instead of fantasizing that he had written them.

*The Mail* was an attractive place for him to work. Barbara Belford writes:

> Stoker found a group of friends there who were . . . every bit as disreputable as those in the theater. Shabby and smoke-filled, the news room was a raucous all-male bastion, offering the kind of camaraderie Stoker enjoyed so much at college.[8]

Stoker became a busy young man: part college student, part civil servant, part bachelor about town. "Tall and graceful, he was much in demand as a dance partner; his waltzing expertise was noted with approval at the season's balls," says Belford.[9] One woman describes how she longed to dance with him because he represented "triumph, twirling, ecstasy, elysium, giddiness, ices, and flirtation!"[10]

What is missing in the account of these bright green years, is evidence of Stoker's amorous involvement with women. Though he liked playing the Dutch uncle to young women, he was very careful to lay down the limits of his feelings for those who asked his advice. To one, he wrote:

> since I have your permission may I talk to you like a father. I am not a bit spoony about you. I say this lest you should ever misconstrue my purpose in writing so often. . . . A correspondence which is neither business, amatory or platonic requires some preliminary explanation.[11]

In 1876 Henry Irving was back in Dublin, this time playing Hamlet. And now there was a young drama critic named Bram Stoker, who fell all over himself praising Irving's performance in *The Mail,* calling Irving "a histrionic genius." With the lavish praise, there were mixed some minor negative comments meant to display the independence of his mind. "Irving's voice lacks power to be strong in some tones. . . ."[12]

Just the same, Irving was pleased by the review and invited its author to dinner at the Shelbourne Hotel, not once, but twice. On the first evening, the two men discovered an affinity that kept them talking almost all night. On the occasion of the second dinner, the overwhelming event that was to change and, in the perception of some, to mar Stoker's life forever took place.

Irving, it should be recalled, was

> now thirty eight-years-old. . . . Bram found him an awkwardly tall, spare man, whose long hair swept back from a broad brow and flowed over the back of his collar . . . a lean, sensitive face, piercing eyes . . . bushy eyebrows. . . .[13]

On the occasion of that second dinner, Irving, as a way of acknowledging that he and his young admirer were on the same wavelength, decided to read a poem by Thomas Hood—the same Thomas Hood who had written "The Song of the Shirt" and "The Bridge of Sighs," two of the most melancholy and lachrymose poems in the English language. This night Irving recited Hood's poem "Eugene Aram," a bathetic tale of murder.

The poem's protagonist, Eugene Aram, is an usher (a minor official in an English court of law), who has been made "very lean/And pale, and leaden-eyed" by overmuch study. Sitting in a sun-lit field, Aram sees a boy engrossed in a book that tells the story of Cain and

Abel. The tormented Aram sits beside the boy, to whom he recounts his most recent dream, in which he saw himself murdering an old man for his money. It does not take readers long to guess that Eugene Aram's dream was not a dream at all:

> That very night, while gentle sleep
> The urchin eyelids kissed,
> Two stern-faced men set out from Lynn,
> Through the cold and heavy mist;
> And Eugene Aram walked between,
> With gyves upon his wrist.[14]

One might expect that Irving's recitation of this soppy poem should have produced laughter. But we are dealing with the Victorian Age, in which moral posturing, particularly among men, was a serious pursuit. Even so, what happened after Irving's recitation is bizarre. Stoker tells us:

> That experience I shall never—can never—forget . . . such was Irving's commanding force, so great was the magnetism of his genius, so profound was the sense of his dominance that I sat spellbound. Outwardly I was as of stone . . . here was incarnate power, incarnate passion . . . Here was indeed Eugene Aram as he was face to face with his Lord; his very soul aflame in the light of his abiding horror . . . the awful horror on the murderer's face as the ghost in his brain seemed to take external shape before his eyes. After the climax of horror the Actor was able by art and habit to control himself to the narrative mood whilst he spoke a few concluding lines of the poem.
>   Then he collapsed half fainting.[15]

Irving's collapse may simply have been the result of that expenditure of feeling that actors can summon up at will. Or, as Irving's grandson suggests, it might have been a brilliant piece of Machiavellianism. He writes: ". . . perhaps he had some ulterior purpose in doing so [reciting the poem] . . . the effect of his recitation on Stoker was all that Irving had hoped. . . ."[16] Stoker's response to Irving's collapse is an altogether different matter.
   He tells us disingenuously:

> I can only say that after a few seconds of stony silence following his collapse I burst into something like hysterics.

Let me say . . . that I was no hysterical subject. I was no green youth; no weak individual, yielding to a superior emotional force. I was as men go a strong man, strong in many ways . . .

I was a very strong man. . . . When, therefore, after his recitation I became hysterical it was distinctly a surprise to my friends; for myself surprise had no part in my then state of mind. Irving seemed much moved by the occurrence.[17]

When Irving recovered from his collapse,

. . . he went into his room and after a couple of minutes brought me out his photograph with an inscription on it, the ink still wet: "My dear friend Stoker. God bless you! God bless you!! Henry Irving. Dublin, December 3, 1876."[18]

Stoker clearly took that picture—and the tribute of that wet ink as an accolade—as letters written in flame. In *A Dream of Dracula*, I commented on this exchange:

I want to convey something of Stoker's energetic unconsciousness about the true nature of manhood, which requires no such elaborate apology for the experience of falling in love, even when it happens between men.[19]

With Barbara Belford's biography before me, it is less clear that what was taking place between the two men was a simultaneous recognition of love of the sort that is classically exemplified by lovers like Romeo and Juliet glimpsing each other for the first time across a crowded space. Stoker may have thought that soul had looked into soul. Irving, more likely, recognized a useful instrument in Stoker.

But to illuminate a little, what had been happening to Stoker in the years before this event, one needs to go back to Stoker's experience at Trinity where, under the tutelage of Edward Dowden, one of his professors at the university, Stoker was introduced to the work of the American poet Walt Whitman. Stoker's response to Whitman was overdetermined much in the same way as was his reaction to Irving.

On February 18, 1872, Stoker sat down to write Whitman a letter, which he did not mail until four years later. It was an unguarded and revealing letter in which he poured out his heart to the good gray American poet, whose warm praises toward the comradeship of men, especially in the series of Calamus poems, had touched a hidden nerve in Stoker. Calamus is the name for an especially tough, long-speared, and fragrant grass. Whitman himself never publicly acknowledged the homerotic content of the poems. Barbara Belford says that in that letter, Stoker's youthful prose "reeked of adoration and insecurity."[20] If a puppy could write with the fervor of its wagging tail, we might get something like Stoker's letter to Whitman.

Stoker describes himself artlessly, to Whitman as

> six-feet two inches high and twelve stone weight naked . . . I am ugly but strong and determined and have a large bump over my eyebrows. I have a heavy jaw and a big mouth and thick lips—sensitive nostrils—a snubnose and straight hair.[21]

Stoker is not only posturing, he is preening.

Anyone seeing pictures of the young or middle-aged Stoker—even of the aging Stoker—would be impressed by the ordinariness of his good looks. He would fit nicely into any room where establishment power brokers meet, whether stockbrokers, bankers, or tenured professors. What seeps through the coded diction of Stoker's letter is a cry of gratitude for a writer who has confronted his homosexuality. Stoker admitted that he read Whitman behind locked doors, and then went on:

> You are a true man, and I would like to be one myself, and so I would be toward you as a brother, and as a pupil to his master. . . . You have shaken off the shackles and your wings are free. I have the shackles on my shoulders still—but I have no wings.[22]

It is easy enough to laugh at this gawky and unrestrained letter, but it would be kinder to see in it the first signs of the denial that would characterize the rest of Stoker's life and that would turn it into a pilgrimage of pain.

Whitman's response was both whimsical and affectionate. "You did well to write me so unconventionally, so fresh, so manly, and so affectionately. . . ." He was especially pleased by Stoker's description of him as "father, and brother and wife to his soul."[23] Whitman understood shrewdly enough that Stoker was not writing to Whit-

**Bram Stoker**

man, the American poet, but that this was a letter from Stoker to himself.

Now let us turn again to Dublin and the climactic events in the Shelbourne Hotel. Whatever had taken place there had its consequences two years later, when Stoker received an abrupt summons from Irving to join him in Glasgow, where he would assume duties as Irving's acting-manager.

Meanwhile, Stoker, dazzled by Irving as he was, was courting Florence Balcombe. Beautiful but poor, she was the daughter of a military man, Lieutenant-Colonel James Balcombe, and the third of five daughters in a family of seven. Born on July 17, 1858, she was eleven years younger than Stoker. "The pretty, but penniless neighbor who lived at Number One on The Crescent. . . . Her dowry was ethereal beauty. Tall at five feet eight, with a Parisian profile, gray-blue eyes, and fine brown hair, who was fragile where he was robust, talkative where he was shy, curious where he was distracted."[24]

Here we get one more of those strange turns of fate, which no doubt gave rise to the Portuguese proverb, "God writes straight with crooked lines." Before Stoker courted her, the pretty Florence Balcombe had been courted by Oscar Wilde. David Skal says that Wilde became enamored by her in the summer of 1875, when she was a ravishing seventeen-year-old. "He escorted her to church, drew her portrait, wrote her poetry and by Christmas presented her with a small gold cross inscribed with their names."[25] Wilde would always have warm feelings for Florence. When she married Bram Stoker three years later, Wilde wrote to ask her to return the cross to him.

Stoker's suit prospered, and Florence and Bram were married on December 4, 1878, when she was nineteen and he was thirty-one. With a brand-new bride, Stoker gave up his sinecure at Dublin Castle, the Irish civil service, in which he had written the dreary manual *The Duties of Clerks of Petty Sessions in Ireland*, to link his life and his fortunes with Henry Irving and the newly refurbished Lyceum Theatre in London.

It is worth lingering over Stoker's decision for a little while. Its heroism and courage have not been sufficiently emphasized by Stoker's biographers. If we see Stoker as a young man dutifully performing his dreary work at Dublin Castle, while he haunts the theaters at night; if we see his encounter with Henry Irving as suddenly opening for him a vista of the life of the imagination for which clearly he had been longing in his years as a civil servant, we must see his decision to join Irving in London as the moment when he cast the die in favor of the dangerous life of the imagination. And he did indeed enter that life, though on terms and in ways that were finally demeaning. But in 1879, we have a plucky Stoker, risking his new marriage, abandoning his pension, to follow his dream. His father spent fifty years drudging away, and it is not too much to see in Stoker's decision a stalwart rejection of his father's passivity in the face of reality. It was a leap toward life.

The Lyceum Theatre could seat 1,500 patrons and with Henry Irving as the owner and theatrical lodestar, it would become the jewel in the crown of London theaters. Irving had had the theater completely redecorated:

changing [its] mood. . . . In their new decor, sage green and blue predominated, emulating the shimmering peacock; the ceiling was pale blue and gold; gaslit candles in wine-colored shades flickered off gilt moldings; escalloped shells shielded the footlights' golden glare. From the vestibule to the ascending staircase to the gilded auditorium, the Lyceum atmosphere was half museum, half church, unlike any other theater in Victorian England.[26]

Stoker's job as acting manager, for which he received £22 a week (a generous salary at the time), is not easy to define. He was, in fact, a combination of gofer, front man for Henry Irving, glorified secretary, accountant, speech writer and theater manager; but, most importantly, he was available to Irving as a sounding board, an unthreatening companion. A man who could give up endless evenings at home with his wife, to spend them in the company of the actor who, wired after his performances, could not sleep and relied on Stoker to be with him through his wakeful hours.

Stoker tells us: "I shall be very well within the mark when I say that during my time of working with Henry Irving I have written in his name nearer half a million than a quarter of a million letters."[27] When the Lyceum company was on tour, Stoker booked the train travel, arranged for the accommodations of the staff, of which there were fifty-four members, and soothed bruised feelings. Stoker and the other members of the staff always referred to Irving as the Chief or the Governor. When the company went to the United States, as it did four times during Stoker's tenure, Stoker did the advance work, inspected the theaters, dealt with the press, and soothed Irving's ego endlessly and forever. That Irving was an egotist should come as no surprise; for an artist of any sort, self is the primary implement. George Bernard Shaw is said to have quipped that Henry Irving "would not have left the stage for a night to spend it with Helen of Troy."[28]

Irving married Florence O'Callahan shortly after the death of his one true love, Nellie Moore, whose photograph was found in his pocket at his death. Florence Irving did not find happiness with her actor husband and he, without much struggle, removed himself from the domestic ménage and lived in bachelor quarters. There is a dreadful story of domestic incompatibility told of the couple by Laurence Irving, Irving's grandson. Irving and his wife were returning from the opening-night performance of *The Bells*, at which

Irving had received the wild applause of the audience — a performance that was hailed later by the critics. Thinking to please his
wife, Irving said to her:

> "Well, my dear, we too shall soon have our own carriage and pair!"
> Florence was no doubt very tired. Incapable of sharing her hus-
> band's misfortunes or hopes, she now rebelled against the adulation
> conceded to him by his friends. Her smoldering and jealous temper
> lowered her guard on her tone. "Are you going on making a fool of
> yourself like this all of your life?" she asked.[29]

In the James Bond series, Ian Fleming invents a concept he calls
the "insult quotient": the degree of toleration people accord each
other before they take final umbrage at insult. In the lives of couples, doomed to separate, one or another of them exceeds the tolerable insult quotient, as Florence Irving did here. No one can blame
Henry Irving for what he did:

> Without a word he got out [of the carriage] and left his wife to con-
> tinue the journey alone. He never returned to his home and he never
> spoke to her again.[30]

Laurence Irving writes perceptively:

> "Brodribb [Irving], scarred and wounded by the hard years and the
> bitterness of estrangement of his mother, his lover and his wife, must
> in future be invisible and invulnerable to his fellow men."[31]

The Stoker menage, on the other hand, seems to have been
steadfast, without being warm. We know even less about Florence
Stoker than we do about Bram. Stoker spent so little time with the
beautiful Florence that she had to depend on W. S. Gilbert of
Gilbert and Sullivan fame to be her escort to social events. When
she referred publicly to her husband's work at all, Florence Stoker
never called him anything else but a barrister. Stoker worked out
what we might call a stable unsatisfactory marriage, in which both
he and Florence got on with their lives without interfering overmuch with each other.

In *Hollywood Gothic*, David J. Skal writes: "It would become
almost a cliché among his chroniclers that Stoker's 'real' marriage

was to Irving and not to his bride."[32] And Daniel Farson, Stoker's great-nephew, is willing to carry judgment even further:

> Florence Stoker was a beauty, and aware of it. This may explain why she was a cold woman. My family, speaking of her, gave me the impression of an elegant, aloof woman, more interested in her position in society than she was in her son. Her granddaughter, Ann, Noel's daughter, confirms this. She told me that she doubted if Granny Moo, as Florence was called, was really capable of love. "She was cursed with her great beauty and the need to maintain it. In my knowledge now, she was very anti-sex. After having my father [Noel Stoker] in her early twenties, I think she was quite put off."[33]

Leaving aside the infelicities of judgment that haunt that paragraph—what kind of authority can a granddaughter be said to have about her grandmother's sex life?—there is enough family folklore in it to confirm our sense of Stoker as having his emotional priorities elsewhere than in his home.

There is another element to be considered when we try to understand Stoker's life: the degree of pleasure he felt in moving in the unaccustomed heights of London society, to which, as Irving's shadow, he and his wife now had access. His social ambitions had been considerably gratified back in Dublin, when he was admitted to the chic circle, at whose center were Sir William and Lady Jane Wilde, Oscar's parents. Lady Wilde, a brilliant and eccentric woman, presided over the most glittering salon in Dublin. In her home on Merrion Square, "Stoker breathed in the latest cultural and political cross-currents. Irish hospitality welcomed everybody and anybody as long as they contributed scabrous wit."[34] In London, Stoker and his wife found themselves even higher socially. As Horace Wildham put it:

> To see Stoker in his element was to see him standing at the top of the theater stairs, surveying a "first-night" crowd. . . . There was no mistake about it—a Lyceum *Premiere* did draw an audience that really was representative of the best of that period in the realms of art, literature, and society.[35]

If Stoker's relationship to Irving was based on masculine sympathies, his relationship with Ellen Terry reveals another aspect of

Stoker's character. Ellen Terry, who was Irving's most famous leading lady at the Lyceum Theatre, was married at sixteen to a painter
named Watts. Evidently, it was a sexless marriage. She divorced
Watts to marry Charles Wardle. She joined Irving at the Lyceum
on July 23, 1878. There followed a six-year liaison with Edward
William Godwin, with whom she had two children: Edith and
Edward Gordon Craig.

As we gather from the brief summary of Terry's relationships,
she, too, had her share of love failures. Stoker would say of her that
"she had to the full in her nature whatever quality it is that corre-
sponds to what we call virility in a man."[36] It is clear that Terry used
Stoker as a confidant, and that may be why she inscribed a signed
photograph of herself to him, "To my 'MA'—I am her dutiful child."
Terry, who for some years was Irving's mistress, would say that he
"lacked knowledge of *womenfolk*. It is almost ludicrous his ignorance
on that one subject. He has, I think, never given it his consideration."[37] This from a woman who should know.

The portrait that emerges of master and man is of two lonely men
who have no taste or talent for relationships with women, sitting
comfortably before the fire of the Beefsteak Room of the Lyceum
Theatre, jogging on silently through life; one of them endlessly emo-
tionally needy, the other endlessly provident.

An important influence on Stoker's life were the extended tours
that the Lyceum Theatre cast made in America. These were strenuous affairs. The troupe traveled to an extraordinary number of
American cities, including New York, San Francisco, New Orleans,
Boston, Detroit, and Philadelphia. Barbara Belford writes: "The
train journeys from city to city delighted Stoker; he thrived on the
strenuous schedule and the romance of the railroads. . . ."[38] Everywhere Irving and his company went, there were fervent audiences
awaiting them.

On the first American tour, Stoker was disappointed at not being
able to meet Walt Whitman, with whom, as we have seen, he had
corresponded some years before. On March 20, 1884, during the
second tour, he finally met the Gray Eminence. If Stoker fantasized
a deeply personal and private meeting with the poet to whom he
had sent his adulatory letter, he was to be disappointed. Henry Irving insisted on joining Stoker at his first meeting with Whitman.
However, Stoker was gratified when Whitman recognized his
name. Whitman is reported to have said of Stoker, "Well, well; what
a broth of a boy he is! . . . He's like a breath of good, healthy,

breezy sea air."[39] There was no hint that there was any talk of the love that dares not speak its name.

What comes through about the two men is that Whitman really liked Stoker and took him at face value as a bluff, candid, energetic Irishman. Stoker left his first meeting with the poet convinced that Whitman was as wonderful as he had imagined him to be.

The Lyceum's American tours produced a friendship with Mark Twain that would prove to be enduring. They also turned Stoker into an Americanophile who, when he got back to England, would write a pamphlet about America. Moreover, he did not hesitate to accept speaking engagements in England, in which he interpreted the American continent and culture to ingenuous English audiences.

Meanwhile, the broth of a boy had become like the protagonist of Budd Schulberg's novel, *What Makes Sammy Run?*, a man in a dreadful hurry. Even in the midst of the life he led as Irving's factotum, he nurtured timeless ambitions. He was writing fiction and beginning to have it published. That fact that these early works were third-rate, scribbled off in the midst of his frenzied existence, seems not to have daunted him. Twenty-five years ago, it seemed to me that,

> The novels before and after *Dracula*, while they are not unreadable, are not in any literary sense important except as they shed light on Stoker himself. They are terribly sincere books. Invariably sentimental, they breathe the humid air of British Decency. The men in them are (except when they are villains) gallant or dutiful or honorable or long-suffering, or patient. The women are not particularly complex either, but there is a difference. Whatever the sum of their positive virtues is, Stoker's women are stronger, smarter, braver and more believable than the men. Not only that, with a nagging frequency that has to be more than coincidental, their given names begin with the letter "M": Maggie, Minna, Marjorie, Margaret, Mimi (though, in a novel called *The Man*, the heroine's name is Stephen!).[40]

About the frequency of those letter "M"s, Barbara Belford is willing to hazard the guess that they "are a tribute, perhaps, to 'Mother' and sisters, Matilda and Margaret."[41]

If the novels are not distinguished in any literary sense, the manner in which their plots are executed give us intriguing glimpses into the nether reaches of Stoker's mind.

Before *Dracula,* Stoker had published three novels: *The Snake's Pass* (1889), *The Watter's Mou'* (1894), and *The Shoulder of Shasta* (1895). *The Snake's Pass* is a tale of love and adventure, the sort that a "manly man" would write. Set in Ireland, it features a hunt for buried treasure and an Irishman whose brogue is considerably more authentic than Van Helsing's Anglo-Dutch speech. *The Watter's Mou',* a tale of smuggling and self-sacrifice, is notable mostly for its breathless romanticism and for Stoker's appreciation of the landscape in the vicinity of Cruden Bay, a rocky seacoast fishing village on the northeast coast of Scotland. Cruden Bay has the further distinction of being where Stoker dreamed the dream out of which the novel *Dracula* would be spun.

*The Shoulder of Shasta,* set in the vicinity of California's Mount Shasta, answers this question, as the radio-soap-opera announcers of the 1930s might put it: "Can a delicate, sensitive young woman find true love in the arms of a crude mountain man named Grizzly Dick?"

After *Dracula,* there was a spate of novels beginning with *Miss Betty* (1898), in which an heiress teaches the man who rescued her from drowning how to be a patient suitor. This was followed by *The Mystery of the Sea* (1902), which I'll discuss soon, and *The Jewel of the Seven Stars* (1903), which borrows from H. Rider Haggard's *She* (1887), exploiting the theme of reincarnation. Stoker's story involves the mummy of a great Egyptian queen and the tender love between Margaret Trelawney and Malcolm Ross. As the book ends, Margaret has absorbed the queen's soul. In 1905 Stoker published *The Man* (called in America *The Gates of Life).* This is the novel in which the female protagonist has a man's name and the plot turns on shifting gender roles.

Harry Ludlam describes *Lady Athlyne* (1908) as "a happy parcel of romantic reading with plenty of love and blushes."[42]

In *Lady of the Shroud* (1909), the theme of vampirism is revisited tangentially. In this novel, the hero is Rupert St. Leger, a seven-foot-tall Englishman who becomes the leader of the Balkan people in The Land of the Blue Mountains, in their fight against oppression. In it we get hints of the kinky sexuality that will become the main characteristic of the last of Stoker's novels, *The Lair of the White Worm* (1911).

In *The Mystery of the Sea* (1902), an American heroine is betrothed secretly to Archie, a handsome young barrister. On the day before their wedding, to outwit some Spanish bad guys who want to kidnap her, Marjory dresses as a boy. She and Archie meet in the forest, then mount bicycles for a three-hour ride from Cruden Bay to Aberdeen. In Aberdeen, Marjory changes clothes, and then the affianced couple take a six-hour train trip to Carlisle. After nine hours of strenuous exertion, they rest in separate rooms in Carlisle, then meet at St. Hilda's Church, where they are married. But there is no such thing as consummation—not yet. At 12:53, they take another six-hour train ride to Aberdeen, where they once again mount their bicycles for the three-hour ride back to Cruden Bay. Twenty-eight hours from the time this hegira began, they are back in the forest from which they started. There, Marjory gives Archie, "a kiss and a hug that made [his] blood tingle," after which they part. Stoker has Archie conclude, "it was not like a wedding day or a honeymoon at all." Indeed it was not. Nor is that all.

That wedding night, Archie hacks at the rock floor of a cave beside the sea hour after hour. Later, in that same cave, Marjory and Archie are trapped by the incoming tide. For a while, their lives seem to be in terrible danger. Facing death, the two young people finally kiss. Lest my readers worry about these two pure souls, let me reassure them that Archie and Marjory are saved. Not only that, but Archie gets to kiss Marjory's foot which, under the circumstances, seems a considerable reward.

The curious sexual reticence that can make us smile in *The Mystery of the Sea* yields to something utterly different in Stoker's *The Lair of the White Worm*, where the kind of graphic detail over which Stoker lingers obsessionally raises questions in our minds about his own mental health. First, one should say that the word "worm" in the title carries the medieval meaning of "dragon."

Stoker's "worm" is Lady Arabella March, who moves with a quick, gliding motion and who

> . . . was clad in some kind of soft white stuff, which clung close to her form, showing to the full every movement of her sinuous figure. . . . Coiled round her throat was a large necklace of emeralds whose profusion of color dazzled when the sun shone on them. Her voice was peculiar, very low and sweet, and so soft that the dominant note was of sibilation. Her hands, too, were peculiar—long, flexible, white, with a strange movement as of waving gently to and fro.[43]

Like tentacles, no doubt. We are told that she lives at the bottom of a thousand-foot hole and that in her serpentine form, she is 200 feet long. As a woman, she is given to swift, decisive, and cruel gestures. She tears a mongoose that senses her serpentine nature and follows its instincts to attack her, to bits with her bare hands. When Oolonga, the black servant of her neighbor, Edgar Caswell, expresses his love for her, she wraps her white arms around him and drags him down, "into the noisome depths of her hole."[44] Stoker's descriptions of that place leave a reader simultaneously queasy and inclined to nervous laughter. Adam, the clean-cut young hero of this novel, slips "on the steps on some sticky, acrid-smelling mass and falling forward felt his way into the inner room where the well-shaft was not."[45] The well-shaft has

> a queer smell—yes! Like bilge or a rank swamp. It was distinctly nauseating. . . . [The smell] was like nothing that Adam had ever met with. He compared it with all the noxious experiences he had ever had—the drainage of war hospitals, of slaughterhouses, the refuse of dissecting room . . . the sourness of chemical waste and the poisonous effluvium of the bilge of a water-logged ship whereon a multitude of rats had been drowned.[46]

Meanwhile, Adam cannot bring himself to propose to the beautiful Mimi, and he asks his uncle, Sir Nathaniel, to do the proposing for him. Sir Nathaniel, who plays the role of Van Helsing in this fiction, defines the problem that Adam has vis-à-vis the serpent: ". . . being feminine, she will probably over-reach herself. Now, Adam, it strikes me that, as we have to protect ourselves and others against feminine nature our strong game will be to play our masculine against her feminine."[47] Sir Nathaniel and Adam are the team confronting evil. Their enemy, in her serpent form as she inhabits her hole, has the shape

> . . . of what seemed to be a long white pole, near the top of which were two pendent white masses, like rudimentary arms or fins. . . . By degrees, as their eyes got their tight focus, they saw an immense towering mass that seemed snowy white. It was tall and thin . . . the hidden mass at the base of the shaft was composed of cast coils of the great serpent's body, forming a base from which the upright mass rose . . .[48]

One has to wonder what readers did with passages like these before Freud opened our eyes to the other meanings of concave and

convex, but let us return to *The Lair of the White Worm*. Guided by
Sir Nathaniel, Adam fills the hole with dynamite and many yards of
sea sand. At some moment, a lightning spark explodes the dynamite
and the novel comes to what, in the most literal sense, is its climax.

> From [the well hole] agonized shrieks were rising, growing ever
> more terrible with each second that passed. . . . Once, in a sort of lull
> or pause, the seething contents of the hole rose . . . and Adam saw
> part of the thin form of Lady Arabella, forced up to the top amid a
> mass of slime . . .[49]

It is interesting to see how closely this orgasm-explosion scene
resembles a deleted passage in *Dracula*. I am grateful to Barbara
Belford for printing it in her biography. It is a passage that, she tells
us "someone, at the last moment, deleted." It reads:

> As we looked there came a terrible convulsion of the earth so that we
> seemed to rock to and fro and fell to our knees. At the same moment,
> with a roar which seemed to shake the very heavens, the whole cas-
> tle and the rock and even the hill on which it stood seemed to rise
> into the air and scatter in fragments while a mighty cloud of black
> and yellow smoke volume on volume in rolling grandeur was shot
> upwards with inconceivable rapidity. . . . From where we stood it
> seemed as though the one fierce volcano burst had satisfied the need
> of nature and that the castle and the structure of the hill had sunk
> again into the void. We were so appalled with the suddenness and
> grandeur that we forgot to think of ourselves.[50]

*The Lair of the White Worm*, then, can be seen as a spasmodic
replay of the metaphors which, in *Dracula*, worked toward the creation of meaningful myth, but which here lie squirming sympto-
matically before the eyes of the reader.

Some years ago, when I first tried to deal with *The Lair of the White
Worm*, I blamed its bizarre imagery on the intellectual and emotional
decline that might be the consequence of Stoker's advancing age, but
I have had to change my mind for two reasons. First, sixty-four is
hardly an advanced age. Second, since that time I have had occasion
to read a short story of Stoker's written nearly ten years before *Dracula* that makes it clear that the disorder in his mind was already there
in 1887.

In the Christmas 1887 issue of *The Theatre Annual*, there appeared a short story by Stoker called "The Duelitists." There may not be anywhere in the world a story quite as grotesque or as repulsive or as garish or as nasty as this one. The story's tone is meant to be whimsical. The story opens with the line, "There was joy in the house of Bub." We are told that after a ten-year wait, Ephraim and Sophonisba Bub are about to become parents. Chapter 1 ends with the doctor's announcing: ". . . allow me to congratulate you—to offer twofold felicitations. Mr. Bub, sir, you are the father of twins!" The twins, Zerubbabel and Zacariah, grow apace. As Chapter 2 ends, they are three years old. In Chapter 3, we are told that Harry Merford and Tommy Santon live nearby. They are such close friends that "Compared with these two youths, Castor and Pollux, Damon and Pythias, and Eloisa and Abelard are but tame examples of duality or constancy and friendship."[51]

For Christmas, these two had each been given knives which "were their chief delights." The boys hack and cut and carve and slash and nick and rip anything and everything that they can reach with their knives. In Chapter 5, we learn that the boys proclivities have expanded beyond knives. "Spoons and forks were daily flattened. [Candlesticks and candy dishes] were used as weapons in the crusade of hack."[52] In short, the boys destroy everything within reach that can be destroyed. In Chapter 6, having destroyed whatever inanimate objects they could find, they commenced

> a work of mystery, blood and gloom. First they destroyed rabbits. When the supply of rabbits was exhausted they turned to white mice, dormice, hedgehogs, guinea pigs, pigeons, lambs, canaries . . . and so on. . . . At last, however, all the animals available were sacrificed.[53]

But the hunger to hack continued to grow.

In Chapter 7, Harry and Tommy catch a glimpse of the twins, Zacariah and Zerubbabel, who have escaped from their nurses. Stoker can hardly contain his glee as he describes what Harry and Tommy then do to Zerubbabel and Zacariah. They squash their noses and cheeks. Then they carry the twins to the roof of the stable, where one of the twins is lifted up and then dropped so that he falls with stunning force on the supine form of his brother. The scene is witnessed by their parents, Ephraim and Sophonisba. "Wildly did Ephraim, mounting on the shoulders of his spouse, strive, but in vain, to scale the stable wall,"[54] to no avail. Though Ephraim shoots at the murderous boys, he misses. When the smoke has cleared, he sees Harry and Tommy waving the trunks of the twins high into the air. "The fond father had blown the heads completely off his own offspring."[55]

Two of Stoker's short stories deserve special mention. "The Judge's House" (1914) and "The Squaw" (1914) are short, frightening fictions that continue to hold honorable places as classic tales of terror. "The Squaw," inspired by a visit to Nuremburg in 1892, has as its protagonist, Elias P. Hutcheson of Nebraska. Being American means that he is friendly, open, and stupid. Having demonstrated to a couple visiting Nuremburg Castle the effects of the law of gravity, and thereby inadvertently killing a kitten before its mother's eyes, the American meets what seems to be a not-entirely-undeserved fate in the embrace of the Iron Maiden. At the story's end, we have some deft borrowing from Edgar Allan Poe's "The Black Cat": "Sitting on the head of the poor American was the cat, purring loudly as she licked the blood which trickled through the gashed sockets of his eyes."[56]

Influenced heavily by Le Fanu's "Mr. Justice Harbottle," "The Judge's House" is a story of a student who is driven to his death by the ghost of a cruel magistrate, in the form of a huge rat.

---

Stoker began obsessively making notes for *Dracula* as early as 1890. He worked in the Circular Reading Room of the British Museum Library, where he gathered the material he used to describe Transylvania, where he had never been. Much of what he learned he got from one of those remarkable travel books written by hardy Englishwomen in the nineteenth century. *The Land Beyond the Forest,* by Emily Gerard, which I discussed earlier, introduced him not only to the appropriate terrain, but also to the folklore of the vampire that he would need for his novel.[57]

In 1890 the Stokers spent part of their summer on holiday in Whitby, a Yorkshire town on England's east coast. Whitby, once a fishing village, was a favorite holiday resort in Stoker's time, and still is. In 1890, when Stoker and his family were there, it had a population of 13,261 inhabitants. Stoker was so taken with the town's theatrical setting that, more or less stick by stone, he reproduced it in *Dracula:*

This is a lovely place. The little river, the Esk, runs through a deep valley, which broadens out as it comes near the harbour. A great viaduct runs across, with high piers, through which the view seems somehow further than it really is. The valley is beautifully green, and it is so steep that when you are on the high land on either side you look right across it, unless you are near enough to see down. The houses of the old town—the side away from us—are all red-roofed, and seem to pile up one over the other anyhow, like the pictures we see of Nurenberg. Right over the town is the ruin of Whitby Abbey, which was sacked by the Danes, and which is the scene of part of "Marmion," where the girl was built up in the wall. It is a most noble ruin, of immense size, and full of beautiful and romantic bits; there is a legend that a white lady is seen in one of the windows. Between it and the town there is another church, the parish one, round which is a big graveyard, all full of tombstones. This is to my mind the nicest spot in Whitby, for it lies right over the town, and has a full view of the harbour and all up the bay to where the headland called Kettleness stretches out into the sea.[58]

Though Barbara Belford says that the Stoker's three weeks' visit to Whitby in 1890 "marks the creative genesis of *Dracula*," [59] we have no indication that there was any emotional or interior churning going on in Stoker's life in the nearly seven years it took him to write his novel. Certainly the sea lore he gathered from the local fishermen kindled his imagination; as did Whitby itself, with its dramatic ruined abbey and its spectacular location overlooking the sea. He did learn that a Russian ship named the *Dmitry* had gone aground in Whitby on October 24, 1885. And he was impressed by the variety of dialects the inhabitants spoke, as I was when I visited Whitby in 1971.

In Whitby, Stoker was busy making notes. From them we learn that his vampire's name started as Count Wampyr. His story did not emerge clearly in his mind right from the start. His notes show that he considered including a painter named Francis Aytown and a scene in which invited guests contribute plot elements to the story. The notes indicate that Stoker contemplated using

a detective, a psychical-research agent, a German professor, and an American inventor called Brutus M. Morris (later Quincey Morris). At first Dracula's castle employs a deaf mute woman and a silent man as servants.[60]

*Contemporary view of Whitby Harbor*

Barbara Belford and Nina Auerbach are willing to believe that Stoker might have been influenced by his meeting with George du Maurier, whose novel *Trilby* was published in 1894. Belford writes: "Both deal with the fear of female sexuality and the loss of innocence, and with brave men who rescue the mother figure from a foreigner's embrace."[61] The trouble for me is that almost any Gothic novel deals with the same elements.

Published by Constable, *Dracula* appeared in May 1897 and, mimicking the notorious *Yellow Books* of the day, *Dracula* sported a yellow cover. It cost six shillings, and it was published in an edition of 3,000 copies. It did not appear in the United States until two years later, where, owing to an oversight on Stoker's part, it was never copyrighted.

The reviews of the book were mixed. The *Athenaeum* of June 26, 1897 treated the the book rather coolly. Such a "fantastic and magical" book, it sniffed, was one more addition to a spate of books dealing with the supernatural, "a reaction—artificial, perhaps, rather than natural, against late tendencies in [scientific] thought." The review complained: "*Dracula* is highly sensational, but it is wanting in the constructive art as well as in the higher literary sense. It reads at times like a mere series of grotesquely incredible events." The *Athenaeum* conceded that the book had "An immense amount of energy, a certain degree of imaginative faculty, and many ingenious and gruesome details. . . ." However, the reviewer did not like Stoker's characters, complaining that they had "no real individuality or being." Mistaking the Dutchman Van Helsing for a German, the reviewer wrote: "The German man of science is particularly poor, and indulges, like a German, in much weak sentiment." The review concludes with faint praise: "[Mr. Stoker's] object is fairly well fulfilled. Isolated scenes and touches are probably quite uncanny enough to please those for whom they are designed."[62]

*The Spectator* of July 31, 1897 contented itself with giving its readers a thumbnail sketch of Stoker's

> clever but cadaverous romance. Its strength lies in the invention of incident, for the sentimental element is decidedly mawkish . . . but we think his story would have been all the more effective if he had chosen an earlier period. The up-to-dateness of the book—the phonograph diaries, typewriters, and so on—hardly fits in with the medieval methods which ultimately secure the victory for Count Dracula's foes.

The reviewer for *The Bookman* of August 1897 chose not to give his readers a plot summary because it "would shock and disgust" his readers. He confessed, however, that, though "here and there we hurried over things with repulsion, we read nearly the whole with rapt attention." The reviewer's final warning to the reader must be read as high praise for Stoker: "Keep *Dracula* away from children, certainly; but a grown reader, unless he be of unserviceably delicate stuff, will both shudder and enjoy" the book.[63]

Bram Stoker's mother wrote to him about his book, praising it ecstatically:

> My dear, [*Dracula*] is splendid, a thousand miles beyond anything you have written before, and I feel certain will place you very high in the writers of the day— . . . no book since Mrs. Shelley's *Franken-stein* or indeed any other at all has come near yours in originality, or terror—Poe is nowhere.[64]

She also told him that the book would make him a lot of money, a prediction that turned out to be mistaken. Though it had a steady small sale, in Stoker's lifetime, it did not earn enough to change the Stokers' standard of living.

Indeed, in the years after *Dracula*'s publication, the Stokers seemed to have entered a period of financial distress and had to borrow £600 from Hommy Beg (Hall Caine), Stoker's best friend. The Lyceum, too, ran into trouble. On February 18, 1898, the theater's storage bins were destroyed by fire, a financial loss that was incalculable. Unable to deal with it, Henry Irving turned the theater over to a syndicate.

In October 1899, Stoker and Irving went to the United States for their sixth American tour. Stoker loved the hundred-mile-an-hour hurricane their ship encountered. This time, in America, Stoker, as the author of *Dracula,* was considerably less in Irving's shadow. But the fortunes of the troupe were changing ineluctably. Ellen Terry, getting ready to leave the company, was also put off by Irving's new mistress, Eliza Aria. Eliza's effect on Stoker was not good either. The comfortable—if peculiar—relationship between the two men suffered a sea change.

The Lyceum Theatre, without Ellen Terry and with an aging Irving, was no longer what it had been. Stoker continued with his duties and with his writing and set his goal at a novel per year, but as we have noted, after *Dracula,* nothing quite fell into place.

As if they were already hearing finale music, Irving and Ellen Terry had the following exchange:

*Ellen Terry*: And the end . . . how would you like that to come?
*Irving* (snapping his fingers): Like that![65]

On Friday, October 13, 1905, Irving appeared in a performance of Tennyson's *Becket.* When Edith Wynne Matthison, who played Rosamund misspoke the word "armed" by treating it as a single syllable, Irving corrected her: "Armèd, my dear, armèd." When he recited Becket's last words, "Into thy Hands, oh Lord, into thy Hands!" Irving fell with his head upstage, contrary to his usual practice. The curtain was rung down and a dazed Irving was helped offstage. He managed to take a cab back to his hotel. There, in the lobby, he stumbled. Tended by a country doctor who happened to be in the hotel manager's private room, Irving died in the arms of Walter Collinson, his dresser and assistant.

Barbara Belford writes: "When Stoker arrived, he knelt over the body and put his hand over Irving's heart. The doctor shook his head."[66]

The last words Stoker heard Irving speak on that fateful night was Irving's gentle admonition to him back at the theater as Stoker was leaving: "Muffle up your throat, old chap! It is a bitterly cold night—you have a cold—take care of yourself. Good night. God bless you."

With Irving dead, Stoker's life lost its savor. From that fateful night in the Dublin hotel when, as Stoker put it, "Soul had looked into soul," Irving had been the anchor of Stoker's being. It's true that, for twenty-seven years, he had been at the actor's beck and call, but it was not a servitude beneath which he chafed. If that lonely, egocentric master exacted service from his assistant, he paid Stoker for it with more than money.

If one must point to an oversimplified explanation of how a life gets lived, one ought to see what Stoker saw as his options when Irving called him to his side. One option the young civil servant had was clearly before his eyes: the image of his father, Abraham Stoker, plodding away for fifty years at his musty bits of paper. Stoker, the author of *The Duties of Clerks of Petty Sessions in Ireland*, could tell a hawk from a handsaw and could look far down the bleak tunnel of his father's days. The alacrity with which he rushed to join Irving, dragging his new bride after him to London, ought to be proof enough that Stoker was saving his own life.

It does not seem to me that Stoker was in any way vampirized by Henry Irving, as has been suggested. Belford among others has identified Irving as the model for Dracula. At one point she says that "somewhere in the creative process, Dracula became a sinister caricature of Irving as mesmerist and depleter, an artist draining those about him to feed his ego. It was a stunning but avenging tribute."[67]

I object to such a reading on the ground of common sense. If Dracula is meant to represent Irving, why are neither Irving nor Stoker, who spent some twenty-seven years in each other's company, ever on record—Stoker for saying spiteful things about his employer, or Irving for hearing or sensing them. And why, after the publication of the novel, did not some so-called friend, seeing Irving maligned in it, call his attention to the unflattering portrait. No one did. Not Ellen Terry, nor—a more likely candidate to have spotted Stoker's "vengeance"—Eliza Aria, Irving's mistress during his final years. Not a single journalist. No *Punch* satirist. No one.

In 1906 Stoker published the kind of biography of his friend that one might expect from a man who could say of himself, "Looking back, I cannot honestly find any moment in my life when I failed him [Irving], or when I put myself forward in any way."[68] It is a doting and affectionate biography. Bizarrely enough, Oscar Wilde's name does not appear among the list of the 1,000 important people who had been entertained at the Lyceum. Or, since Stoker never commented publicly on Wilde's arrest and trial, the omission may not be so odd if, as seems clear to me, Stoker was protecting the door to the closet in which he hid his own sexual identity.

For a while after Irving's death, Stoker worked as an acting manager for a musical version of Oliver Goldsmith's novel, *The Vicar of Wakefield*. The show closed after two months, after which Stoker's life took on the quality of a man living at loose ends, moving from project to project. For a while he worked on the literary staff of the *Daily Telegraph* and wrote profiles that were published in the New York *World* and the London *Daily Chronicle*. Evidently unaware, or at least unwilling to confront the erotic content of *Dracula*, he lent his voice to the call for censorship of pornography.

After a performance of Shaw's play, *Captain Brassbound's Conversion*, that was part of a celebration of Ellen Terry's Golden Jubilee in the theater, Stoker suffered a stroke that affected his walk and his eyesight. He was afflicted, too, with Bright's disease, a kidney ailment. Meanwhile, his income continued to suffer. From being the belle of the ball, Florence was now reduced to scrabbling to make ends meet. In May 1909, Stoker suffered a second stroke and was put on an arsenic-and-soup diet, even as he was working on his book, *Famous Impostors*. In 1911, his financial situation was such that he applied to the Royal Literary Fund for a grant-in-aid. In support of his application, he wrote:

> At the beginning of 1906, I had a paralytic stroke. Fortunately the stroke was not a bad one and in a few months I resumed my work. Just a year ago I had another break-down from overwork which has incapacitated me ever since. The result of such a misfortune shows at its worst in the case of one who has to depend on his brain and his hands.[69]

He was given a grant of £100. In 1911, to save money, the Stokers moved to a smaller flat. During this period, Stoker wrote the unsettling horror novel, *The Lair of the White Worm*, in only three months and nine days.

On April 20, 1912, with his wife and his son at his side, Bram Stoker died at the age of sixty-four. Again, we are indebted to Daniel Farson for an unnecessary speculation about whether

Stoker died of the syphilis he may have contracted from the prostitutes he visited because of his cold marriage.

Barbara Belford, however, points out that the attending physician listed three causes for Stoker's death: "Locomotor Ataxy 6
Months, Granular Contracted Kidney. Exhaustion."[70] Farson, also
distressed by the frantic writing I have called attention to in my
comments on *The Lair of the White Worm*, consulted a physician, who
interpreted the term "Locomotor Ataxy" as being a euphemism for
tabes dorsalis, General Paralysis of the Insane, or tertiary syphilis.[71]
Belford writes: "Stoker was never the classic demented, psychotic
personality associated with tertiary syphilis. . . . We shall never
know whether Stoker ever had syphilis, but the medical evidence
argues against his dying from that disease."[72] She cites various medical experts to support that conclusion.

I think that the syphilis question is irrelevant. Oscar Wilde died
of it. Syphilis was endemic in Victorian England. And it can be contracted from men as well as from women. Besides, by now it should
be an exploded myth that people go to prostitutes because of some
sexual lack in their domestic partners.

There is plenty of reason to think that Stoker's life was tragic,
but the explanation for it is not to be found in the name of the illness that killed him. What is tragic is Stoker's lifelong inability to
come to terms with his own identity; his inability to face the fact
that he was a homosexual; his refusal to move past the moment of
near-courage of his letters to Whitman, or to see the implications of
his own work.

Many years ago, Robert Duncan, the American poet and a
friend, made a fine distinction about sexual orientation: "It is not
whom you sleep with that determines whether you are a heterosexual or a homosexual, it is whom you dream of sleeping with." If it
was hard to be a heterosexual in the Age of Victoria, it was a hundred times harder to be a homosexual for whom being closeted was
the only option. However, against all the odds, men found each
other and so did women. Stoker's tragedy is that he not only lived in
the closet, he also died in it without ever having expressed the love
that mattered most to him.

What transcends even the tragedy of Stoker's life and his death is
the mystery of his greatness as a novelist. There is no way of knowing what life forces acted on Stoker that produced the nearly obses-
sional concentration and focus that enabled him to create *Dracula*.

What makes a writer of mediocre skills and mediocre vision somehow reinvent himself?

I have offered my own tentative explanations. I have suggested that even a mediocre mind, when it is seized by a great fear, can, like someone carrying a family member down the stairs of a burning building, have access suddenly to the intellectual adrenaline he needs to outdo oneself. Before and after Stoker wrote *Dracula,* his work expressed the thoroughly mediocre man he was.

But *Dracula* obsessed him. Stoker spent nearly seven years readying himself for the task of the novel; and, whether he was or was not aware of the polymorphous perverse nature of his central symbol, his luck held, and he was able to create the image that haunts us as it haunted him.

Besides, Stoker had role models for writing well. He had spent a lifetime working for Henry Irving in England's busiest and most famous theater. He heard fine prose or poetry being spoken daily, and had the image of the dynamic Henry Irving—as a model of dramatic energy, not of vampirism—constantly before his eyes. His subconscious understood what he was doing perhaps better than the stalwart six-foot two-inch red-haired Irishman who prided himself on having a sound mind in a sound body.

Some fifteen years ago, at the University of Buffalo, when I carelessly observed that Stoker was a second-rate writer, Leslie Fiedler brought me up short by reminding me: "A second-rate writer who writes a great novel is a great writer." It was well said then, and it is the last word on the matter now.

# In Which the Author and His Connoisseur Readers Remember Stoker's Dracula Together

*". . . we saw a whole mass of phosphorescence which twinkled like stars. We all instinctively drew back. The place was becoming alive with rats."*

. . . WHICH WAY SHALL I FLY
INFINITE WRATH AND INFINITE DESPAIR?
WHICH WAY I FLY IS HELL; MYSELF AM HELL;
AND IN THE LOWEST DEEP A LOWER DEEP,
STILL THREAT'NING TO DEVOUR ME, OPENS WIDE,
TO WHICH THE HELL I SUFFER SEEMS A HEAVEN.

—JOHN MILTON, PARADISE LOST, BOOK IV, LINES 73-78

he Gothic elements in *Dracula* are easy to spot. There are craggy mountains, a ruined castle, and a ruined abbey. It has, too, a glowering foreigner pursuing English womanhood with wicked intent, and it has the requisite mixture of realism and the supernatural that is the hallmark of Gothic fiction.

There are, however, important differences involving numbers. Stoker's *Dracula* has not one, but two endangered young women. And the decent, sexually unthreatening young man whose role in the Gothic novels is to rescue the maiden, is here cloned into an entire committee of five: Dr. Van Helsing, Lucy's three suitors, and Jonathan Harker. Not only that, Stoker's protagonists have to confront a villain who threatens their very souls as well as their lives.

Stoker borrowed the form of his fiction from Wilkie Collins's best-selling novel, *The Woman in White.* That story is a construct of several personal narratives, a technique Collins adapted in turn from the eighteenth-century authors like Henry Fielding and Samuel Richardson, who wrote epistolary novels in which characters both advance the plot and reveal their own or other people's character through the letters they exchange. We have seen how Maturin's *Melmoth the Wanderer* is also organized like nested boxes. In *Dracula,* we get the story as it emerges from our reading of what purport to be diaries, journals, letters, and even the transcript made from phonograph recordings and telegrams. The result is that there is no single point of view from which the story is told; and there is no omniscient third-person narrative anywhere in the fiction.

This means that in some way every document we read illuminates the character of the writer. More than that, we hear these various voices speaking in the very heart of their high-tech nineteenth-century world.

One more thing. Readers will find that Stoker's mosaic plot structure gives it a singularly filmic quality. It is as if Stoker instinctively knew all the techniques—flashbacks, smash-cuts, close-ups and tracking shots—that would later be invented by the film industry.

The novel has a theatrical organization, which suggests discussing it as if it were divided into four acts, each one of which is focused on a different character. Act I belongs to Jonathan Harker (Chapters 1–5); Act II to Lucy (Chapters 6–16); Act III to Mina Harker (Chapters 17–21); and Act IV (Chapters 22 to the end), the climactic Act, to Dracula.

## ACT I: JONATHAN, CHAPTERS 1–5

As the book opens, we find Jonathan Harker, a young British solicitor, on his way to a destination somewhere in Transylvania, where he is to conclude an intricate real estate transaction with a Count Dracula. Harker's being a solicitor is of some importance because solicitors prepare legal cases for barristers, who try them in the courts. Harker, as we will learn later, has the lowest social status of any of the characters with whom he will become allied. We learn from Jonathan's journal that he has been traveling from Munich, through Vienna to Budapest, then Klausenburg, where he spent the night, sleeping fitfully, after which he went on from there to Bistritza.

> All day long we seemed to dawdle through a country which was full of beauty of every kind. Sometimes we saw little towns or castles on the top of steep hills such as we see in old missals; sometimes we ran by rivers and streams which seemed from the wide stony margin on each side of them to be subject to great floods. . . . At every station there were groups of people, sometimes crowds, and in all sorts of attire. Some of them were just like the peasants at home or those I saw coming through France and Germany, with short jackets and round hats and homemade trousers; but others were very picturesque. The women looked pretty, except when you got near them, but they were very clumsy about the waist. . . . The strangest figures we saw were the Slovaks, who are more barbarian than the rest, with their big cowboy hats, great baggy dirty-white trousers, white linen shirts, and enormous heavy leather belts, nearly a foot wide, all studded over with brass nails. . . . (5)[1]

He arrives in Bistritza and stays the night in the Golden Crone Hotel. Jonathan's hostess at the Golden Crone, knowing that his destination is Dracula's castle, pleads with him not to go. "Do you know what day it is? . . . It is the eve of St. George's Day. . . . Do you not know that tonight, when the clock strikes midnight, all the evil things in the world will have full sway?" (7–8)

Harker, however, is all business and insists on going his way. Just the same, he allows the agitated woman to place a crucifix around his neck. Later, we see Harker in the coach passing from the congenial *"mittel land"*—the middle land—to the barren crags, among which rises Dracula's castle.

Harker tells us that the coach is traveling at an unwarranted pace "through mighty slopes of forest up to the lofty steeps of the Carpathians themselves." Harker notes the appearance of roadside crosses. Various peasants in the fields are kneeling before the road-side shrines. When Harker thinks of getting down from the coach to walk, the driver deters him. " 'No, no,' he said: You must not walk here, the dogs are too fierce.' " (13) Meanwhile, the coach goes plummeting through the night, until it reaches a point over-looking the Borgo Pass. Harker leaves the coach to get into the small carriage waiting for him at the top of the pass.

Once again there are howling wolves in the vicinity, but the dri-ver commands them, and they fall back. The upward journey is resumed. Then, abruptly, "the driver was . . . pulling up the horses in the courtyard of a vast ruined castle. . . ." (17)

The meeting between Jonathan Harker and Count Dracula is one of the most momentous and theatrical in the book:

Then there was the sound of rattling chains and the clanking of mas-sive bolts drawn back. A key was turned with the loud grating noise of long disuse, and the great door swung back. Within, stood a tall old man, clean-shaven save for a long white moustache, and clad in black from head to foot, without a single speck of colour about him anywhere. He held in his hand an antique silver lamp in which the flame burned without chimney or globe of any kind, throwing long quivering shadows as it flickered in the draught of the open door. The old man motioned me in with his right hand with a courtly ges-ture, saying in excellent English, but with a strange intonation:—

"Welcome to my house! Enter freely and of your own will!" He made no motion of stepping to meet me, but stood like a statue, as though his gesture of welcome had fixed him into stone. The instant, however, that I had stepped over the threshold, he moved impassively forward, and holding out his hand grasped mine with a strength which made me wince, an effect which was not lessened by the fact that it seemed cold as ice—more like the hand of a dead than a living man. Again he said:—

"Welcome to my house. Come freely. Go safely. And leave something of the happiness you bring!" . . . I said interrogatively:—

"Count Dracula?" He bowed in a courtly way as he replied:—

"I am Dracula . . ." (22–23)

The entire encounter is rigidly formal—indeed, ritualistic—because it is an exchange governed by the tradition that the Devil can have no power over anyone who resists him. "Get thee behind me, Satan" is the formula for sending the Fallen Angel about his business. In Goethe's *Faust,* Mephistopheles, in the guise of a poodle, is invited by Faust into his home. In Coleridge's *Christabel,* the monstrous Lady Geraldine is unable to cross the threshold of Baron Leoline's castle and must be carried in by Christabel. Dracula always requires the help of a mortal creature to give him access to his victims. Here, once Harker steps across the threshold, Dracula has received permission to act.

If the atmosphere in the castle is that of a fairy tale, Harker soon discovers that the castle's lord is an ogre. Dracula has pointed ears like a wolf's; his bushy eyebrows meet over the bridge of his nose. His fingernails are long and fine, cut to a sharp point; his canine teeth are long and protuberant. Most disturbing of all, hair grows at the center of his palms.

This voivode who traces his ancestry to Attila the Hun is planning, with Harker's help, to relocate his home to England, where, as he puts it, he is eager "to go through the crowded streets of your mighty London, to be in the midst of the whirl and rush of humanity, to share its life, its change, its death, and all that makes it what it is." (28)

Soon Harker, who has been treated affably by the Count, takes note of several peculiar things: first, there are no mirrors to be seen anywhere in the castle; second, when Harker cuts himself while shaving, the Count is weirdly drawn to a drop of blood that appears on Stoker's neck and is prevented from grabbing at his throat only when the crucifix Harker is wearing brushes the Count's hand. Finally Harker discovers that all the doors that might lead him out

of the castle are locked. As he notes in his journal: "The castle is a
veritable prison, and I am a prisoner." (35)

Meanwhile, Dracula, as if he were Bluebeard talking to his latest
wife, warns Harker:

> "Let me advise you, my dear young friend—nay, let me warn you
> with all seriousness, that should you leave these rooms you will not
> by any chance go to sleep in any other parts of the castle . . ." (46)

Then, in the course of a very beautiful moonlit night, Harker
looks out of a window and sees

> . . . the whole man slowly emerge from the window and begin to
> crawl down the castle wall over that dreadful abyss, *face down.*" (47)

Horrified and by now desperate, Harker, violates Dracula's
injunction and starts off to explore his part of the castle. Finally he
finds a door that is not locked. Harker has pushed his way into a
dust-filled but beautiful room that he believes must once have been
some woman's boudoir. He lies on a couch there and, in a state
between sleep and waking, he sees three women:

> Two were dark, and had high aquiline noses, like the Count, and
> great dark, piercing eyes, that seemed to be almost red when con-
> trasted with the pale yellow moon. The other was fair, as fair as can
> be, with great masses of golden hair and eyes like pale sapphires. . . .
> All three had brilliant white teeth, that shone like pearls against the
> ruby of their voluptuous lips. . . . I felt in my heart a wicked, burning
> desire that they would kiss me with those red lips. (51)

When one of the dark women urges the fair one, " 'Go on! . . . He is
young and strong; there are kisses for us all,' " Harker, though pre-
tending to keep his eyes closed gloatingly takes in the scene through
slightly parted eyelids. (52)

The fair woman gets down on her knees beside Harker and "as
she arched her neck she actually licked her lips like an animal, till I
could see in the moonlight the moisture shining on the scarlet lips
and on the red tongue as it lapped the white sharp teeth." (52) One
can almost hear the director of a porno film urging his actress to
pantomime the words that follow:

Lower and lower went her head as the lips went below the range of my mouth and chin and seemed about to fasten on my throat. Then she paused, and I could hear the churning sound of her tongue as it licked her teeth and lips, and could feel the hot breath on my neck. Then the skin of my throat began to tingle as one's flesh does when the hand that is to touch it approaches nearer—nearer . . . I closed my eyes in a languorous ecstasy and waited—waited with beating heart.

Lower and lower . . . nearer and nearer . . . the churning sound of her tongue . . . I closed my eyes in a languorous ecstasy and waited. (52)

In that pause during which the blonde woman's tongue is churning and Harker's inchoate horrified and passionate hopes explode, we can guess the lascivious details withheld from us by the text. Details imagined by the inert man who has three moist-lipped women kneeling beside his couch while he dreams the word "suck" and waits—with beating heart.

Now, that's pretty kinky even today, but Stoker, back in 1897, insists on dragging us even farther toward the wilder shores of love. Just as Harker, telling himself that it isn't his fault, is ready to drift off toward his passive ecstasy as the center of attention of three women, there is the equivalent of a thunderclap. The Count enters the room. Harker says:

Never did I imagine such wrath and fury, even to the demons of the pit. His eyes were positively blazing. The red light in them was lurid, as if the flames of hell-fire blazed behind them. . . . In a voice which, though low and almost in a whisper, seemed to cut through the air . . . he said:—"How dare you touch him, any of you? . . . Back, I tell you all! This man belongs to me! Beware how you meddle with him, or you'll have to deal with me." (53)

When the women, in the tone of wives who have had a long, bilious experience of marriage, reply, "You yourself never loved; you never love!" the Count, though he seems to be replying to their accusation gazes into Harker's face attentively and says, "in a soft whisper:— 'Yes, I too can love; you yourselves can tell it from the past, is it not so? Well, now I promise you that when I am done with him you shall kiss him at your will.' " (53)

There are two euphemisms buried in that last sentence: "kiss" stands for whatever it is the vampire women had in mind to do with Harker before Dracula, the outraged father figure, burst in upon them; and "when I am done with him" is a very lightly veiled reference to the homoerotic delights Dracula has reserved for himself and Jonathan Harker.

Stoker brings the impasse between the outraged Dracula, the sexually frustrated women, and the disappointed Harker, who is feigning sleep, to an end by creating a monstrous diversion. Keeping in mind that all the characters who are onstage just then are in a state of tumescence, Stoker relieves the tension by having one of the women complain, "Are we to have nothing tonight?" The sympathetic husband/father/nurturer Dracula, who has frustrated his wives once more, lets them have his game bag within which some creature is stirring. As the women close around it, Harker's notebook tells us: "If my ears did not deceive me there was a gasp and a low wail, as of a half-smothered child." (53)

At this point in the novel, Harker knows only that the Count and his women are monsters but their kind of monstrosity, though it evidently involves the death of infants, is not yet clear to him. A few days later, Harker climbs down the face of the castle wall and makes his way to what he supposes is the Count's room and from there to a ruined chapel in the lower levels of the castle where, lying in one of fifty coffins, he sees the Count.

> He was either dead or asleep . . . for the eyes were open and stony, but without the glassiness of death — and the cheeks had the warmth of life through all their pallor, and the lips were as red as ever. But there was no sign of movement, no pulse, no breath, no beating of the heart. (63–64)

Six days later, on June 30, Harker, who has overheard the Count promising the dreadful women that they can have their prey "tomorrow night," makes his way once more to the Count's resting place:

> There lay the Count, but looking as if his youth had been half renewed, for the white hair and moustache had been changed to dark iron-gray; the cheeks were fuller, and the white skin seemed ruby-red underneath; the mouth was redder than ever, for on the lips were gouts of fresh blood, which trickled from the corners of the mouth and ran over the chin and neck . . . It seemed as if the whole

awful creature were simply gorged with blood; he lay like a filthy leech, exhausted with his repletion. (67)

Now fully aware of the nature of the beast and clear about the Count's reasons for moving to England, Harker seizes a shovel meaning to destroy the monster. He brings his weapon down but as he does "... the head turned, and the eyes fell upon me, with all their blaze of basilisk horror." (67) The blow Harker meant to be deadly glances off Dracula's forehead, leaving a gash. Meanwhile, Harker is aware that the Count's gypsy servants have arrived and are loading the fifty boxes of earth. Soon the Count will be on his way to London

> ... where, perhaps for centuries to come, he might, among its teeming millions, satiate his lust for blood, and create a new and ever-widening circle of semi-demons to batten on the helpless. (67)

Knowing that he soon will be alone in the castle with the ghastly women, Harker decides to risk his life in an attempt to escape down the castle wall.

> And then away for home! away to the quickest and nearest train! away from this cursed spot, from this cursed land, where the devil and his children still walk with earthly feet! (69)

## ACT II: LUCY

As Chapter 5 begins, in a smash cut worthy of Hollywood, Stoker transports us to England and we find ourselves reading a letter from Mina Murray to Lucy Westenra. Mina is Jonathan Harker's fiancée. Her letter lets us know that she is an assistant schoolmistress; Lucy is both her former pupil and now her friend.

One needs here to pause for a moment to consider Mina Murray (later Mina Harker). Of all the characters Stoker created for his fiction, with the exception of Dracula himself, Mina is easily the most interesting. She is a composite of all the virtues which a nineteenth-century Englishman who has very little feeling for women might wish to endow the woman of his dreams. She studies shorthand and typing so that she can be a helpmeet to her fiancé. She is so industrious and orderly that she thinks nothing of transcribing

and typing a sixty-two-page manuscript overnight. One thing more needs to be kept in mind about Mina. She works for a living as a schoolmistress while her former pupil, Lucy Westenra, is a spoiled and self-indulgent daughter of wealth.

Four months away from her twentieth birthday, Lucy is a good-hearted bubble head who preens herself on having had three proposals in a single day—"Isn't it awful!" The first was the twenty-nine-year-old Dr. John Seward, "the lunatic-asylum man, with the strong jaw and the good forehead," who, in the course of his proposal, "kept playing with a lancet in a way that made [Lucy] nearly scream." (75)

Number two "came after lunch ... an American from Texas." Quincey P. Morris talks the way nineteenth-century British readers might imagine a Texan would talk when he is proposing to the woman he loves: "Won't you just hitch up alongside of me and let us go down the long road together, driving in double harness." (77)

The third—and successful—suitor is Arthur Holmwood, the "tall, handsome curly-headed man," whose character Stoker hardly develops at all beyond making him a scion of a noble family and very rich. Strangely enough, it is this one-dimensional character who will be at the center of one of the most powerful scenes in the novel.

Later we meet one of Seward's mental patients, the fifty-nine-year-old R. M. Renfield whose symptoms are only vaguely indicated. He is, Seward says, "morbidly excitable; [and has] periods of gloom ending in some fixed idea which I cannot make out." (81)

Renfield will have a major role in the action of the novel, but Seward's diary entry about him gives us a revealing glimpse of Seward himself as a man neurotically inclined to introspection.

Lucy's three suitors are actually old friends who have been adventurers and comrades-in-arms together in far-flung parts of the world.

With Chapter 6, the scene shifts abruptly once more, this time to Whitby, a seaside town in Yorkshire on the northeast coast of England where Mina Murray has gone to be Lucy Westenra's house guest.

Mina's entries, in which her fiancé Jonathan's name is hardly mentioned, are almost entirely devoted to a close and affectionate description of Whitby, a charming seaside resort. Mina describes the view of the town overlooking its harbor in great detail, but Stoker's best writing in this chapter is devoted to the long passages in which Mina describes a local character named Mr. Swales, a crusty centenarian who has a long memory of other people's foolishness and a loose tongue of his own. Among the tales the old man tells Mina and Lucy is one about George Canon, whose tombstone has served Lucy as a congenial place to sit. Mr. Swales scoffs at the inscription on the stone which says that Canon died falling from the rocks at Kettleness. The truth, says Swales, is that Canon was a cripple who committed suicide to keep his mother from getting the proceeds of an insurance policy she had bought on his life.

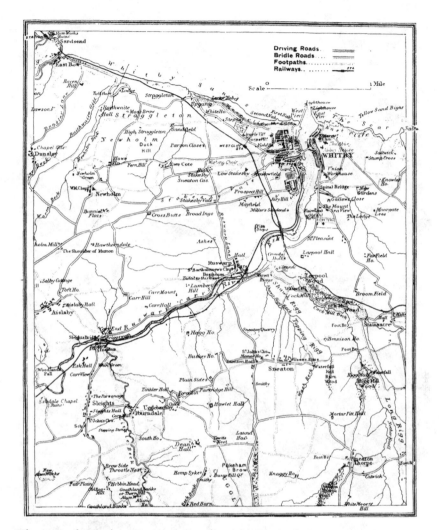

*The town of Whitby, Dracula's first home in England.*

Dr. Seward's diary extracts over a period of five or six weeks elaborate Renfield's madness for us. He is a zoophagous patient who believes that if he can ingest living creatures, he will acquire their life force. He defends his swallowing a blowfly, for example, with the observation "that it was life, strong life, and gave life to him." (92)

By now it is late July, and Mina is properly worried about Jonathan. Meanwhile, we learn from her journal that Lucy Westenra has resumed her old habit of sleepwalking. If readers glance at the calendar in the Appendix, they will notice that Lucy's sleep-

*Ruins of Whitby Abbey*

walking coincides with the approach of the schooner *Demeter,* which is bearing Count Dracula to England. This is important because it lets us know that, among his other powers, the Count is able to project his hypnotic will over great distances.

Soon he is much closer. The Russian schooner *Demeter,* whose chief cargo is Dracula, crashes ashore at Whitby. A great dog leaps from the bow and heads for the churchyard. Swales is found the next day on the suicide's seat with his neck broken. By now, even if we did not know the folklore that says a suicide's grave is a congenial resting place for a vampire, we are likely to have put two and two together: Dracula has arrived and is alive and well in Whitby.

Mina, writing in her journal at 3:00 A.M. on August 11 tells us that in the course of that night she woke to find that Lucy was not in her bed nor in the house at all. It was then 1:00 A.M. Worried about her friend and guessing that Lucy in her sleepwalking state might have gone to the suicide's seat, Mina bravely goes there. As Mina nears the seat, she sees a strange dark figure bent over Lucy's recumbent white-clad form. By the time Mina reaches Lucy, the dark thing with its "white face and red, gleaming eyes" is gone. Lucy herself, still asleep, is breathing stertorously.

Stoker's description of how Mina gets Lucy, who is clad only in her nightgown, back to the house contains some of the novel's best

*The Suicide Seat, Whitby Harbor.*

writing. This is the first time that we see Dracula at his bloody work, and Stoker, by giving us just enough—but not really precise—detail gives the moment an air of mystery colored strangely with a vague eroticism. There is a balletic formality in the complementary attitudes Stoker ascribes to the vampire bent in an arc over his victim.

Then, when Mina is leading the still-somnabulant Lucy home, Stoker's use of homely details is masterful. Mina protects not only Lucy's health, but her reputation. Mina tells us that when she realizes that she—Mina—was barefooted, ". . . when we got to the pathway outside the churchyard, where there was a puddle of water . . . I daubed my feet with mud, . . . so that as we went home no one . . . should notice my bare feet." (123)

Now, halfway through August, we have met all but one of the novel's chief characters. The driving dynamics of the plot are fully before us: Dracula, a dark, foreign evil creature armed with supernatural powers has come to England to prey on English womanhood. The force for evil is here, but the force for good is yet to come.

On a bright moonlit night, Dracula gets to Lucy once more, perhaps with her connivance. Mina, returning from a solitary walk looks up to see ". . . Lucy with her head lying up against the side of the window-sill and her eyes shut. . . ." (126) Beside her there crouched "something that looked like a good-sized bird." Understandably, after such a visitation, Lucy "was languid and tired." (127)

While Lucy's health declines before our eyes, Mina hears from Jonathan Harker, who has been lost to sight for nearly 60 pages. He is in a hospital in Budapest, and Mina travels posthaste to join him there.

Now the focus of the novel shifts to Dr. Seward's patient, Renfield, in his London lunatic asylum. Seward's diary entry is dated August 19, some days after Dracula has sent his boxes to London. Renfield now seems utterly uninterested in the ingestion of life and has begun to make oracular utterances like "I don't want to talk to you: you don't count now; the Master is at hand" (132) and,

The bride-maidens rejoice the eyes that wait the coming of the bride, but when the bride draweth nigh, then the maidens shine not to the eyes that are filled. (134)

Renfield escapes from his cell and is found cowering against a ruined chapel on the grounds of the Carfax estate, now Count Dracula's property.

Renfield speaks in the language of religious devotion:

I am here to do Your bidding, Master. I am Your slave, and You will reward me, for I shall be faithful. I have worshipped You long and afar off. Now that you are near, I await your commands, and You will not pass me by, will You, dear Master, in Your distribution of good things? (135)

Renfield's devotional language and the crudely capitalized "Yous" are meant to give us the clues we need to see that he has been cast by Stoker in the role of an anti-John-the Baptist figure announcing, and offering to aid and abet, the coming of Dracula in the role of the Antichrist. Five days after the events described above, Jonathan Harker is married to Mina from his Budapest hospital bed.

Meanwhile, back in Whitby, Lucy's health miraculously improves, which coincides with Dracula's removal to London. But when she returns to London with her mother, her nightmares and physical weakness begin once more. At the same time, we are reminded that Lucy's mother *and* Arthur's father are ill.

Lucy's fiancé, Arthur Holmwood, no doubt too distracted by his father's condition to have paid much attention to Lucy, finally notices that she is also sick. He writes to his friend, Dr. John Seward, and asks him to examine her. Baffled by her condition, Seward sends for his friend from Amsterdam, the Dutch physician-metaphysician, Dr. Van Helsing, whose favorite student Seward once was.

With the entry of Dr. Van Helsing into the story, the novel's cast of characters is complete and the story assumes its combat mode. Until now, the Dragon, in the form of Dracula has inhabited the fiction pretty much untrammeled while Good has been either passive or defeated. Now, at last, St. George, in the guise of Dr. Van Helsing, has arrived.

In Seward's description, Van Helsing is a medical paragon of the first order. On the evidence of his first letter to Seward, he is also a somewhat ridiculous figure who writes and later speaks a clownish English that must have tickled Stoker's funny bone as much as it annoys a contemporary reader. Tucked into that first letter is an astonishing bit of news. The first bloodsucker in this novel is not Dracula, as we have supposed, but Dr. Seward himself. Van Helsing writes:

> Tell your friend [Holmwood] that when that time you suck from my wound so swiftly the poison of the gangrene from that knife that our other friend, too nervous, let slip, you did more for him when he wants my aids and you call for them than all his great fortune could do. (148)

We now enter the phase of the novel that we might call the Battle for Lucy. Dracula is on one side, and Dr. Van Helsing, helped by Seward and later by Holmwood and Quincey Morris, is on the other. The battle rages back and forth. Dracula visits Lucy; she loses blood; there is a blood transfusion; Dracula visits Lucy; she loses blood; another transfusion. Then Van Helsing, who has intuited what he is battling, sends for and receives aid not prescribed in any pharmacopoeia: a great bundle of garlic flowers out of which he fashions a wreath which he puts around Lucy's neck. He rubs handfuls of the blossoms around the doors and windows of her room, and even around the fireplace.

That night, Van Helsing's precautions are rendered useless when Lucy's mother, thinking to freshen her daughter's room, removes the garlic wreath and opens a window. In the morning, Van Helsing and Seward find a Lucy all but beyond help.

"Again, the operation; again the narcotic; again some return of color to the ashy cheeks." (174) This time, it is Van Helsing's blood in her veins that restores Lucy to life, while poor Seward asks himself, "What does it all mean? I am beginning to wonder if my long habit of life amongst the insane is beginning to tell upon my own brain." (174)

But then, on September 17, Dracula contrives the escape of a wolf named Berserker from the London Zoo. At Dracula's instigation, the wolf crashes through the window of the bedroom where Lucy Westenra and her mother lie sleeping:

> The window blind blew back with the wind that rushed in, and in the aperture of the broken panes there was the head of a great, gaunt grey wolf. Mother cried out in a fright . . . and clutched wildly at anything that would help her. Amongst other things, she clutched

the wreath of flowers that Dr. Van Helsing insisted on my wearing round my neck, and tore it away from me. . . . (183)

Already fatally ill, Lucy's mother dies of fright, and Dracula subjects Lucy to her final bloodletting.

The air seems full of specks, floating and circling in the draught from the window, and the lights burn blue and dim. . . . My dear mother gone! It is time that I go too. Good-bye dear Arthur, if I should not survive this night. God keep you, dear, and God help me! (184)

Once again we went through the ghastly operation. (189)

This time, Quincey Morris is the donor.

After the transfusion, Lucy can hardly be said to be recovering. She is desperately weak, and once seems to be obedient to a telepathic message from Dracula when she tears up the diary entry she made on the night the wolf invaded her room. Her body, too, seems to be changing: "Whilst asleep she looked stronger, although more haggard, and her breathing was softer; her open mouth showed the pale gums drawn back from the teeth, which thus looked positively longer and sharper than usual. . . ." (193)

Dr. Seward's September 20 diary entry records Lucy's final hours. Dracula, in the form of a bat at her window, clearly commands her to tear the garlic flowers from her throat. At 6:00 A.M., Van Helsing announces, "She is dying . . ." Arthur is sent for. For a while, the sleeping Lucy "looked her best, with all the soft lines matching the angelic beauty of her eyes. . . ." But when she wakes from sleep, "Her breathing grew stertorous, the mouth opened, and the pale gums, drawn back, made the teeth look longer and sharper than ever . . . she opened her eyes which were now dull and hard at once, and said in a soft, voluptuous voice . . . 'Arthur! Oh, my love, I am so glad you have come! Kiss me!' " (201)

Arthur hastens to obey, but Van Helsing "[caught] him by the neck . . . and actually hurled him almost across the room. 'Not for your life!' he said; 'not for your living soul and hers!' " (201) For a moment, Lucy's face registers rage. Then

putting out her poor, pale, thin hand, [she] took Van Helsing's great brown one; drawing it to her, she kissed it. "My true friend," she said. . . . "My true friend, and his! Oh, guard him, and give me peace!" (202)

Moments later, she is dead. Amazingly, the marks on her throat disappear.

Meanwhile, in an entry from Mina Harker's journal, there is news from London where Mina and Jonathan have caught a glimpse of Dracula, "grown young" in Piccadilly Circus.

That entry is followed by the King Laugh episode recorded in Dr. Seward's diary on September 22. There we read that Van Helsing nearly choked with suppressed laughter when Arthur observed "that [since the blood transfusion] he felt . . . as if they two had been really married and that [Lucy] was his wife in the sight of God." (217) When Seward demands that Van Helsing explain himself, the answer we get on the nature and uses of laughter is couched in some of Stoker's loftiest prose. Encapsulated in it are two important pieces of information about Van Helsing that critics have by and large overlooked. He is the father of a son, now lost to him—a son who much resembled Arthur Holmwood; and, like Charlotte Brontë's Rochester in *Jane Eyre*, Van Helsing has a still-living mad wife.

We now learn that toddlers have been molested in the neighborhood of Hampstead Heath; they have been found with slight wounds in their throats. The children report that they have been lured away by a "bloofer lady," Stoker's baby talk for a "beautiful lady." We soon understand that the lady is Lucy, who has just begun her new—and as yet incompetent—career as a vampire.

A week after Lucy's death, to prove to Seward that the wounds in the molested children's throats were made by Lucy, Van Helsing takes him on a night visit to her tomb. There he unscrews the coffin's lid and shows Seward that the coffin is empty. A while later, Seward sees a white figure making its way toward Lucy's tomb. Though an unhurt sleeping child is found nearby, Seward is willing to concede only that Lucy's tomb is empty.

A second daytime visit to Lucy's vault follows on the first. This time, when Van Helsing opens the coffin,

There lay Lucy, seemingly just as we had seen her the night before her funeral. She was, if possible, more radiantly beautiful than ever; and I could not believe that she was dead. The lips were red, aye redder than before; and on the cheeks was a delicate bloom. (245)

Van Helsing now invites the men who loved Lucy to join with him and Seward in a visit to Lucy's tomb, where he plans to prove that she has become a demon and must be destroyed. Of those who listen to the outrageous proposal, Arthur Holmwood, naturally, is the one most offended, but he agrees finally: "I shall go with you and wait."

The next night, about midnight, Van Helsing leads the young men to Lucy's coffin. There he pries off the lid. Seward writes:

> . . . we all looked in and recoiled. The coffin was empty! (254)

With that much demonstrated, Van Helsing seals the tomb against Lucy's reentry with a paste made of a crumbled sanctified Host. For a while, the men wait. Coming toward the tomb, they see "a dim white figure, which held something dark at its breast." (256) It is Lucy, once more carrying a child victim. Lucy, "but yet how changed. The sweetness was turned to adamantine, heartless cruelty, and the purity to voluptuous wantonness." (256) When Van Helsing lifts his lantern, the men see that her "lips were crimson with fresh blood. . . ." Seeing Arthur among the men, Lucy flings the child carelessly to one side and moves toward him, saying, "Come to me, Arthur. Leave these others and come to me. My arms are hungry for you. Come . . . Come, my husband, come!" (257)

The macabre eroticism of the scene can hardly escape us. Nor Lucy's utter shamelessness as she reiterates before the watchers, the classic bedroom cry: "Come . . . come . . . come . . . come." Of course Arthur is spellbound. Of course he opens his arms.

And of course Dr. Van Helsing leaps between the would-be lovers wielding his little golden crucifix. Seward writes:

> Never did I see such baffled malice on a face . . . the beautiful color became livid, the eyes seemed to throw out sparks of hell-fire . . . and the lovely, blood-stained mouth grew to an open square, as in the passion masks of the Greeks and Japanese. (258)

At last Arthur is persuaded. When Van Helsing asks, "Am I to proceed in my work?" he replies, "Do as you will, friend. . . . There is no horror like this ever anymore!" (259)

The next day, at about 1:30 in the afternoon, the men, with Van Helsing leading them, are beside Lucy's tomb which Van Helsing opens once more. Lucy lies there and the men see "the pointed teeth, the bloodstained, voluptuous mouth." (260)

Like a good workman, Van Helsing arranges the tools he has brought with him: surgical knives, a soldering iron, and a wooden stake. Curiously enough, in no Dracula film has anyone shown a stake with the dimensions Stoker gives us:

> . . . some two and a half or three inches thick and about three feet long. One end of it was hardened by charring in the fire, and was sharpened to a fine point. With this stake came a heavy hammer, such as in households is used in the coal-cellar for breaking the lumps. (260)

After a brief pep talk by Van Helsing in the form of instruction in the lore of vampirism, and the dangers that would have ensued if, for instance, Arthur

> had met that kiss . . . or when you open your arms to her, you would in time, when you had died, have become *nosferatu* [undead] and would all time make more of those Un-Deads . . . (261)

Now Arthur steps forth from the shadows in which Stoker has kept him:

> Arthur took the stake and the hammer, . . . his hands never trembled nor even quivered. Van Helsing opened his missal and began to read, and Quincey and [Seward] followed as well as we could. Arthur placed the point over . . . the heart, and as I looked I could see its dint in the white flesh. Then he struck with all his might. . . .
> The Thing in the coffin writhed; and a hideous, bloodcurdling screech came from the opened red lips. The body shook and quivered and twisted in wild contortions; the sharp white teeth champed together till the lips were cut and the mouth was smeared with a crimson foam. But Arthur never faltered. He looked like a figure of Thor as his untrembling arm rose and fell, driving deeper and deeper the mercy-bearing stake. (262–63)

This is the central thematic image of the book. A wise old man teaching three incompetent young men how to deal with a voluptuous woman who flings her arms out and calls, "Come . . . come . . . come . . . come . . ." The penetrating stake is the right way to drive the Dracula taint out of her because it was Dracula, representing Satan, who eroticized her and transformed her from an innocent hoyden to a pleasure-promising whore.

Every conceivable sort of sexual violence or perversion is implied in this scene: bridal defloration as Arthur, Lucy's fiancé, armed with a master phallus, penetrates Lucy. Voyeurism, sadism, necrophilia, and a symbolic gang rape are all happening here.

When it is all over and the holy chanting stops, the body "lay still. The terrible task was over." Understandably, Arthur "reeled and would have fallen had we not caught him. . . . It had indeed been an awful strain on him." (263) When, a few moments later, the men look towards the coffin, they see that in it there "no longer lay the foul Thing that we had so dreaded and grown to hate . . . but Lucy as we had seen her in her life, with her face of unequalled sweetness and purity." (264)

That dreadful task accomplished, the implacable Van Helsing reminds the men that "there is a terrible task before us, and once our feet are on the ploughshare, we must not draw back." (265)


## ACT III: MINA

Lucy's second death takes place at the end of Chapter 16. The focus of the narrative now shifts to Mina.

Since Chapter 14, we have been aware that the Mina-Jonathan story has been approaching the one that involves Lucy, her suitors, and Dr. Van Helsing. Now, in Chapter 18, the two strands of the story are entwined.

It is a deft bit of symmetrical plotting. Mina replaces Lucy as the object of the men's affections, but, while Lucy was their romantic target, the married Mina is designated carefully as an erotically out-of-bounds mother figure.

Meanwhile, the indefatigable Mina has created a vast manuscript in which she has incorporated transcriptions from Jonathan's diary, Seward's journal, Lucy's diary, and clippings from various newspapers; and Seward, somewhat belatedly, has come to the realization that "the very next house might be the Count's hiding-place," and that his patient Renfield's outbreaks "were in some way linked with the proximity of the Count." (273–274)

By September 30, all the members of Van Helsing's team have read all of Mina's documentation. In the meantime, the ever-motherly Mina asks Seward to let her talk with Renfield. During the interview, Renfield appears surprisingly sane. As she takes her leave of him, Renfield says to her, "Good-bye, my dear. I pray God I may never see your sweet face again. May He bless and keep you!" (284) The tone of rationality that has marked their conversation and this ambiguous farewell are the clues we need that Renfield's relationship with Dracula may be changing. The disciple has begun to distrust the Master.

The good guys, with Van Helsing at their head, now constitute themselves as a holy band dedicated to the destruction of the vampire. The men make two fateful decisions: they will look for Dracula in Carfax Abbey, the house next door; and, in order to protect Mina, she will be left behind in a room in Seward's establishment. She writes:

> Manlike, they had told me to go to bed and sleep; as if a woman can sleep when those she loves are in danger! I shall lie down and pretend to sleep . . . (294)

At that critical moment, Renfield makes a desperate—and remarkably sane, but futile—effort to persuade Seward to release him. He cries:

> "By all you hold sacred . . . take me out of this and save my soul from guilt! . . . Will you never learn! Don't you know that I am sane and earnest now; that I am no lunatic in a mad fit, but a sane man fighting for his soul." (298)

Later, armed with silver crucifixes, garlic flowers, and portions of the sacred wafer, as well as flashlights, a revolver, and a knife, the men go off to Carfax Abbey in search of Dracula. There, in the dust-filled and cobwebbed ruins, they poke about from room to room until they come to a place that has an awful smell:

> But as to the odor itself, how shall I describe it . . . it was composed of all the ills of mortality and with the pungent, acrid smell of blood. . . . Every breath exhaled by that monster seemed to have clung to the place and intensified its loathesomeness. (302)

There they find the Count's boxes, but there are only twenty-nine out of the original fifty. As they stand perplexed, they see "a whole mass of phosphorescence which twinkled like stars. . . . The whole place was becoming alive with rats." (303)

Ignorant of Mina's deepening peril, the men continue their search for Dracula's other boxes.

Meanwhile, Mina is growing paler; and Seward, after another

interview with Renfield, realizes: "Merciful God! the Count has been to him, and there is some new scheme afoot!" (325) Even as Seward and Van Helsing are digesting this possibility, they are informed that Renfield has been found "lying on his face on the floor, all covered with blood." (327) His back has been broken, and his right arm and leg and the whole side of his face are paralyzed. Dr. Van Helsing performs a trephining operation (without an anesthetic!) on the spot.

Renfield tells the doctors that Dracula has been at Mrs. Harker.

"So when He came to-night, I was ready for Him . . ." Renfield grabbed at Dracula, but it was an unequal battle: "When I tried to cling to Him, He raised me up and flung me down . . ." (335)

The men, who now know the worst, leave Renfield to die alone and, armed once more with their supernatural aids, belatedly hurry off to protect Mina, whose bedroom door they break down.

The scene they come upon is the most unforgettable of the entire novel:

On the bed beside the window lay Jonathan Harker . . . as though in a stupor. Kneeling on the near edge of the bed . . . was the white-clad figure of his wife. By her side stood a tall, thin man, clad in black . . . we all recognized the Count. . . . With his left hand he held both Mrs. Harker's hands . . . his right hand gripped her by the back of the neck, forcing her face down on his bosom . . . a thin stream [of blood] trickled down the man's bare breast. . . . The attitude of the two had a terrible resemblance to a child forcing a kitten's nose into a saucer of milk to compel it to drink. (336–337)

A note in *The Essential Dracula* reads:

"This extraordinary scene bears comparison with the moment in Castle Dracula where Harker, flat on his back, peeps out at the three beautiful brides of Dracula more than half hoping that they will do their worst. In that scene . . . it is Dracula who bursts into the room precisely like an outraged father-husband-lover to prevent the longed-for consummation. Here, a full Victorian committee, representing the supine Harker, is in time to create scandal if not *interruptus*.

Just what is going on here? A vengeful cuckoldry? A ménage à trois? Mutual oral sexuality? The impregnation of Mina? Stoker, no doubt would be horrified by these suggestions and yet each of them is in some way valid. (337)

Now, more than twenty years since those words were written, the scene is as rich in perverse meaning as ever. Perhaps richer. Among recent critics, the notion that this scene masks a "closeting" of homosexual male bonding has achieved considerable currency.[2]

What authorizes our speculations is the meaning of the blood transfers in this novel. Remember that Arthur Holmwood was the first to claim that, because he was Lucy's blood donor, he was, in one sense, her husband, a suggestion which set off the King Laugh episode. It ends with Van Helsing saying that then poor Lucy must be guilty of polyandry, since she had the blood of four men, including his own, in her veins.

Focusing on that idea alone, what do we have here? First, there is Dracula, who took Lucy's blood, which was mixed progressively with the blood of all the men who were her donors. Is he now, following Van Helsing's logic, "married" not only to Lucy, but to all the men whose blood flows in *his* veins. Then there is Mina. Now that she has drunk from Dracula's veins in which is mixed the blood of every man in the room but Jonathan's, to *whom* is she married?

Which perhaps is why Mina cries out, "Unclean, unclean! I must touch him or kiss [Jonathan] no more." (339)

Readers may fairly question whether one is entitled to deduce so much meaning from a scene in a vampire fiction in which, after all, blood taking is a vampire's only business. However, the blood-is-marriage idea was introduced by Stoker in the King Laugh episode, not by readers or critics. And Stoker reemphasizes the idea via Dracula himself.

Back to our story. Armed with their holy artifacts, Van Helsing and his companions drive the Count, in the form of a thin vapor, from the room. What is left onstage is a group of profoundly embarrassed friends surrounding the married couple, whose shame is so great that there seems to be no way to console them.

Mina tells the men how she woke and became aware first of a strange mist in the room, and then of her husband sleeping beside her so deeply that he appeared to be drugged. Out of the mist there stepped Dracula, who told her:

"First, a little refreshment to reward my exertions . . . it is not the first time, or the second, that your veins have appeased my thirst!" . . . strangely enough I did not want to hinder him. . . . He placed his reeking lips upon my throat. . . . Then he spoke to me mockingly. . . . "And you, their best beloved one, are now to me, flesh of my flesh;

blood of my blood; kin of my kin; my bountiful wine-press for a
while . . . (342–343)

Dracula's language is borrowed from Genesis 2:23–24, in which
Adam, on first seeing Eve, says of her:

"This is now bone of my bone, and flesh of my flesh: she shall be
called Woman. . . . Therefore shall a man leave his father and his
mother, and shall cleave unto his wife: and they shall be one flesh."

It is also language that is echoed in the Catholic marriage cere-
mony:

So also ought men to love their wives as their own bodies . . . for we
are members of His body, of His flesh, and of His bones . . . For this
cause shall a man leave his father and mother, and shall cleave to his
wife; and they shall be two in one flesh.[3]

The next day, before setting out to lead the hunt for the Count's
remaining boxes, Van Helsing tries to ensure Mina's safety while
they are gone by touching her forehead with a piece of the sacred
wafer. As he does so, "There was a fearful scream. . . . As he had
placed the Wafer on Mina's forehead, it had seared it — had burned
into the flesh as though it had been a piece of white-hot metal." (352)
 Readers with a long memory and a sense of symmetry will recognize, in this branding scene, Dracula's satanic revenge against
Jonathan Harker for having scarred *his* forehead with a shovel
back in Castle Dracula.
 Once more, Mina cries, "Unclean! Unclean! Even the Almighty
shuns my polluted flesh . . ." (353) The men, whose lack of foresight
exposed her to that violence, now turn to what men always turn to in
a quandary: work. They find and poison the coffins at Carfax Abbey
against the Count's return, then go to the house in Piccadilly where
his other boxes are. There, by the simple expedient of hiring a lock-
smith to open the door, they break into the house and seal the boxes
they find. Then they settle down to wait for the Count.
 He does not disappoint them. He swoops down on their ambush
with the energy of a great warrior:

Suddenly with a single bound he leaped into the room, winning a
way past us before any of us could raise a hand to stay him . . . (363)

And though Harker lashes out at him with his great kukri knife, he succeeds only in slashing his coat so that the Count's banknotes and a stream of gold fall out. Never at a loss, the Count snatches money up from the floor and leaps through a closed window, leaving behind shards of glass and a frustrated group of hunters, whom he taunts:

> You think to baffle me. . . . You think you have left me without a place to rest; but I have more. My revenge is just begun! . . . Your girls that you all love are mine already . . . Bah! (365)

## ACT IV: DRACULA

But even as Dracula exults in his triumph, his fortunes begin to change. His enemies know what species of creature he is and, what has not been true until now, all of the men now know what he looks like. From having been the hunter, the King Vampire finds himself now to be fully the hunted as Act III ends and Act IV begins.

Though Dracula has succeeded in ravishing Mina, Mina discovers that, because she shares Dracula's blood, she has a psychic tie to him that can prove useful to her men in their hunt for the vampire. Under hypnosis, she reveals that the single earth-box still left undiscovered is in the hold of a ship that is weighing anchor. Vowing that Dracula shall not escape, the men plan their pursuit. With Mina's hypnosis-induced information to guide them, coupled with close scrutiny of Lloyd's Registry, they deduce that the Count and his box are on a ship named the *Czarina Catherine*, bound for the Rumanian port of Varna.

Here we may pause for a moment to savor the joke Stoker has perpetrated with the names he gave to the ships that brought Dracula to England and then carried him back to Rumania. Inbound, the ship was named the *Demeter*; and outbound, the *Czarina Catherine*. Demeter, it will be recalled, was the earth goddess and therefore a symbol of fruitfulness. She was also the mother-in-law of Pluto, the ruler of the kingdom of the dead. As Stoker and all of Europe knew, the name of the outbound ship, the *Czarina Catherine*, belonged to a woman of unbridled sexuality. These ships' names resonate with the implications of Stoker's plot: the *Demeter* bearing Dracula whose harvest is death; the *Czarina Catherine* bears Dracula, who eroticizes women.

We are now fully into Chapter 25. Still in London, Van Helsing's team lays out a plan to pursue the monster. Knowing that he is being taken to Varna by a ship, they plan to outwit him by getting to Varna faster by train. Their task has taken on an urgency because it is now clear that Mina Harker has been infected by the blood exchange with Dracula. Her canine teeth are lengthening perceptibly, and her eyes occasionally take on a harder look. There are times when it is clear she is under—or else is fighting—Dracula's hypnotic powers, which reach her even at a great distance.

Knowing herself to be to be vulnerable to Dracula, Mina first extracts a promise from the men that they will no longer include her in their councils; then she demands of them something graver still:

> "When you shall be convinced that I am so changed that it is better that I die that I may live. When I am thus dead in the flesh, then you will, without a moment's delay, drive a stake through me and cut off my head; or do whatever else may be wanting to give me rest!" (391)

There are five men in the room as she makes this request. Four of them have already been accomplices in Lucy's second death. Now these high-minded four promise to do to Mina what they have already done to Lucy. What happens next—or, better, what does not happen next—reveals Stoker's delicate reticence. Though he has Mina insist that Jonathan, too, take the oath the others have sworn, we note that Jonathan hangs back and, in fact, does not swear along with the others. Good wife that she is, Mina does not insist. To save Jonathan's face, she asks Van Helsing to promise that *he* will see to it that Jonathan does his duty.

The chase now takes the chivalric band, accompanied by the endangered Mina, by train and boat from London to Paris and from there, by train, to the Rumanian port city of Varna.

Van Helsing and his Christian knights, with Mina in their midst, reach Varna in time—they think—to intercept the *Czarina Catherine* there. It is now October 15. For nearly ten days, they cool their heels in Varna. Then a telegram reaches them that the *Czarina Catherine* has been sighted passing through the Dardanelles. Three days later, they learn, to their consternation, that Dracula has eluded them. His ship has bypassed Varna and sailed some 130 miles northward to the port of Galatz, on the Prut River.

There, Mina—resourceful, logical *and* intuitive—deduces that the Count in his box must have taken a water route back to his castle in Transylvania. The most likely river, she concludes, is the "Sereth [which] at Fundu, is joined by the Bistritza which runs up round the Borgo Pass." (417)

When she has finished her analysis, the men are ecstatic. Dr. Van Helsing says, "Our dear Madam Mina is once more our teacher. Her eyes have seen where we were blinded. (417)

Now, it is the men's turn to act. They divide themselves into three bands: Godalming (Holmwood), accompanied by Jonathan Harker, will take a steam launch and follow the Count's boat up the river; Quincey Morris and Dr. Seward, on horseback, will ride along the river bank to intercept the box in case it is put ashore; Meanwhile, Dr. Van Helsing and Mina will go by train to Bistritza and then, following Jonathan's route, will make their way to Dracula's castle.

Several elements in the pursuit elicit admiration; most important, the way that Stoker violates the governing principle of the well-made novel, which requires that there be a long rising action leading to a climax, and that the climax must be followed by a shorter falling action, or denouement. Instead, Stoker, having a sort of pseudo-climax with the scene of the Mina-Dracula blood exchange now gives us a new rising action, whose real climax comes literally moments before the novel ends, leaving us with a denouement that is all but perfunctory.

The conception and execution of the chase are superb. This, the novel's concluding sequence, has all the exhilaration of an operatic finale. Most of the excitement derives from the way Stoker has linked the exigencies of the pursuit of Dracula with the perceptible spread of the vampire taint in Mina. While the physical chase unwinding before us moves from one changing geography to another, and from peril to peril, readers are simultaneously being goaded by two anxious questions that keep them turning pages: In addition to "Will the good guys catch the demon?" they also have to worry whether the good guys will catch him in time to save Mina's soul.

There is another, subtler element in the plot that deserves notice and praise: During this final phase of the novel, when everything and everyone is in constant motion, Dracula himself is inert to the penultimate moment. The subliminal effects on a reader of that contrast between kinetic and potential energy are incalculable.

Four vectors of action now point toward Dracula's castle: Dracula, in his box being borne by Slovaks and then gypsies; Godalming and Jonathan on the steam launch; Seward and Morris on horse-back; Van Helsing and Mina heading toward the castle via train and carriage.

Mina is growing increasingly lethargic as Dracula's power over her increases. Van Helsing notes, "Something whispers to me that all is not well." (429) His concern grows when he notices that "she looks in her sleep more healthy and more redder than before." (431) And she is becoming more charming than ever!

In sight of Dracula's castle, Van Helsing, anticipating the worst, encloses Mina in a circle he sanctifies with a holy wafer and learns that she has no power to move out of it. There, at night, by the light of Van Helsing's campfire, they are visited by the three loathsome, lovely women who call to Mina, "Come, sister. Come to us. Come! Come!" (434) just as the vampirized Lucy had called to Godalming. Though Mina and Van Helsing are safe in their holy circle, in the presence of the monsters, the poor carriage horses die of fright.

Back on the river, Godalming and Jonathan, stranded by an accident to their steam launch, have taken horses and are riding toward Dracula's castle, hoping to join Morris and Seward. They know that Dracula's box, on a leiterwagon guarded by gypsies, is somewhere ahead of them.

While they are riding pell-mell, Stoker shifts our attention back to Van Helsing and Mina. Van Helsing, in daylight, has made his way into the castle where he finds the three voluptuous women in their coffins. Though he confesses that their beauty gave him pause, he finally nerves himself to his "wild work . . . butcher work" and destroys them.

Now the weather takes a hand. Snow begins to fall. Then Mina and Van Helsing hear the howling of wolves in the distance, just as, from their shelter on the slope of a mountain, they see the leiter-wagon bearing Dracula's body hurrying toward them. They also see "two horsemen follow fast," then "two other men, riding at break-neck pace."

All the elements of the chase now converge: the sun is setting, wolves are "gathering for their prey," snow is "driven with fury," two sets of horsemen are pursuing the Gypsy-guarded leiterwagon. Dr. Van Helsing loads his rifle, Mina, her pistol. The scene takes on the character of an event seen through a lens that is closing down.

Van Helsing's knights cry, "Halt!" The leader of the gypsies, "a splendid-looking fellow who sat his horse like a centaur" (441), waved them back. The good guys rush forward; the gypsies assume an attitude of undisciplined battle. Impetuous and heroic, Quincey and Jonathan ride through the ring of gypsies. "In an instant [Jonathan] jumped upon the cart, and, with a strength which seemed incredible, raised the great box, and flung it over the wheel to the ground." (442) In the ensuing melee, Quincey Morris, wielding his great bowie knife, receives a fatal wound. Though the gypsies make no further resistance, the battle is not over. The sun has not yet gone down.

Mina Harker writes:

> I saw the Count lying within the box upon the earth . . . He was deathly pale, just like a waxen image, and the red eyes glared with the horrible, vindictive look which I knew too well.
>
> As I looked, the eyes saw the sinking sun, and the look of hate in them turned to triumph. (443)

Then Jonathan's kukri knife and Morris's bowie simultaneously do their work. The kukri knife shears through the Count's throat, and the bowie plunges into his heart.

With the death of Quincey Morris and the knowledge that Mina's forehead is now as white as the driven snow, the novel is effectively over.

There is however, a final "note," in which we are told that Mina and Jonathan are the happy parents of a boy who was born a year to the day on which Quincey Morris died. The child bears the names of all the members of the happy band.

I cannot resist noting my dissatisfaction with Stoker's Note. If one considers how supine Harker has been throughout most of the novel, and compare him to the vibrant Dracula, it is hard to resist the supposition that baby Quincey's true father was Dracula and that the child was begotten in the blood exchange in Chapter 21. The problem is, that the bloodletting took place on October 3, and the child was born on November 6, one year after Quincey Morris died. Hoping that the devil's children might have a longer gestation time than mortals, I consulted Anton LaVey, a Satanist who, to my disappointment, informed me that Satan's offspring required the same nine months *in utero* as mortal babies.

It seems too bad.

## CHAPTER 9

# In Which We Look at Some of Dracula's Fictional Descendants

*"The count suddenly stopped . . . and cowered back."*

THEY RECKON ILL WHO LEAVE ME OUT:
    WHEN ME THEY FLY, I AM THE WINGS;
I AM THE DOUBTER AND THE DOUBT,
    AND I THE HYMN THE BRAHMIN SINGS.

—RALPH WALDO EMERSON, "BRAHMA"

In the century since *Dracula* was published, hundreds of vampire stories have appeared, but the world has yet to see a vampire who can compare with the count for stature, power, menace, and memorability. As Renfield put it sadly about Mina Harker when he sensed that Dracula had been taking blood from her, it is as if the teapot had been watered—i.e., by comparison with Stoker's *Dracula*, the vampires in twentieth-century fiction have been fairly anemic.

Just the same, our century has seen some notable vampire stories.

One of the best of the vampire genre's authors is the German Hans Heinz Ewers, who wrote the novels *Vampir* (1921) and *Alraune* (1911) and the short story "The Spider" (1921). He also wrote *The Student of Prague* (1924)—not a vampire novel, but a Faustian tale on which the great silent film of that name was based.

Written long before the Third Reich was established, *Vampir* tells the story of Frank Braun, a German who goes to America during World War I to make fund-raising speeches in aid of the German war effort. There he discovers that he is most eloquent after he has drunk some of his Jewish mistress's blood. Lotte, his mistress, offers herself willingly to him, telling him, "You are going down the path I made for you—the way to the Homeland . . . my blood flows in you."[1]

It's a weird vision of how Jewish and German destiny might be joined together, and, in light of the history Jews and Germans shared during the Hitler years, particularly macabre.

Ewers's *Alraune* does not have a blood-drinking vampire protagonist, but his Alraune is one of those magnificently imagined succubi who, though she does not steal blood, brings disaster to everyone who loves her. Every male who has ever had anything to do with her suffers, including, at her birth, the surgeon who performs minor surgery on her. Her tiny fingernail scratches him, and he dies of blood poisoning. As the story comes to its end, Professor ten Brinken, who, along with Frank Braun continued her creation, also falls madly in love with her. Ten Brinken, sixty years older than she is, suffers the fate of all the others who have ever loved her.

Ewers's prose is almost cloyingly sensual. Like *Dracula*, it has the erotic power of fiction pushing its way through layers of a repressed sensibility in which the horror and delight of sexuality are tangled inextricably.

Parenthetically, Alraune's name was chosen carefully. *Alraune* is the German word for the mandrake root, about which we are likely to remember only that John Donne makes strange mention of it in his "Song" that begins:

> *Goe and catche a falling starre,*
> *Get with child a mandrake root,*
> *Tell me, where all past yeares are,*
> *Or who cleft the Devil's foot,*

The mandrake root, which has a forked, vaguely humanoid shape, is believed to grow at the foot of a gallows, where it is fertilized by the sperm ejaculated by men at the moment of their final spasm at the end of the rope. Folklore says that the mandrake shrieks when it is uprooted, and that it is an aphrodisiac and will promote a woman's fertility. We may remember that in the biblical story of Rachel and Leah, wives of the patriarch Jacob, the barren Rachel bought mandrake roots from Leah by yielding up to her as payment a connubial night with Jacob.[2]

The creation of Ewers's Alraune, while not quite so magical, is most unusual. She was born of the artificial insemination of Germany's most hot-blooded whore with the sperm of Germany's most ferocious murderer. Like Mary Shelley's Creature, she is less guilty of evil than the men who created her.

---

In America, though there have been scores of vampire novels whose gaudily emblazoned paperback covers make brief appearance on the "Horror" shelves of our bookstores, a few names stand out: Dion Fortune's *The Demon Lover* (1927), Richard Matheson's *I Am Legend* (1954), Theodore Sturgeon's *Some of Your Blood* (1961), Raymond Rudorff's *The Dracula Archives* (1972), Fred Saberhagen's

*The Dracula Tape* (1975), and Whitley Strieber's *The Hunger* (1975).

Three novelists seem destined to be associated forever with the vampire genre: Stephen King, Chelsea Quinn Yarbro, and Anne Rice.

In 1975, Stephen King published *Salem's Lot*, the second novel of his career. *Carrie* (1973) was the first. Those two, along with *The Shining* (1977), seem to me to be the best of his many books.

*Salem's Lot*—the name is a contraction of Jerusalem's Lot—is a vampire fiction set firmly in America. In addition to being a master plot maker, one of the things King does best is rendering the feel of American small-town life. In this novel one of those small towns, Salem's Lot, is invaded by a vampire named Barlow who, like Dracula, has left Europe in search of juicier prey in America. Like his Transylvanian predecessor, Barlow must have a mortal open doors for him. That doorman is Straker, an elegant, bald man whose name, I'd guess, is derived from Stoker himself. These two come to Salem's Lot, where they buy the Marsten House, a huge structure in which a Mafioso murdered his wife and then hanged himself, and in which his ghost is reputed to walk.

Barlow and Straker open an antique shop in the village. Not much later, the horrors begin as, one by one, beginning with the Glick family, villagers are vampirized. The care with which the king creates the villagers for us *before* they are vampirized is wonderful. He lets us see them as a cross section of humanity. In another context, they would be the inhabitants of Peyton Place: child abusers, adulterers, drunkards, as well as kindly teachers, doctors, and children.

King, who makes good use of Stoker's plot, creates, as he does, a band of good guys who combat Barlow. The members of the band include Father Callahan, a priest; a twelve-year-old Mark Petrie; Ben Mears, a young novelist; Matthew Burke, a teacher; Jimmy Dodds, a doctor; and Susan Norton, with whom Ben falls in love. And, as in *Dracula*, one of the characters, Mark Petrie, is smarter and more effective than the others.

Partly because King, taking his cue from Stoker, keeps Barlow, his vampire, out of sight or sound for most of the book, it takes the band some little while to identify the vampire, who seems to have found in Salem's Lot a particularly easy killing field.

One by one, the villagers die. Meanwhile the good guys, in the great tradition of horror fiction (and film), though they know the vampire is inert by day, manage to do their antivampire chores so inefficiently that, time after time, they are in range of the vampire after dark.

Some of the scenes in *Salem's Lot* are candid replays of those in *Dracula*. When the good guys find Susan Norton's vampirized body, we are told:

> Death had not put its mark on her. Her face was blushed with color, and her lips, innocent of makeup, were a deep and glowing red. Her forehead was pale but flawless, the skin like cream. Her eyes were closed, and the dark lashes lay sootily against her cheeks. Yet the total impression was not of angelic loveliness but a cold, disconnected beauty.[3]

And when Ben Mears, who loved her, is given the stake and the hammer with which to give her her quietus, it is as if we were seeing a replay of Arthur Holmwood wielding the merciful stake over the equally beautiful and undead Lucy:

> The stake that had been a simple baseball bat four hours before seemed infused with eerie heaviness, as if invisible yet titanic lines of force had converged on it. . . . Something was put into Ben's other hand—years later he still did not remember which of them had put it there. The hammer. The Craftsman hammer with the rubber perforated grip. The head glimmered in the flashlight's glow.
> "Do it quickly" Callahan said, "and go out into the daylight. . . ."
> "God forgive me," Ben whispered.
> He raised the hammer and brought it down.
> The hammer struck the top of the stake squarely and the gelatinous tremor that vibrated up the length of ash would haunt him forever in his dreams. Her eyes flew open, wide and blue, as if from the very force of the blow. Blood gushed upward from the stake's point of entry in a bright and astonishing flood splashing his hands, his shirt, his cheeks. In an instant the cellar was filled with its hot, coppery odor.[4]

King's borrowing from Stoker is respectful, but his remake of the scene is uniquely his own. That Sears Roebuck hammer is as masterful as Stoker's coal-breaking hammer in Holmwood's hands.

Chelsea Quinn Yarbro's vampire novels featuring the Count Saint-Germain are in a completely different fictional country. King's vampire is still very much in the great tradition: a wicked blood drinker who threatens decent folk.

With Chelsea Quinn Yarbro's vampire Count Saint-Germain, who was introduced to the world in her novel *Hotel Transylvania* (1977), we are millions of miles away from Count Dracula. Saint-Germain is a nobleman who is also a truly noble man. The most common adjectives Yarbro uses for him in that novel are "distinguished," "gentle," "gallant," "tender." He is not tall or dark or handsome. Instead, he is described as stocky, but with exceptionally delicate, small hands. He is also supremely good, coming to the aid of the poor and the oppressed whenever he can. Though he needs blood to live, he needs no more than about a wineglass full and he takes it only from willing women of whom there have been a great many in the course of his four-thousand-year existence. Sometimes, if a woman insists on it, he will turn her into a vampire herself so that she can keep him company for a time.

Among other talents, Saint-Germain is an alchemist, a part-time painter, and a musician, a skilled hypnotist, a powerful swordsman and horseman. Though he is a vampire, he is in no way demonic and, in *Hotel Transylvania,* he fights the good fight against the devil's disciples. To Madelaine, the young woman he loves, he says of the vampiric embrace: "You are right to compare it with Communion. It is that when there is love . . ."[5]

Apparently he is bounded by only a few of the usual rules supposed to govern the lives of vampires. He goes about by day. He handles—he actually wears—a crucifix. And, though he has never been seen to eat, he has a gourmet's appreciation for the food he serves his guests. Like Dracula, he never drinks wine.

If Stoker's Dracula is seen by modern readers as an atavistic creature whose animality turns women on, Saint-Germain turns them on because he is a supremely gifted and sophisticated lover.

In *Hotel Transylvania* the blood exchange between Saint-Germain and Madelaine takes place like this:

"This is my life. I give you my life." His voice, deep and low, stirred the strongest yearnings of her heart. Without a word, she bent to put her lips to the wound he had made, trembling as his body arched at the touch of her mouth. His hands sought out her desires, drawing response on response from her, until the very air shook with the force of her love. Passion blinded her, so that there was only Saint-

Germain and the glory of his ravishment. All her soul was contained in his small hands, fused by the white-burning ardor they shared. The fierce sweetness of her heart opened to him as she felt his inexpressible loneliness thaw in the radiance of her fulfillment.[6]

And this is how he how he treats Gudrun, the woman he loves in *Tempting Fate* (1982). They are in bed, where Saint-Germain

gave her numberless kisses, on her face, her breast, the curve of her hips, her inner thighs. He touched her, felt her tremble, tighten, and give a sobbing laugh as her spasm shook her. He was glad for her, pleased that she could find such pleasure in so bleak a world. . . . She was unwilling to think, for it detracted from the warmth that washed through her, setting all her skin afire, sensitive to the least brush or lightest caress. She was weak with the fervor he offered her. Never had she been so roused, so deeply responsive to the least nuance of lovemaking. She trembled like the strings of a violin. . . . [He] began a feather-light caress of the petal-soft rosy folds between her legs . . . with those small, beautiful hands working their enchantments on her and his lips awakening and soothing . . . [Gudrun] rejoiced, her body, her soul, a glorious paean . . .[7]

These scenes are the literary equivalent of one of those moments in which Frank Langella as Dracula embraced his Lucy in the 1979 stage production of *Dracula*. James V. Hart, the author of the screenplay of Francis Ford Coppola's *Bram Stoker's Dracula*, tells me that he heard a woman in the audience sighing, "What woman wouldn't risk a little damnation to be kissed like that?"

With *The Vampire Chronicles* of Anne Rice, we come to the most imposing literary achievement of all in twentieth-century vampire fiction.

First, however, a personal observation. My own relationship to Anne Rice's literary fortunes is brief, interesting, and tangential. Sometime in the early 1960s, Anne Rice and her husband, Stan, were students of mine in a night literature class in the extension division of San Francisco State University. Stan Rice, then a young poet, later became one of my colleagues at the university, where he taught poetry writing in the Creative Writing Department, as did I. In 1972, when my first book on Dracula, *A Dream of Dracula*, was published, I had no idea that Anne Rice was also interested in the vampire phenomenon. Then, in the fall of 1975, Anne came to my office bringing with her a manuscript of a novel about vampires which, she said, had been turned down by a couple of publishers. She wondered whether I would mind giving her book a critical reading.

Of course I did not mind. I read her book with pleasure and made notes of the changes I would suggest that I thought would tighten the story line and would make her narrative flow more smoothly.

It may have been a week or two later, as I was at my desk in the very act of checking her manuscript against my notes, when Anne came into my office, beaming. Knopf had taken *Interview with the Vampire*.

There is a concept in the Jewish tradition for which the Yiddish word *nakhes* is used. *Nakhes* is the mixture of pride and joy one feels at the achievements or triumphs of those for whom one cares. When speaking of *nakhes* one speaks of it as if it were a liquid. The phrase used is *M'n shept nakhes*, meaning that one scoops up the joy by the ladleful. The day when Anne Rice announced that Knopf had taken her book gave me one great gush of *nakhes*. Her career since then has been dazzling.

Only recently I learned that *Interview with the Vampire* (1976) had its origins as a short story that followed on a piece of introspection:

> "I was just sitting at the typewriter wondering what it would be like if a vampire told you the truth about what it was like to be a vampire. I wanted to know what it really feels like. I wanted to see through the vampire's eyes and ask the questions I thought were inevitable for a vampire who had once been human, to ask. What do you feel when you drink blood? Is it erotic? Is it glorious? Is it spiritual? I followed my imagination and my instinct."[8]

One notices immediately that the three-part question she put to herself about blood takes for granted that all the answers have ecstasy of the body, mind, and soul implicit in them and throughout the five novels that would eventually make up the *The Vampire Chronicles*, ecstasy in all three states are her frequent theme.

The protagonist of her ur-story, which for some years was unpublished, was an Oscar Wilde character, quippy and ironic. Then, in 1972, Michele Rice, the Rices' six year old daughter, died of leukemia. The loss of her daughter to a disease of the blood affected Rice's imagination in ways that are evident but, finally,

**Anne Rice**

incalculable. Immediately what she produced was *Interview with the Vampire*. She says that in the creation of that fiction, she was "in the guise of Louis, . . . able to touch painful realities. Through Louis's eyes, everything became accessible."[9]

As *Interview* begins, we find Louis telling his life's story to a "boy" journalist in San Francisco. We learn that Louis was born in the eighteenth century in New Orleans and that Louis had a brother whom he loved dearly. That unnamed brother was a spiritual boy who, when he was fifteen years old, reported receiving visions of St. Dominic and the Virgin Mary. The saints tell him that Louis must sell the family's plantations and houses and invest the money to do God's work in France. Though he loves his brother, Louis cannot believe in his visions. He refuses his brother's requests and laughs at him. Shortly thereafter, his brother dies, leaving Louis a prey to profound feelings of guilt. For a while, he takes to drink. Then — one night — he is attacked by a vampire. When Louis has nearly recovered from that attack, the vampire Lestat returns and offers a despairing Louis vampiric immortality, which he accepts. The year is 1791.

In 1794, Lestat, in order to bind Louis to him, vampirizes a five-year-old girl named Claudia, whom they find weeping beside the corpse of her mother. We then have a family of vampires, in which Louis, who cares deeply for Claudia, looks after her and is a sort of mother figure to her while Lestat, who made her a vampire, is her father.

Claudia is a curious figure. Once vampirized, she is a swift and cruel killer. Rice is quoted as saying:

> I saw Claudia as a woman in a child's body. . . . There are women who are eternally called girls — cute, sweet, adorable, pinchable, and soft — when in fact they have a strong mind that's very threatening.[10]

The vampire family, who share the same coffin, live through a series of adventures over a period of sixty-five years. Then Claudia, who, presumably, has been nursing her resentment against Lestat all that time, "kills" him. She and Louis head for Europe to look for others of their kind. Their European wanderings are fairly joyless. Central European vampires seem not much higher in the scale of undead evolution than zombies.

Louis and Claudia go on to Paris, where they discover the Theater of the Vampires and vampires more like themselves. In Paris, Claudia persuades Louis to vampirize Madelaine, the doll maker, so that she may have a real mother figure. Then Lestat arrives in Paris. He persuades the resident vampires that Claudia, by contriving his "death," has broken a vampiric law and must die. Claudia and Madelaine are trapped in an airshaft and are destroyed by the action of the rising sun.

Louis finds his way to San Francisco, where the novel ends as it began, with Louis telling his story to the "boy" reporter.

*Interview* is a dense and complex narrative conceived, I think, as a single work. However, once it became apparent both to Rice and to her publishers that they had a gold mine on their hands, Rice, whose capacious imagination was up to the task, expanded her primary vision to accommodate the series of novels we now have in which she re-creates, volume by volume, the history of the vampires, beginning with 4000 B.C. "before the fall of Jericho," when we meet Akasha and Enkil, the ur-parents of the race. These two become Those Who Must Be Kept after they go into their trance in the year 3000 B.C.

Akasha becomes the center of interest in *The Queen of the Damned* (1988). She plans to destroy the world of men as a way of improving the status of women.

In *The Tale of the Body Thief* (1992), Lestat inhabits a mortal body. Here, for the first time in the five-volume chronicles, a male vampire gets to use a phallus since he is in a human body. In their usual state, vampires do not use their genitals since they procreate—when they do—by the oral-oral method. One needs to keep this in mind when, later, I will argue that one of the attractions of the vampire's embrace to some readers is that it is a nonphallic coupling.

In *Memnoch the Devil* (1995), the chronicles come to their end. This last volume is perhaps the most demanding of the five because it is conceptually the most audacious.

But first we ought to see how Lestat, one of the most verbal creatures in all of vampire literature and perhaps in the whole damned world, sees himself. He is the narrator of *The Vampire Lestat, The Queen of the Damned, The Tale of the Body Thief,* and *Memnoch the Devil.* He describes himself in *The Vampire Lestat* (1985):

> I'm six feet tall, which was fairly impressive in the 1780s when I was a young mortal man. It's not bad now. I have thick blond hair, not quite shoulder length, and rather curly, which appears white under fluorescent light. My eyes are gray, but they absorb the colors blue or violet easily from surfaces around them. And I have a fairly short narrow nose, and a mouth that is well-shaped but just a little too big for my face . . .[11]

In *The Tale of the Body Thief,* his eyes have changed color. Here he says that he has

> full and beautiful blond hair, sharp blue eyes, razzle-dazzle clothes, an irresistible smile, and a well-proportioned body six feet in height

that can, in spite of its two hundred years, pass for that of a twenty-year-old mortal.[12]

In *The Queen of the Damned*, he describes himself as

The vampire who became a super rock star, the one who wrote the autobiography? [sic] The one with the blond hair and the gray eyes, and the insatiable desire for visibility and fame?[13]

Finally, in *Memnoch the Devil*, we read that he is

a blond, blue-eyed, six-foot Anglo-Saxon male. A vampire and one of the strongest you'll ever encounter.[14]

Having begun with the story of Louis's brother, who dies in the very midst of his dreams of reconverting the world to Christianity, *The Vampire Chronicles* end with the story of Dora who, when she is given Veronica's veil by Lestat, is able to begin her work of saving the world. Between the stories of these two visionaries, there stretches what has by now become a vast surging and sometimes horizonless sea of vampire fiction within which there are islands of intensely lyrical prose.

Rice has managed to build on the fusion of love and death that is the central element of the vampiric embrace a series of novels steeped in *volupté*. She writes:

The blood is all things sensual that a creature could desire; it's the intimacy of that moment—drinking, killing—the great heart-to-heart dance that takes place as the victim weakens and I feel myself expanding, swallowing the death which, for a split second, blazes as large as life.[15]

Sensual, vast, and wild. As might be expected from a writer who deluges the world with language, the five volumes of *The Vampire Chronicles* are often awash in speech that is disciplined only loosely within the confines of her bold—even brazen—plots. Rice is perfectly willing to have her Memnoch teach God about orgasm:

in the moment when I lay with her, and she with me, and we knew that pleasure together, that small flame did roar with a sound very like the songs of the Most High.

Our hearts stopped together, Lord. We knew in the flesh eternity, the man in me knew that the woman knew it. We knew something that rises above all earthly expectations, something that is purely Divine.[16]

There is nothing Rice's characters do that is not animated by the enormous vitality of the forbidden. In her work, gorgeous, unimaginable couplings are everywhere. Men with men, men with women, mothers with sons. The vampire Lestat gives his dying mother the Dark Gift of immortality by performing the Dark Trick. He asks:

"DO YOU WANT TO COME WITH ME INTO THIS NOW? . . ."
    With her whole being she said Yes.
    "Yes!" she screamed aloud suddenly, drunkenly . . .
    "Yes!" . . . I leant forward and kissed the blood on her open lips. It sent a zinging through all my limbs and the thirst leaped out for her and tried to transform her into mere flesh . . .
    And jetting up into the current came the thirst, not obliterating but heating every concept of her, until she was flesh and blood and mother and lover and all things beneath the cruel pressure of my fingers and my lips, everything I had ever desired. I drove my teeth into her, feeling her stiffen and gasp, and I felt my mouth grow wide to catch the hot flood when it came.[17]

As I've said, the most audacious—if also the most fatiguing—of Rice's five novels is *Memnoch the Devil.* Like an immortal Job, Memnoch bothers God who, at one point, replies mildly, echoing the voice that spoke to Job out of the whirlwind:

"Memnoch, can you count for me all of the stars? Do you know their name, their orbits, their destinies in Nature? Can you give me a rough calculation, Memnoch, of the number of grains of sand in the sea?"[18]

But Memnoch however has no shame. He challenges God to put on man's flesh and endure the crucifixion. Amazingly, God accepts the challenge. He goes down to earth and gets crucified.
    When the Vampire Lestat, having visited Hell in Memnoch's company, returns to this world bearing with him, in the folds of his

garment, Veronica's veil with the image of Christ imprinted on it, he finds his way back to Dora, the evangelist whose father he murdered. Dora, who is menstruating, greets Lestat tenderly:

> "Darling, darling." She kissed me.
>
> "Forgive me, forgive me," I whispered, and my tongue broke through the thin cotton of her panties, tearing the cloth back from the soft down of pubic hair, pushing aside the bloodstained pad she wore, and I lapped at the blood just inside her young pink vaginal lips, just coming from the mouth of her womb, not pure blood, but blood from her, blood from her strong, young body, blood all over the tight hot cells of her vaginal flesh, blood that brought no pain, no sacrifice, only her gentle forbearance with me, and my unspeakable act.[19]

All this, with Veronica's veil pressed to his bosom!

Blood, sex, and theology! A much more riveting formula than Hollywood ever imagined. Rice's readers are always within sight or sound of spiritual—if heretical—discourse. It is this mix of body-mind-soul talk that allows millions of law-abiding middle-class citizens to cling to their respectability even as they enjoy her tumescent prose as it describes the adventures of her race of brilliant and beautiful—always beautiful—killers.

There have been hundreds of short stories about vampires published in the century that has passed since Stoker wrote *Dracula*. In fact, I have only recently finished collecting and editing an anthology of representative vampire short fiction, a task that has given me a pragmatic perspective about what has been published in that time.

As I worked, I noticed that the stories fell into the following categories:

1. **The classic adventure tale,** in which, as in *Dracula*, a vampire pursues innocent victims to drink their blood: M. R. James's "Count Magnus" (1904), F. Marion Crawford's "For the Blood Is the Life" (1911), and E. F. Benson's "Mrs. Amsworth" (1920) are examples.

Crawford tells the story of a young Calabrian named Angelo,

whose father Alario dies after burying a treasure which is then stolen by some unscrupulous stonemasons. When they realize that they have been seen by the gypsy girl, Cristina, they kill her and bury her in the deep hole they have dug along with the stolen treasure.

Meanwhile, with his father's treasure gone, Angelo is suddenly impoverished and is therefore no longer welcome as a suitor for the young woman he loves. He lives alone and "cooked his miserable meals for himself and from being sad became melancholy and morose."[20]

The he begins to have strange waking dreams of Cristina who "whispered strange sweet things in his ear. . . . He felt her sharp kisses upon his white throat, and he knew that her lips were red."[21] With the help of a priest, Angelo finds Cristina's grave and drives a stake made from a piece of driftwood into her heart and as he did so he hears "a woman's shriek, the unearthly scream of a woman neither dead nor alive . . ."[22]

The experience is too much for Angelo, who "went to South America and has not been heard of since."[23]

**2. The psychic vampire.** It should not surprise us that, in the age of Freud, there should have emerged a category of fiction in which the vampire is not a blood drinker, but rather a parasite on other people's energy. All but unknown in the nineteenth century, such stories proliferate in the twentieth. Some examples are Mary Wilkins Freeman's "Luella Miller" (1902), Edith Wharton's "Bewitched" (1925), Fritz Leiber's "The Girl with the Hungry Eyes" (1949), John Cheever's "Torch Song" (1970), and Joyce Carol Oates's "The Bloodstone" (1980).

In Mary Wilkins Freeman's "Luella Miller," Luella has the effect of making people want to care for her, to look after her. "Luella used to just sit and cry and do nothin'."[24] And one by one, all of the caretakers died.

One of the best of the psychological vampire tales I know is Fritz Leiber's "The Girl with the Hungry Eyes." The story, whose title is modeled on Honoré de Balzac's "The Girl with the Golden Eyes," is written in a fairly graceless prose, but its theme is scary and its ending is powerful. Its vampire is a smashingly beautiful photographer's model, all of whose victims die, though the cause of their death is uncertain. The narrator tells us:

There are vampires and vampires, and the ones that suck blood aren't the worst . . . she's the smile that tricks you into throwing away your money and your life . . .[25]

As the story ends, the vampire confides to the narrator what it is that she wants from her victims:

"I want you . . . I want everything that's made you happy and everything that's hurt you bad . . . I want your first girl. I want that shiny bicycle . . . I want your mother's death . . . I want your wanting me. I want your life. Feed me, baby, feed me."[26]

**3. The science fiction vampire.** Some examples: C. L. Moore's "Shambleau" (1933), Leslie Roy Carter's "Vanishing Breed" (1970), and, best of all, Suzy McKee Charnas's "The Unicorn Tapestry" (1980).

"The Unicorn Tapestry" is a marvelously literate, subtle story whose grace, sophistication, and astute insights have already made it a classic. Charnas creates a woman psychiatrist, one of whose patients, Weyland, believes himself to be a vampire. Despite her training, despite her ethics, the therapist, a woman in her forties, becomes involved with her patient, who has been sent to her to be cured of his delusion by the college that employs him before it will let him teach again.

Charnas's story ends with an insight as the therapist wonders, ". . . am I simply no longer fit for living with family, friends and work? Have *I* been damaged by *him*—by my marvelous, murderous monster?"[27]

**4. The nonhuman vampire.** As the title suggests, these are stories about blood-drinking creatures who are not human. Examples are Hans Heinz Ewers's "The Spider" (1921), Roger Zelazny's "The Stainless Steel Leech" (1963), and Tanith Lee's "Bite-Me-Not or Fleur de Feu" (1984).

In Ewers's short story "The Spider" (1921), the fear of women and a fascination with women are interwoven with that of the voluptuous joy of yielding up one's will to a superior force. Richard Bracquemont, a young medical student, moves into a room whose three previous tenants have each committed suicide. We get the details of what happens to him from his journal.

Like Gautier's more benign vampire in "Love and Death,"

Ewers's destroying female is named Clarimonda, "light of the world." There is a remarkable scene in the story in which the vampire Clarimonda stands before a window across the courtyard from the window in which Bracquemont is facing her. She makes a series of movements, which he then imitates.

> Clarimonda makes a movement and I resist it as long as I can. Then I give in and do what she wants without further struggle. I can hardly express what a joy it is to be so conquered; to surrender entirely to her will . . . It is a sort of oppressive terror which I would not want to avoid for anything in the world. Its grip is irresistible, profoundly cruel, and voluptuous in its attraction.[28]

**5. The heroic vampire, or sympathetic vampire.** This is a category of vampire fiction to which an ever-increasing number of stories belong. Examples are Ray Bradbury's "Homecoming" (1946), Laura Anne Gilman's "Exposure" (1990), and Jewelle Gomez's "Joe Louis Was a Heck of a Fighter" (1991).

Ray Bradbury's "Homecoming" is Bradbury at his best. He tells the story of the bittersweet life of a boy who is the only nonvampire in a vampire family. Talking to his pet spider, the boy says:

> "I've just got to go to the party, Spid," said Timothy. The spider whirled at the end of its silk, and Timothy felt alone. He would polish cases, fetch toadstools and spiders, hang crape, but when the party started he'd be ignored. The less seen or said of the imperfect son, the better.[29]

Bradbury's is a skewed perspective that produces a gush of sympathy for the poor boy who has to sleep in a bed instead of a coffin.

**6. The comic vampire.** Examples are Charles Beaumont's "Blood Brother" (1961), Woody Allen's "Count Dracula" (1966), and Frederic Brown's "Blood" (1955).

Perhaps for the obvious reason that blood is so precious, there are not many first-rate comic vampire tales. But there are some. Frederic Brown's "Blood" is a short short story whose punch line I would not dream of revealing. In the face of a solar eclipse, Woody Allen's Count Dracula acquires the same nebbish qualities that have made Allen America's most famous Jewish ditherer.

As our century comes to a close, the distance between Stoker's *Dracula* and the types of vampires that have been imagined in the last fifty years has grown incalculably. Count Dracula is an unambiguous monster. Old, when we meet him, and always evil, powerful, and bestial. The vampires imagined by Anne Rice and Chelsea Quinn Yarbro, as well as by a clutch of younger writers, are more and more frequently Byronic figures: handsome, dynamic, and profoundly lonely (mostly) men.

In one of the most recently published anthologies, sadomasochism, which has always been a subtext in vampire fiction, is treated graphically, indeed, enthusiastically. In *Love in Vein*, an anthology edited by Poppy Z. Brite, we find vampires with needles in their tongues, and others who feed on orifices where one does not expect blood. The worldview of the stories is nasty and brutal, reminiscent of the extravagances of *American Psycho:*

> A set of cuffs, a fashionable ceiling bolt, a butt plug set to placehold for his cock, and the laying on of lashes at breast and buttocks sufficiently rough to recall fathers trying to whip sense into them —these made them happy and tenderized them for the unexpected descent and feeding of himself [the vampire] and his wives.[30]

Late twentieth-century vampire fiction can be seen to be taking two directions. Both of them are expressions of a tenacious romanticism. On the one hand, we have what we might think of as the revisionist Draculas, as we get them in the fiction of Chelsea Quinn Yarbro, Suzy McKee Charnas, and Anne Rice. These vampires are elegant, superior iconoclastic folk with whom Byron would have been comfortable. The other direction, exemplified by the stories in the Poppy Z. Brite anthology are gritty tales that assume that their readers are young people who haunt the Gothic scene, are familiar with drug experiences, and feel themselves exiled from the common ruck of middle-class, middlebrow respectability.

If we remember that the late eighteenth-century Gothic fiction, with its emphasis on sensation, sexuality, and violence, was part of the nascent Romantic movement, then this corrosive new fiction will seem more like nostalgia rather than a move in a new and shocking direction.

In either case, the elegant vampire or the Marquis de Sade with a hypodermic needle for a tongue are both a far cry from Count

Dracula, the white-haired, moustached old man with the bad breath and hair in the palms of his hands. What the twenty-first-century vampire writers will imagine for a descendant yet to come is no doubt working in the mind of a teenager surfing one of the countless vampire-related websites on the Internet. Perhaps website http://www.dracula.com.

## CHAPTER 10

# The Movie Draculas: All About Celluloid Dreams and Sex

*"He have done this all alone; all alone! From a ruin tomb in a forgotten land."*

VAN HELSING [TO AUDIENCE]: JUST A MOMENT, LADIES AND GEN-
TLEMEN! JUST A WORD BEFORE YOU GO. WE HOPE THE MEMORIES OF
DRACULA AND RENFIELD WON'T GIVE YOU BAD DREAMS, SO JUST A
WORD OF REASSURANCE. WHEN YOU GET HOME TONIGHT AND THE
LIGHTS HAVE BEEN TURNED OUT AND YOU ARE AFRAID TO LOOK
BEHIND THE CURTAINS AND YOU DREAD TO SEE A FACE APPEAR AT
THE WINDOW . . . WHY, JUST PULL YOURSELF TOGETHER AND
REMEMBER THAT AFTER ALL THERE ARE SUCH THINGS.

—CURTAIN SPEECH, 1931 STAGE PERFORMANCE OF
DRACULA

arlier in this book, I pointed out that the organization of Stoker's novel, the pretense that it is a collection of journal and diary entries, letters, and memoranda, allowed Stoker to present the action from several points of view, a technique which filmmakers would later develop to a high degree. The book was "filmic" long before the film industry was very far developed.

The film industry discovered very early that *Dracula* has the two essential ingredients which, when exploited properly, put money in the bank: sex and violence. The violence was the most obvious element in Stoker's story; but its sexual content—especially the ambiguous meanings of the vampire's embrace—passed all but unnoticed by the book's first readers and reviewers.

F. W. Murnau, who directed *Nosferatu,* the very first film based on *Dracula,* understood immediately that there was more going on in that tale than met the Victorian readers' eyes, and filmmakers ever since have been alert to its eroticism. From *Nosferatu* to *Dead and Loving It,* movie audiences have been informed ever more explicitly that the vibrant dark vampire, male or female, hovering over a recumbent victim had blood—and something more—in mind. In 1970, a character in a movie finally blurted out, "Are you trying to tell me that a girl sucking blood from a man's neck can induce orgasm?"[1]

Nothing in Murnau's *Nosferatu,* is ever as crass as that. Murnau got at the eroticism by hints and indirection, by keeping the camera focused a bit too long on one scene, or one facial expression, but he never lost sight of the fact that the story he was telling was about a wicked man who desires—and gets—another man's wife.

In a catastrophic misjudgment, Murnau thought that he could evade paying for the film rights to the book by changing the theme of the novel, the names of its characters, and the setting. When Stoker's widow, Florence, heard of Murnau's film, she immediately appealed for help to the London Society of Authors, which sued Murnau on her behalf and prevailed. Prana Films, the studio that produced *Nosferatu* went bankrupt, and, according to the judgment of the German court, all copies of the film were to have been destroyed. Fortunately for us, fugitive copies escaped the scrutiny of the court. The masterpiece that is Murnau's *Nosferatu* will be seen by generations still to come.

My good luck is that I have seen the film many times and have learned to appreciate a greatness that is not always apparent to viewers who see it either for the first or only a few times. Twenty-five years ago, I wrote:

> I felt that I was not the ideal spectator of this much-admired film. I was wearied by the silent shrieks and spastic implications hurried at me by a determined director. Though I appreciated Murnau's skill as a manipulator of textures, I began finally to feel surrounded by them: as if fog and velvet were twitching in every corner of my eye. . . . Watching *Nosferatu* I began to feel like a man exiled to a country of moths flickering around a candle I was probably *not* carrying — feelers, wings, dust and a soft, fluttery dreadfulness everywhere.[2]

Now, writing in 1997, I can see how precisely those things that troubled me in 1972 are the marks of Murnau's achievement. The softness, the fuzziness, the sense of being surrounded by textures are what help to turn the film into the dream-document that it is.

Despite the shoddy effort to disguise it, the story of *Nosferatu* is essentially Stoker's. A young, newly married real estate agent named Hutter is sent from Bremen in Germany to Transylvania to transact some business with a Count Orlok. We follow Hutter through a series of scenes like those through which Jonathan Harker lived: Hutter, too, stays at an inn where he is urged not to go on. Looking out of his window, he notices that the domestic animals are agitated. The screen titles tell us: "Men do not always recognize dangers beasts can sense." When Hutter goes to bed, he reads about vampires from a book he has found in his room.

Later, when Hutter arrives at Orlok's castle, the film, which until then has been entirely realistic, suddenly turns surreal when he meets Orlok. The creature he sees can have no link to the human species as we know it. As played by Max Schreck, Orlok is pale, tall, grotesquely round shouldered. He has huge pointed ears, thin clawlike hands, and wide staring eyes. When he looks down at a

*Max Schreck as Count Orlok in* Nosferatu *(1922)*

picture of Hutter's wife, the screen title says, "Your wife? What a lovely throat."

In the novel, Dracula can project his psychic energies halfway around the world. Here, it is Hutter's wife Ellen, whose deep sympathy with her husband saves his life. Though she is in Bremen when Orlok hovers over the sleeping Hutter's bedside in Transylvania, her prescient shudder is felt by Orlok and drives him off.

Like Dracula, Orlok embarks on *his* journey of destruction. The screen titles tell us that the Count "leaves his castle to haunt the world . . . wherever he emerges, rats swarm out and people fall dead." Meanwhile, like Jonathan, Hutter escapes from the monster's castle.

Now Murnau begins to braid for us the ambiguity of Orlok's and Hutter's journeys to Bremen. Orlok travels by boat, Hutter on horseback. But Murnau's camera moves from Orlok to Hutter to Ellen longing for her husband. Or is she longing for her demon lover?

Back in Bremen, Hutter is welcomed by his wife. Moments later, in one of film history's greatest moments, and one that Werner Herzog, in his version of *Nosferatu* (1979) would imitate, we see Orlok's ship drifting, prow first, into Bremen harbor. Then we see Orlok himself, rising from the ship's hold, as rigid as an upended ironing board. Later, we see him in a boat that moves without visible propulsion. Looking amazingly like Charon crossing the River Styx, he is holding his coffin before him at a 45-degree angle to his chest; we know that he is on his way to some hiding place.

That place turns out to be the house just opposite the Hutter residence. We are treated then to some lovely camera work as our attention is directed back and forth to focus on Ellen staring out of her window in Orlok's direction, and then on Orlok staring back. The look in Ellen's eyes is that of a fascinated bird looking into a serpent's eyes. Orlok's are aflame with desire. Finally, we see him making his way down *his* stairs while Ellen, who has sent her husband away, readies herself to receive the monster.

We must understand that Ellen is about to offer up her body and her virtue for the sake of accomplishing a greater good. She—and the film's audience—know that Orlok is the creature who has been spreading death by plague throughout the country. From having been shown a book about vampires, she knows, too, that sunlight can destroy him. This final climactic scene possesses layers of meanings. On one level, we have a French bedroom farce, with the husband sent away so that the wife can receive her lover; on

*Klaus Kinski as Count Dracula in* Nosferatu *(1979 remake)*

another, there is a Gothic woman-endangered-by-a-vampire scene as Orlok comes into her room; finally, there is the holy temple prostitute offering herself up in order to save mankind.

By some trick of light and shade, all of this, intensified profoundly in the minute and a half of screen time that the scene lasts, makes this moment in a silent film feel especially *silent*. When the camera finally cuts to a shot of a crowing rooster, we can almost hear the triumphant cackling of the old lecher Orlok even as we know that for him it is the sound of the crack of doom because, with sunrise, his evil days are over.

Nearly ten years would pass before *Dracula* would be filmed again. This time, Universal Pictures paid Florence Stoker for the right to make the movie. Directed by Tod Browning and starring Bela Lugosi in the role of the Count, the film was released in 1931. Many actors were considered for the role of Dracula: Lon Chaney, Conrad Veidt, Ian Keith, William Courtenay, Chester Morris, and even Paul Muni. Finally, the choice was Bela Lugosi, who had played the role in the Balderston-Deane production of the play on Broadway. Lugosi, who had lobbied, bowed, and scraped and in every way possible humbled himself to get the role, was hired for the paltry sum of $500 a week for a seven-week shooting schedule.

Nosferatu *(1979)*

Tod Browning, a problematic, alcoholic, but brilliant director was chosen as the film's director. David Skal who has traced the history of how Dracula reached the movies in his *Hollywood Gothic,* writes:

> To many cineastes, Browning is a major *auteur* in a minor key; others, however, point out that his technical execution rarely does justice to the brilliance of his concepts. His films *should* be good. But more often than not the Browning end product is an unholy mess.[3]

For most people who are not familiar with Murnau's *Nosferatu,* Universal's *Dracula* is the first of the Dracula movies. Though it is hardly a "mess," it is pretty much received wisdom that Browning's *Dracula* is not a particularly good film. Nevertheless, for several reasons, it has become the signature film. It has given us the Count Dracula who has become imprinted on our collective unconscious. The one to which our minds recur when we hear the word Dracula spoken. We have heard other actors saying, "Listen to them, [the wolves] the children of the night, what music they make." And "I do not drink—wine." But they have never quite produced the frisson we have each time we hear Lugosi saying them.

*Dracula* begins, endearingly enough, with the music of Tchaikovsky's *Swan Lake* on the sound track as we follow the young English solicitor on his way to Castle Dracula. Here, he is named Renfield, instead of Jonathan Harker. As in Stoker's novel, we get the scene in Bistritza, at which the people at the inn plead with the young man not to pursue his journey. His reply, "I've explained to the driver . . . it's a matter of business with me," defines him precisely as the rational Englishman plunked down in a land of medieval superstition.

We watch Renfield (Dwight Frye) swaying in the coach as it climbs the rocky road upward into the mists and craggy mountains. The camera cuts to the interior of Dracula's castle and we see a hand emerging from a cut-rate coffin. Suddenly we have a glimpse of the Count and his three ghostly women. Then we are back again with Renfield in the coach.

At the Borgo Pass, the coachman flings Renfield's luggage out into the road and drives off pell-mell toward Bukovina, leaving Renfield nonplussed. Just then the Count's carriage appears, driven by a man whose face is muffled. Renfield gets into the carriage, and they take off. Startled by the carriage's speed, Renfield leans

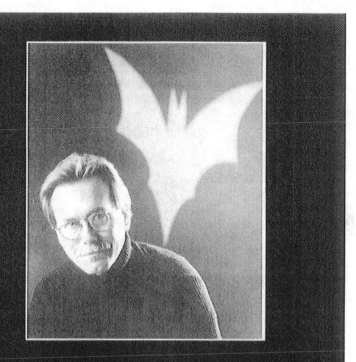

## AN INTERVIEW WITH
## DAVID J. SKAL:

ON VAMPIRES, BRAM STOKER, AND *DRACULA*

*David J. Skal is the author of the superb* Hollywood Gothic *(1990), a study of the fortunes of* Bram Stoker's Dracula *in Hollywood, and of the making of the 1931 Universal Pictures* Dracula, *starring Bela Lugosi. He is the author, too, of the* Monster Show: A Cultural History of Horror *(1993) and, most recently, of* V Is for Vampires *(1996), an A-to-Z compendium of vampire-related lore.*

In an age where we're told we can't be sexual, the vampire is omni-sexual, utterly unafraid of body fluids and blood contact. The vampire has also become a kind of all-purpose caricature. Almost anybody who feels disaffected, disconnected from society, or simply not in the mainstream now has ample opportunity to identify with the exploits of the undead outsider.

The symbol of the vampire is a veiled symbol. It represents something that we don't want to look at too directly. Like it or not, human beings prey on each other in literal and figurative ways.

Stoker was much influenced by the popular theories about "degeneration" that arose throughout Europe in the wake of Darwinism. Evolutionary theory rattled the Victorians as it still rattles many people today. *Dracula* is civilization's shuddering acknowledgment of the unpleasant biological interdependency of all living things. Stoker bargains with the materialist Darwin, conceding that we're animals, but he gives us an option: If we're all animals, so be it—we'll just be animals with a new kind of immortal afterlife.

The character of Dracula engages our imagination, like one of those optical illusions that keep an image shifting. The image keeps us fascinated because it's incomplete and ambiguous. It does not make logical sense, but it does make dream-sense, and that's very compelling. Stoker was one of those writers who had an ability to produce prose with a facility akin to automatic writing. He wrote quickly as the characters came into his work, combining and recombining in his mind the way shapes do in dreams. If you look at the working notes of *Dracula*, you see all of these characters mixing together and splitting apart almost like literary amoebas. The process he started hasn't stopped. To this day film makers keep recombining Stoker's cast of characters. I think if he had worked it all out, the book would have been much less interesting.

Stoker started working on *Dracula* around 1890 and kept working at revising, revising, revising. I think he probably wanted to create something worthy of Henry Irving, his employer, but he was not a playwright and those who have read the soon-to-be published Lyceum adaptation of *Dracula* for the stage know it's terrible, at least as drama. It comes to life in a few places, but one can readily see why Irving turned it down. Stoker thought that Dracula would be a character combining all of Irving's showiness, experience, and classical ability, but the novel falls terribly short of that. Dracula is mostly an off-stage character throughout the book—no doubt an affront to an actor of Irving's stature.

The final composition of *Dracula*, interestingly enough, coincided with the trial of Oscar Wilde, who became the focus of all late Victorian England's obsession with this idea of degeneration. Even H. G. Wells said that the Wilde trial was a partial inspiration for the *Island of Dr. Moreau.*

This idea of degeneration came out of Victorian science and even more from Victorian pseudo-science. Certainly women were considered to be congenitally prone to degeneration, as were homosexuals. Dracula is a foreigner who brings out the degenerate animal tendencies in the novel's women. And the homo-erotic aspects of the novel have inspired some of the richest recent *Dracula* criticism.

Obviously there is a homo-erotic component to Stoker's adoration of Irving. Quite likely a lot of it on a level that he'd never consciously admit. He certainly had Wilde's *The Picture of Dorian Gray* in mind when he wrote *Dracula*. He knew Wilde and his circle well. He even married Wilde's youthful sweetheart, Florence Balcombe. In his notes [for *Dracula*] there were some Wildean themes that were not played out in the finished novel. He originally considered having a painter as a major sub-character who tried to paint Dracula, but his image could not be captured on canvas. He thought about introducing the Kodak camera into the book and when someone tries to take a picture of Dracula, he would be revealed as an x-ray, a skeleton. His Dracula, like Dorian, is a corrupt degenerate who remained supernaturally young while destroying the innocent.

## ON *DRACULA* AND FILM

Universal produced *Dracula*, one of the earliest talking pictures, in 1931, the worst year of the Great Depression, and it turned out to be one of the year's biggest money-makers. I don't think the images of dread in *Dracula* and *Frankenstein* would have had the same power had they been set in some other year. The monsters were lightning rods for all kinds of cultural anxieties.

Though the stage play by Hamilton Deane and John Balderston had a lot of intentional humor in it, with many knowing winks to the audience, the Lugosi film is very somber and slow-moving. It's also highly stylized. Lugosi had played the role so much on stage that his film performance was extremely mannered. The result may not be good film acting, but this stylization makes the performance unforgettable.

It was Lugosi's voice and presence more than anything else that made it the signature "Dracula" film of all time.

According to Lugosi's son, his father never really learned to think in English. He was still learning his stage roles phonetically in the late twenties. He didn't begin studying English seriously until his late forties—too late to achieve complete fluency.

Lugosi's theatrical training never left him. On screen, in *Dracula*, he was always acting for the last row of a large theater. The performance has a hell of a kick and you can't get it out of your mind. It is that intensity probably that also doomed his later career. He could not escape his Dracula: No matter who he played, he would sound like Dracula and look like Dracula.

*Nosferatu* has a dreamlike quality, a fairy tale quality. *Dracula* is structured in the same way. It's very much an archetypal quest.

It's interesting that *Nosferatu* is considered a German expressionist film, but it doesn't have a lot of theatrical artifice. It's shot on location. The shadows are real, they're not painted on (as in *The Cabinet of Dr. Caligari*). One can imagine *Dracula* being filmed in that high expressionistic and very theatrical style, but that wasn't what they did with *Nosferatu*. The film was intended as an art film. Albin Grau, the art director, really emphasized the fact that the vampire was a metaphor of the war and its aftermath. That World War I had been a "cosmic vampire" that had sapped the blood of Europe and Germany.

out the window to say something to the driver, but all he sees up ahead is a huge bat flapping over the horse's heads.

The carriage arrives with a clatter in the courtyard of Dracula's castle. Renfield, umbrella in hand, stands before a creaking door that opens to let him enter. We hear wolves howling. As Renfield enters the castle, our eyes see ruin everywhere. We glimpse bats, huge spiderwebs and then, astonishingly, a small family of armadillos that wandered onto the *Dracula* set from a nearby sound stage and which, for some reason, were not edited out of the film.[4] But that distraction aside, we—and Renfield—then meet Dracula as the world has forever after known him: the perfect Gothic villain. A tall, dark, sinisterly handsome European nobleman with a cold, chiseled face and a superbly foreign accent, speaking through curled lips, "I am Dracula."

It is no ordinary moment. It is Bela Lugosi uttering his first screen words, announcing himself to the world—and to himself his destiny as the man whose face would be forever linked with Dracula's. It was an identification that he could never shake and which embittered him for the rest of his life. Understandably nervous, Renfield replies, "I am really glad to see you."

"I bid you welcome," Dracula says. Behind him rises a vast stone staircase hung with thick cobwebs. Outside, we hear the howling of wolves. Again the lilting voice of evil speaks, "Listen to them, children of the night. What music they make."

*Bela Lugosi as Dracula (1931)*

The majestic Count and his guest mount the great staircase, with its aura of bleak vastness, of ancient power and present-day ruin. Renfield is amazed to see that Dracula simply passes through the overhanging cobwebs without disturbing them while he must tear his way through them.

Later, when Renfield is eating the cold dinner that he finds waiting for him, Dracula pours a drugged wine for him, saying, "This is very old wine. I hope you will like it." When Renfield asks his host why he is not drinking, we get the by-now-familiar reply, "I do not drink [significant pause] wine." When Renfield gives himself a paper cut, Dracula leans forward, avidly taking in the sight of the blood oozing from the small wound.

The drugged wine takes effect, and Dracula's three wives, whom we glimpsed at the beginning of the film move eerily toward Renfield. They seem to be floating, sleepwalking, and suffering from acute indigestion all at once. They want Renfield's blood, but are prevented by the interference of Dracula himself, who has reserved first blood for himself.

*Dwight Frye as Renfield, laughing his unearthly laugh, in* Dracula *(1931)*

Now we cut to the ship bearing Dracula to England and to one of the finest film moments in this frequently flawed film. We see Renfield, who has gone mad after his blood encounter with Dracula back in Transylvania, rising up out of the hold of the ship. He does not rise the way Max Schreck did in *Nosferatu*, tilted bolt upright as if he were a board, but comes up quite naturally with the difference that his face is distorted in lunatic grimace and he is laughing a laugh so blood chilling that only Pablo Alvarez Rubio, in the Spanish-language version of this film, has ever improved on it. That laugh is

a low, low chuckle beginning deep in the bowels and rising unwillingly through stages of pain until it leaves the mouth, bedraggled, helpless, lonely.[5]

The laugh marks the end of the film's Transylvanian action. It is by far the most atmospheric, most effective segment of the film. From that moment on, all the action will take place in a modern London with electric lights and taxis and women with marcelled hair. In that setting, the tautness of Stoker's story gives way onscreen to a flabbiness and a turgidity that is all but fatal to the film. Some of the problem can be blamed on Browning's careless direction, but much of it can be ascribed to the fact that he truncated and telescoped the action because he was following the plot of the Balderston-Deane stage play instead of Stoker's novel.

In London, we see Dracula, impeccable in tie and tails, approaching a young woman selling violets in front of a concert hall. We hear a scream. Then a refreshed Count Dracula makes his way into the concert hall where he contrives to meet Lucy Weston (not Westenra, as in Stoker), her friend Mina Seward, and Mina's psychiatrist father, Dr. John Seward.

Browning's cast of characters is different from Stoker's. From having been one of Lucy's three youthful suitors, John Seward is now a middle-aged psychiatrist while Mina, who is an orphan in the novel, is his daughter here. Though Jonathan Harker (David Manners) is still Mina's fiancé, he does not get to marry her. Lucy Weston is still a sprightly hoyden, but in this film, she is unpartnered. That is, until she meets the suave Count Dracula. She is drawn immediately to his accent, his title, his distant castle in Transylvania, and to such aphorisms as "There are worse things than death to be afraid of." She confides her infatuation to Mina and then goes off to the guest room in Dr. Seward's house. Before she

gets into bed, she looks out of her window and sees a very uncon-
vincing large bat flying by. A moment later, the camera watches her
sleeping. All at once, a leering Dracula materializes beside her. He
bends over her, lower and lower and lower—until fade-out.

In the next scene, without a moment wasted, we learn that Lucy
is dead. Baffled by the strange marks at her throat, Dr. Seward calls
in his friend, Dr. Van Helsing.

With Helsing's arrival, the film focuses on the struggle to save
Mina's life and soul.

The rest of Stoker's story is cobbled together. Dracula continues
to feed at Mina's throat, then takes her with him to Carfax Abbey,
where Van Helsing and Harker find his coffin at dawn. Then, in the
tradition of the classical Greek theater, which kept violence off-
stage, we hear a grunt and a groan which signify that Van Helsing
has given Dracula his quietus. Almost at once, the camera finds
Mina, having spasms which tell us that with the death of Dracula,
Mina is no longer under his spell.

There are a number of things wrong with Browning's film. It
feels disjointed and occasionally incoherent because it was edited
awkwardly and haphazardly. There are also the indifferent performances of David Manners (Jonathan Harker), Helen Chandler
(Mina Harker), and Frances Dade (Lucy Weston). Partly the
problem is that the women were cast to be decorative; very little
acting was required of them. As Helen Chandler put it, "In *Dracula*,
I played one of those bewildered little girls who go around pale,
hollow-eyed and anguished, wondering about things."[6]

Another of the film's defects is that it retains the low comedy that
helped make the Balderston-Deane stage play a long-running success. While such scenes may have amused theater audiences, they
interfere with the dominating mood of the film, which is one of
somber portentousness.

What's right about the film is also told quickly. If Lugosi has
imprinted Dracula on our minds, Edward Van Sloan must be credited with having given us an equally unforgettable Van Helsing.
The role of Van Helsing would later be played by such towering talents as Laurence Olivier and Anthony Hopkins (not to mention
Mel Brooks), but no one has left his mark on it the way Van Sloan
has. He embodies Stoker's description of him:

> . . . a philosopher and a metaphysician, and one of the most
> advanced scientists of his day . . . [with] an absolutely open mind . . .

iron nerve, a temper of the ice brook, an indomitable resolution . . .
and the kindliest and truest heart that beats . . .[7]

In one sparkling scene, Van Helsing and Dracula meet and have
a battle of wills, during which Lugosi arches his eyebrows com-
mandingly as he says, "Come here!" to the adamant Van Helsing.
The scene ends with neither of them quite the winner, though Dracula leaves Van Helsing with a complimentary parting shot: "For one
who has lived not a single lifetime, you are a wise man, Van Helsing."

Finally, since I am bestowing accolades, Dwight Frye plays Renfield with an air of innocence that manages to intensify the physical
terror through which Renfield lives in the Transylvania segment of
the film up to—and including—his famous laugh coming out of the
hold of the ship. If Frye's interpretation of the mad Renfield in England turns hammy, the fault lies more with the script than with his
acting. Even there, one catches glimpses under the exaggerated
"crazy" posturing, of authentic moral dismay Stoker's Renfield
exhibits in his moments of sanity. With all the movie's faults the
judgment of the *New York Daily News* film reviewer who saw the film
in 1931 will stand:

> You'll find it creepy and cruel and crazed. It is superbly pho-
> tographed. . . . It is just plain spooky and bloodthirsty. . . . Brrrr!
> We enjoyed it.

Critics like David Skal admire the Spanish-language version of
Universal Studio's *Dracula* far more than the Tod Browning film.
Skal says the film, which was produced by Paul Kohner

> can be read as an almost shot-by-shot scathing critique of the
> Browning version. And whatever else it is, the Spanish *Dracula*
> remains one of the few examples in world cinema of a simultaneous,
> alternate rendition of a familiar classic, richly illustrating the inter-
> pretive possibilities of a single script.[8]

Because he could not speak Spanish, George Melford, the film's
director, relied on an on-set translator to convey his instructions to
his actors. The cinematographer was George Robinson. Dracula
was played by Carlos Villarias, and Barry Norton, né Alfredo

Biraben was Jonathan Harker (Juan Harker) while the role of
Renfield went to Pablo Alvarez Rubio, whose on-screen presence
was longer than Dwight Frye's in the Tod Browning version. Inci-
dentally, his insane laugh lasted longer than Frye's, but it was
equally macabre. Carmen Guerrero played Lucia (Lucy). The film's
ingenue, named Eva instead of Mina, was Lupita Tovar, who was
all of seventeen years old.

Though Universal's publicity for Tod Browning's film trumpeted
that it was about "The strangest love ever known," the Spanish version is sexier in every respect. Like Lupita Tovar, Dracula's three
wives are seen with deep cleavages. Ms. Tovar recalled, "My neg-
ligee was very low-cut. When my grandson saw the film, he said,
'*Now* I know why Grandpapa married you!' "[9] Parenthetically, all
the young women in the Spanish film look real, unlike the decorative cardboard cutouts we get with Helen Chandler and Frances
Dade.

For Kohner, Robinson, and Melford's superior picture, Universal Pictures paid $66,069.35, a small sum of money for a feature
film, even in 1930. It was something of a triumph for which the
Spanish-speaking cast deserved much of the credit. Working at
night on the same sets used by the English-speaking actors by day,
they finished the film in twenty-two days of shooting, compared
with the seven weeks required by the English speakers. In an interview, Lupita Tovar says that the Spanish-speaking actors were
determined "not to let them down. . . . We were all anxious to make
a good film. We wanted our film to be the best, and according to the
critics, I think it was."[10]

———◆———

Considering that *Dracula* was the top-grossing film of 1931, it took a
surprisingly long time before Universal Pictures made the Dracula
sequel for which the film's success cried out. Five years later, in
1936, Universal released *Dracula's Daughter.* George Robinson, who
had been the cinematographer for the Spanish *Dracula* and Garrett
Fort, who wrote the screenplay for the Tod Browning film, worked
on this one as well.

Not as well known as it should be, *Dracula's Daughter,* like *The
Bride of Frankenstein,* violates the rule that sequels of films are neces-
sarily weaker siblings of the films they follow. *Dracula's Daughter* is
simply superb; it gives us, early in the evolution of horror film, a
sympathetic study of an unwilling female vampire. Lambert Hillyer,

the film's director, and Garrett Fort, the screenwriter, understood how to meld the archetypal symbolic power of a father-daughter relationship with that of the equally threatening idea of vampirism. Furthermore, if Tod Browning's film deserves praise for its atmospheric effects, *Dracula's Daughter* far surpasses the earlier movie.

The film opens somewhat awkwardly as it tries to link the story we are about to see with the final scene in Tod Browning's *Dracula*. For a few moments, the film occupies itself with the arrest of Dr. Van Helsing for having driven a stake through Dracula's heart and the activities of young Dr. Jeffrey Garth, who is trying to save him from a murder charge.

Then the real story of *Dracula's Daughter* begins. Gloria Holden, playing the role of the Countess Marya Zaleska, an artist who paints faceless women, shows up at the London morgue. She takes her father's body to a forest clearing where, in an exquisitely conceived and photographed scene, she performs her father's funeral obsequies. Standing in flickering firelight, cloaked in black from head to foot, and holding a crucifix up in one hand, Countess Zaleska stands over her father's body and intones a prayer addressed at once to God and to Satan:

Dracula's Daughter *(1936)*

"Unto Adonai and Azrael, and in keeping with the laws of the Flame and lower pits, I consign this body to be consumed with purging fire. Let all baleful spirits that threaten the souls of men be banished. Be thou exorcised, O Dracula, and thy body, long undead, find destruction throughout eternity in the name of thy dark unholy master.

"In the name of the All Holiest, and through this cross, may the evil spirit be cast out until the end of time."

With that she consigns her father's body to the flames.

Now the Countess's own spiritual hegira begins. For a while, she believes that, with her father's death, the curse of vampirism which has tainted her family has left her. "I can lead a normal life. Think normal things. Even play normal music." But very soon she learns that she is mistaken. When she asks her faithful servant, Sandor, to look into her eyes and tell her what he sees, he replies unequivocally, "Death."

Like any twentieth-century American bewildered by life, she consults Jeffrey Garth, the psychiatrist whom she met at a party. When she has confided her problem to him, his advice is "Don't avoid it. Meet it. Fight it. That's the secret."

That vapid counsel does not keep her from falling in love with Garth. Meanwhile, like a drug addict resolving to kick her habit, she tests her resolve by having her servant, Sandor, bring a model to her studio. The scene in which the Countess, whose victims have always been women, has the model lower her shoulder straps, is delicately homoerotic.

Later, when Garth refuses to run off to Transylvania with the Countess where, she hopes, he will be able to free her from the curse of vampirism, she kidnaps Garth's secretary, Janet, and flies to Transylvania with her. She offers to free Janet if Garth will "remain here with me among the undead." The self-sacrificing Garth accepts the bargain, but by now, the stony-faced Sandor, the Countess's faithful servant who has always loved her and is murderously jealous of Garth, brings the film to its climactic end by firing an arrow at the woman he has loved.

When Dr. Van Helsing looks down at her body, he observes, "She was beautiful when she died—a hundred years ago."

———

The 1930s was a great decade for Universal Studios and its monster movies, especially once it decided to exploit its great monsters by providing them with family. After *Frankenstein* (1931), it released *The Bride of Frankenstein* (1935), and *Dracula's Daughter* (1936). In 1939 it gave the world *The Son of Frankenstein*, after which there was a brief hiatus. Then, in 1943, with World War II still raging, Universal released *The Son of Dracula.*

For the first time, a Dracula film is set in the United States. The film, directed by Robert Siodmak, most unfortunately starred Lon Chaney Jr. in the title role. It is hard to know whether it is the frozen-faced Chaney's performance, Eric Taylor's script, or Robert Siodmak's direction that makes *The Son of Dracula* such a wretched film. Tedious though it is, to sketch the still-evolving film lore of Dracula, we must take this film into account, too.

Katherine Caldwell, a woman with an interest in the occult, has recently returned from Europe to her home in the swamp country of Tennessee. In Europe, she made the acquaintance of a Count Alucard, whom she has invited to Dark Oaks, her family's plantation. She has also brought back with her a gypsy fortune teller named Queen Zimba, who warns Katherine: "I see you marrying a corpse and living in a grave." Even as she speaks, a bat chirps overhead, and she dies of a heart attack.

Not long afterward, Count Alucard shows up. It does not take us long to solve the riddle of his name: Alucard? Alucard? Aha, Dracula spelled backward. But Katherine, we learn has a scheme: She wants to marry Alucard, so that he will vampirize her, thereby giving her eternal life. Once she is immortal, she will have Frank Stanley, her true love, destroy the Count. For a while, all goes well. She marries Alucard; he vampirizes her. Then she explains to Stanley what she has been up to: "Count Alucard is immortal. Through him, I attained immortality. Through me, you will attain it."

Stanley does not find the prospect of eternal life as a vampire attractive. With the help of Dr. Brewster, who has been guided by a vampire expert named Laszlo, he outwits the vampires.

*The Son of Dracula* has its admirers, mostly for the way its director Robert Siodmak sustains its sinister mood, and particularly for a scene in which Alucard's coffin rises from the swamp in which it has been hidden. The Count leaves the coffin in the form of a mist. It turns into Alucard, who then glides toward the shore. I must admit that there *is* something creepy about the densely overgrown Tennessee swamp in which the story is set, with its strange night noises and dark, silent waters. But Katherine's crazy scheme for immortality strains our willingness to suspend disbelief in the film's plot.

The Son of Dracula *(1943)*

In 1958, another Dracula story was set in the United States. In *The Return of Dracula*, Francis Lederer's Dracula comes to California, where his depredations end with his being impaled on a stake at the bottom of a mine shaft.

Dracula's next American appearance was in *Billy the Kid Versus Dracula* (1965), a movie for which I have a particular fondness. We should honor the breathtaking audacity of the filmmaker's decision to fuse two well-established genres: the cowboy movie with the vampire film. And honor, too, the ingenious plot that pits the all-American epic outlaw, Billy the Kid, against Count Dracula, that most evil of Europeans. On top of that, John Carradine's title role provides this film with its one small scrap of splendor.

Perhaps the bleak years for Dracula filmmaking should be dated from 1943, with the release of *The Son of Dracula*. After that, there is a considerable number of years in which films involving Dracula went from bad to deporable. In 1945 Universal released *The House of Frankenstein* on the premise that if one monster was good and two were better, then three would be best of all. *The House of Frankenstein* has a wicked doctor, Dr. Gustav Neiman (Boris Karloff) and Dracula's skeleton with a stake sticking out of it. It also has the lachrymose Lon Chaney, Jr. reprising his role as the Wolfman. The best part of the film is John Carradine playing Dracula.

The next year, Universal employed the formula of three-monsters-in-one-film once again in *The House of Dracula*. This film uses the theme of the reluctant vampire, which made *Dracula's Daughter* such a poignant film. Here, however, the problem is blood chemistry. We are asked to believe that Dracula (John Carradine) suf-

*John Carradine as Dracula in* Billy the Kid Versus Dracula *(1965)*

fers from a blood ailment that he wants cured. For that cure, Dracula (here named Baron Latos) consults Dr. Edelman, played by Onslow Stevens. Edelman tells him, "A sample of your blood reveals the presence of a peculiar parasite." But before the doctor can find a cure for Latos, the vampire taint asserts itself and he vampirizes Edelman. Edelman revives the Frankenstein creature. In the mayhem that follows, everything that could end badly does so. Only Larry Talbot, played with his usual frozen-faced aplomb by Lon Chaney Jr., gets away with a whole skin.

In 1948 there was a glimmer of light when Universal allowed two of filmdom's wisest fools to join its team of monsters in *Abbott and Costello Meet Frankenstein*. Those two zanies would eventually play opposite Jekyll and Hyde and the Mummy. Here they encounter the Frankenstein Creature, the Wolfman, Dracula, and the Invisible Man. In the midst of their high jinks, Bud Abbott summarizes the entire Dracula question: "Count Dracula sleeps in his coffin, but rises every night at sunset. This is awful silly stuff."

The film's plot involves Dracula's decision to put Lou Costello's brain into the skull of the Frankenstein Creature. It's not much of a plot idea, but this film hardly requires one. What comes through best is the sheer silliness of monster folklore when it is as it were, hyperventilated by comedians as brilliant as Abbott and Costello.

———◄○►———

In 1958 Hammer Films' *The Horror of Dracula* marked a major shift in the treatment of the Dracula theme. The film was in color, whose use literally changed the emotional tone of the vampire idea from here on, making it simultaneously more realistic and, because of the way Technicolor works, more romantic.

To appreciate the difference, think for a moment about how black-and-white films work. We do not see the real world in black and white. As a result, the world interpreted by black-and-white photography is already a world of abstraction, lacking the myriad colors in which we usually experience it. That abstraction works to intensify mythic materials, whose plots are already profoundly abstracted. The horror genre, when it works at all, is based heavily on myth. This is why the black-and-white horror film, and emphatically those dealing with Dracula, employing complex manipulations of light and dark, are linked so beautifully to shades of moral meaning and allegory. A bizarre trick of the senses allows us to feel that black and white tells a truer story than color, that it gives us an X-ray image of the emotion of truth. Hammer's shift to color for its horror films opened an entirely new vista.

With *The Horror of Dracula* (1958), the "horror" is made even more problematic because Terence Fisher, its director, abandoned the somber tones of previous Dracula films. Henceforth Hammer horror films would be characterized by resplendent interiors, richly polished wood surfaces, expensive draperies and rugs, and characters whose clothing is invariably tailored beautifully. Fisher also racheted up toward the explicit, the awareness of the eroticism implied in the vampiric blood transfer. More than that, the female leads—victims—will all be splendidly bosomed young women whose décolletage is almost the first thing one is expected to notice about them.

*The Horror of Dracula* is also remarkable because it gives us a second "signature" Dracula: Christopher Lee. Tall, lean, aloof and, most of all, profoundly silent, Lee haunts the film as much by his absence as by his comparatively rare presence. He projects menace. He told me, "What I try to do is to give the audience a sense of anxiety, to make it worry. An audience should ask, 'What's he going to do next?' This is the essence of suspense. . . . What I try to convey is his tremendous *stillness* and the way it combines with his savagery to produce a hypnotic power."[11]

In addition to Lee, the film introduces us to a Van Helsing— Peter Cushing—who will be nearly as unforgettable as Edward Van Sloan. Like Lee, Cushing makes aloofness an enormously attractive characteristic. His Van Helsing knows what he knows without ambiguity and without hesitation, and acts on it.

The plot of the film itself is simple enough. We see Jonathan Harker in Dracula's castle, sitting at a priceless antique desk, writing in his diary. We learn that he is about to catalog Dracula's library. Suddenly there is a knock at the door, and a beautiful young woman comes in who begs Harker to help her because Dracula is keeping her prisoner. Before Harker can be helpful, she is at his throat, with her fangs exposed. Dracula invades the scene, flings Harker to one side, and takes the woman away. As in Stoker's novel, Harker finds Dracula's body in his crypt, as well as the body of the young vampire in her coffin. As the sun is setting, Harker drives a stake through the young woman's heart. Shrieking and writhing, she turns into a toothless old hag before his eyes. But

Harker has delayed too long. The staking of the woman coincides with sunset, and Dracula's eyes pop open. Moments later, he is gone.

We cut to a tavern in Klausenburg, where we find Van Helsing asking for news about his friend Harker. He is met by hostile silence. A kindly chambermaid slips him Harker's diary.

Van Helsing makes his way to Dracula's castle, where he finds the vampirized Harker. He drives a stake into Harker's heart.

Now we cut to the home of Arthur and Mina Holmwood, where Lucy, Holmwood's sister, is feeling poorly. We see Lucy in bed wearing a cross that falls engagingly into her cleavage. But she removes it and snuggles down into a languorous position as she fingers the wounds in her neck. We have the usual confusion about the garlic flowers and the servants who take them away. Then Lucy is dead.

From here on, the film moves with telegraphic speed, as Van Helsing searches for Dracula; the vampirized Lucy takes a ten-year-old girl for a walk; and Lucy encounters Holmwood in front of her tomb. But this time, the "come here" scene has Lucy trying to seduce *an Arthur Holmwood who is her brother.* As in Stoker's pages, Arthur is saved at the last moment by Van Helsing, wielding the cross that sears a mark on her forehead.

Van Helsing and Holmwood leave Mina, Holmwood's wife, as once more they go in pursuit of information about Dracula. When they return, they find to their horror that Dracula's coffin is in the cellar of the Holmwood house, and that Dracula has already tainted Mina's blood. After further alarums and surprises, the good guys pursue Dracula to an abandoned chapel. Dracula and Van Helsing put on a battle royal. Van Helsing, who is no physical match for Dracula, opens the chapel's curtains, letting in a flood of daylight. The discommoded vampire squeals, groans, and roars. Van Helsing pursues his advantage and makes a makeshift cross, with which he advances on Dracula. Before our eyes, the vampire turns into an old man, falls apart, and crumbles to dust. As the dust blows away, the mark of the cross seared in Mina's forehead fades.

Texture, more than mood, characterizes this film. Texture and speed and the careful manipulation of rhythms—coaches drawn by white horses, men running, women walking, clouds scurrying, men in Bond Street clothing, and women in negligees, redefine the Dracula matter as we enter the 1960s.

In 1960, Terence Fisher and Jimmy Sangster were at it again with *The Brides of Dracula*. Despite the film's title, nobody named or resembling Dracula appears in this film. Neither does Christopher Lee. If brother-sister incest was threatened in *The Horror of Dracula*, here we have mother-son incest implied as the film's protagonist, Baron Meinster, vampirizes his mother. When Van Helsing (Peter Cushing) arrives, the scales of justice finally balance, and evil gets what evil deserves.

In 1965, Christopher Lee, who did not want to be typecast as Dracula, appeared once more as the King Vampire in *Dracula, Prince of Darkness*, in an unforgettable scene that I cannot resist dubbing "the instant Dracula scene." Here, Dracula's servant upends and kills Allen, a youth played by Charles Tingwell, over the tomb holding his master's ashes. He cuts the young man's throat, and the gushing blood pours down. The blood suffusing the ashes projects sufficient energy to reconstitute and revivify the King Vampire. In this film Fisher once more touches on symbolic incest when one of the vampire hunters, a priest who is emphatically called Father Sandor, drives a stake through the sculptured bosom of a vampirized and beautiful young woman. The staking scene is memorable because Fisher contrives to have the blood from her wound gush straight into the lens of the camera.

The Hammer formula is firmly established here: sumptuous interiors, frequent carriage rides through forests, bosomy negligee-clad women, and ever-increasing hints of incest and/or sadism.

With *Dracula Has Risen from the Grave* (1968), Hammer Films once more advanced the eroticization on film of the vampire legend. The film's director is Freddie Francis. Here, a priest has fallen through the ice beneath which Dracula's body lies; his blood drifts toward and touches the dead vampire and resurrects him. Once more he is up and around and in the pursuit of luscious young women. He comes to his end impaled on a cross at the bottom of an abyss.

The very next year, Christopher Lee was back with *Taste the Blood of Dracula*, directed by Peter Sasdy. This time, the Dracula legend is set entirely in England. Despite the film's offputting title, this is one of Hammer Films' superior productions. It has a marvelous opening sequence in which we see a scruffy traveling salesman named Wella being thrown from a coach by angry travelers. As he dusts himself off, Wella hears screams nearby. After a brief search, he comes upon a pit, at the bottom of which we see Count Dracula, still skewered on the cross that impaled him in the previous film, *Dracula Has Risen from the Grave*. As Wella watches, the vampire, like the Wicked Witch of the West, dwindles until there is nothing left of him but a pool of blood beside his cloak and a silver brooch bearing his name. The sly Wella gathers up whatever he thinks might be salable, including some of the Count's blood.

From this opening, the film's focus shifts to its apparent theme: bourgeois male hypocrisy. Its hardly disguised real interest is father-daughter incest.

We meet three solid businessmen, Hargood, Secker, and Paxton, who get together in the pursuit of vice once a week. These men buy the Count's relics from Wella. With the help of a young Satanist named Courtney, they use them to resurrect Dracula in an abandoned church. In the process, Courtney is killed. The Count spends the rest of the film avenging himself on the hypocrites by vampirizing their daughters, who then kill their fathers.

Phil Hardy, the editor of *The Overlook Film Encyclopedia of Horror,* says of *The Scars of Dracula* (1970) that Hammer Films "tried to increase the film's commercial appeal by cynically inserting nudity and pointlessly sadistic scenes."[12] As scenes of sadism are an essential element of horror films it seems not quite fair to fault Hammer on this score, but Hardy's comment is pertinent: he recognizes a by-now-perceptible drift of the horror-film genre in the direction of explicit violence as well as explicit sexuality. Later that drift becomes a flow. In any case, *The Scars of Dracula* opens with a nearly hilarious ressurection scene in which chittering bats take turns squirting blood from their mouths, onto a pile of dust which is presumably all that remains of Count Dracula. It is a cartoonish replay of the instant Dracula scene in *Dracula, Prince of Darkness.*

For those who have some knowledge of real vampire bats, the scene recalls the fact, already noted, that the vampire bat, which lives entirely on liquid, is capable of urinating in flight.

*The Scars of Dracula* is a curiously static film, as if Hammer was unwilling to spend much money on sets or on location shots. There are really only three focal points for the action: the inn we see at the beginning of the film, Dracula's castle (mostly its interior), and the forest that lies between the castle and the inn.

The story line involves a young lothario named Paul, his brother Simon, and a young woman named Sarah, who is uncertain which brother she cares more for. After a semicomic interlude in which he has seduced the innkeeper's daughter, Paul is driven from the inn, falls asleep in Dracula's coach, which just happens to be standing nearby, and travels unawares to Dracula's castle, which has already been burned once by the villagers. He is admitted to the castle, which is surprisingly unscathed despite the recent fire. We are once again in exquisitely furnished Hammer Films interiors. Paul is let into the castle by Dracula's servant, Clove, played by Patrick Troughton, who falls in love with the portrait of Sarah.

In the rest of the film, Simon, Sarah, and a priest try to find Paul and battle the vampire. The priest is bitten to death by bats, lightning strikes Count Dracula, and the happy ending belongs to Simon and Sarah.

For me, the real interest in this film lies in the performance of Patrick Troughton, who, I think, steals the film utterly from Christopher Lee. It's rare when a subplot—in this case Clove's struggle to be loyal to his master at the same time that he wants to

The Scars of Dracula *(1970)*

*Christopher Lee and Soledad Miranda in* Count Dracula *(1970)*

save the woman he loves—overwhelms the plot in quite the way that this one does. Marvelously animated and powerful, Troughton's face gives off a sense of reality that is entirely out of keeping with the mood of fantasy that characterizes the Hammer Films. He looks more like Captain Ahab or the face of Christ in the Grünewald German Gothic painting of the crucifixion than a character in a vampire movie. The whipping, which Hardy thought was gratuitous and sadistic, plays a considerable part in rousing our sympathy for the suffering Clove.

In 1970, the same year as *The Scars of Dracula,* Lee starred in a Spanish/Italian/West German–financed production of *Count Dracula.* The film opens with an on-screen note that tells us: "Now, for the first time, we retell [Bram Stoker's *Dracula*], exactly as he wrote [it]." This claim to fidelity to Stoker's text is pretty much just that: a claim. The plot line is pretty much as Stoker wrote it, but the characters have been rearranged. Arthur Holmwood disappears utterly from the story. Instead, Lucy's fiancé is Quincey Morris. Instead of being in charge of and owning his own sanitarium, Dr. Seward becomes Dr. Van Helsing's employee. But—for the first time—the film gives us an aged Dracula at the beginning of the story. It also gives us Klaus Kinski as Renfield. Kinski will play Count Dracula in Werner Herzog's *Nosferatu*.

From the beginning, Renfield was a plummy role. Kinski gives us the first truly subtle interpretation of the role, one to be matched later only by Tom Waits, who played the role in Francis Ford Coppola's *Bram Stoker's Dracula* (1992). Here and in the later *Nosferatu* (1979), Kinski conveys the stillness that characterizes the moments between sanity and madness. The film otherwise is a cut-and-paste affair in which Christopher Lee is the only character who seems to possess any dignity. He brings to his role the attributes that have made him the second great interpreter of Dracula: he projects a cold austerity, an aristocratic contempt for the human race on whom he is forced to feed. In this film, he also has the profound patience of a man in a production from which he would very much like to be released.

In 1970, the same year that Lee was making *Count Dracula*, for Fenix Films Etc., Hammer Films released *Countess Dracula*, directed by Peter Sasdy. As in *Dracula's Daughter*, there is a female vampire. However, this time she is not related to Dracula; the film's title is simply meant to exploit the name recognition of the better-known count. The historical Countess Elizabeth Bathory (1560–1614) believed that bathing in the blood of virgins would keep her youthful. Once again, as in Hammer Films generally, we get a mixture of opulence, pulchritude, and fear. Like Dracula's daughter in the film of that name, the Countess has a loyal helper, a captain of the guard who knows her secret, but does not mind it as long as he shares her embraces. If we are looking for Freudian nuances in the blood exchange, we get one more here. When she runs out of other sources for virgin blood, the Countess attacks her own daughter.

In 1972, Christopher Lee appeared in his last Hammer film, *Dracula A.D.* Hammer, determined to cash in on the sea change in the sensibility of young people influenced by the hippie movement of the 1960s, concocted this film, which was meant to be trendy. Both Christopher Lee and Peter Cushing, that other great interpreter of a Stoker character, were wasted on this film. This is a forgettable movie, so let's forget it.

Dracula A.D. *(1972)*

From the opulence and pulchritude of the Hammer films which, though they were visually pleasing, are not memorable for the creation of character, we turn our attention now to the American films that were elaborating the Dracula myth in the 1970s.

The turbulence of the 1960s included radical self-consciousness about ethnicity in addition to the new sensuality to which young people were drawn because of the hippie revolution. This was, after all, the era of the Black Panthers. In 1972, in keeping with the zeitgeist, and as a profit-making venture, American International Pictures gave the world *Blacula,* which is a much better film than even its makers thought it would be. Its excellence rests neither on plot nor character. This film does not illuminate the relationships between whites and African-Americans, but it offers the magnificent presence of William Marshall as Blacula. He has a dual role. At the beginning of the film, he plays Prince Mumawalde, presumably the ruler of an African country. In 1815 he comes to Transylvania to seek Count Dracula's help in modernizing his country. The Count leers at Mumawalde's wife, Luva, and then makes contemptuous remarks about the inferiority of blacks. When Mumawalde violently resents Dracula's behavior, there is a fracas at the end of which Dracula vampirizes the Prince, puts him in a coffin, and lays a curse upon him:

> "I put the curse of suffering upon you. I will damn you to a living hell . . . A hunger for human blood. I curse you with my name. You shall be Blacula!"

The action now moves to 1972 and Dracula's castle, where a couple of gay American antique dealers buy up the antique furnishings of the castle, including Mumawalde's coffin. Now we cut to Los Angeles and the warehouse in which the coffin is stored and from which Mumawalde rises, to find himself in twentieth-century La-La

**Blacula** *(1972)*

land. Animated by Count Dracula's curse, he finds victims whose blood he drinks. He also finds Tina (Vonetta McGee) who, Mumawalde believes, is the reincarnation of his wife, Luva. The rest of the story is inevitable. Two cops, one black and one white, realize what they have to deal with and pursue Blacula until Mumawalde himself, having lost his Luva a second time, chooses the means of his own destruction.

Watching William Marshall investing this trivial plot with dignity is a real pleasure. Marshall dominates the film with all the stature of an anachronistic Othello and gives resonance to an otherwise-lightweight film.

In *Scream, Blacula, Scream* (1973), a sequel to the profitable *Blacula*, Marshall once again plays the title role.

In 1973, Dan Curtis who in the following year made *Trilogy of Terror*, probably the most frightening TV film ever made, produced and directed his version of *Dracula* for Universal Pictures. This time, however, he cast Jack Palance in the title role. In a hierarchy of memorable interpretors of Dracula, Jack Palance should not be on anybody's list. And yet he made an earnest try, which is rather poignant in some ways.

Though the producers of Christopher Lee's Count Dracula took credit for a faithful re-creation of Stoker's novel, the Curtis-Palance version has a little more right to the claim. At the beginning of the film, Count Dracula is portrayed as an older man, and some effort has been made to identify him with the historical Dracula, Vlad Tepes. Some scenes in the film set are in Transylvania and some in Whitby, England. I complained in print that Jack Palance was badly miscast:

> For one thing, he is so quintessentially American that it betrays all of his efforts to sound like an anciently evil European aristocrat. But beyond even that, he cannot seem to understand either the power or the attraction of the vampire.[13]

Reviewing the film for this book, I have softened my judgment somewhat. The earnestness I complained of seems to me to be invested with a certain dignity. Palance's soft-spoken Dracula sets off light currents of sympathy for him. However, a Dracula film is supposed to be frightening, and Palance has no way of terrifying us beyond hissing furiously or roaring at the top of his voice.

The pacing of the film is lethargic. It seems that by utterly abandoning the Renfield subplot and losing Jonathan Harker for a very long time, Curtis worked hard to create missing opportunities. We never do know what Mina's fate is, though in her last scene, her hand has been burned by the touch of the cross. And why does it takes both daylight *and* Van Helsing's skewer [and such a long, long skewer] to finish Dracula off?

Still, the last we see of Dracula, pinned like a moth to the wall, makes him look like a sad and lonely figure whom life has passed by.

All else aside, this film, like *Blacula*, makes use of the theme of the transmigration of souls, which would be exploited more fully in Coppola's *Bram Stoker's Dracula*.

In 1973, Andy Warhol lent his name to *Andy Warhol's Dracula*, a bizarre production of *Dracula* whose Italian title says: "Dracula Searches for Virgin Blood." The codirectors of the film were Anthony Dawson and Paul Morrissey. The film featured Udo Keir and Vittorio De Sica! Roman Polanski, too, was sneaked in. The film's premise is that Dracula is having a hard time in the modern world because he cannot find virgins whose blood he can drink. Beyond repulsive scenes in which Dracula vomits blood, and the fact that the film is associated with the Andy Warhol legend, I can find very little more to say about it.

The next notable Dracula of the 1970s is Universal's *Dracula* (1979), starring Frank Langella and directed by John Badham. As our century ends and we tot up the Dracula films that have achieved the status of classics, Langella's performance must be included as third in the great line, starting with Max Schreck (1921) and Bela Lugosi (1931). This film blends the resplendent interiors and pulchritude of Hammer Draculas and gives us two key performances of the highest level. Even when he is not on screen, Frank Langella seems to inhabit every frame of the film. He is tall, handsome, dashing, and dynamic—an Errol Flynn with fangs. Langella, who interpreted the role on the Broadway stage, is an actor who gives off enormous erotic energy, which the makers of this film have exploited. In some way, that aura of dynamic sexuality works against the success of this production because one can hardly believe that the female victims of a Dracula so handsome and dynamic are being victimized. Nevertheless, Langella has given us a third signature Dracula: suave, ironic, delicately witty, and vibrantly erotic.

## D R A C U L A   O N   S T A G E

### A N   I N T E R V I E W   W I T H   A N N   S A C H S

*Ann Sachs played Lucy opposite Frank Langella in the 1977 Broadway production of Balderston-Deane's* Dracula.

*Her involvement with the play* Dracula *began in 1973 when she, her husband, Robert Morgan, and John Wolpe, who later produced the play on Broadway, were instrumental in creating the Nantucket Stage Company. Wolpe got the idea to do the play in Nantucket with set and costume designs by Edward Gorey.*

I didn't have any particular interest in *Dracula* except when I read the play I thought that, as a young actress, it would be fun to do it. So I read for it and I got the role.

We did it, and it was such a magnificent piece of work. There was a sense of freedom in the air; a lack of pressure. We entered into the spirit of the piece and created a wonderful evening, which was reviewed by *The New York Times* and *Time Magazine*. They absolutely loved it.

John Wolpe then decided that the play should go to Broadway but four or five years elapsed between that Nantucket stage production and the Broadway play because John had trouble raising the money for it. In the meantime, I had a child, who was two years old by the time we went into rehearsal in New York. I was fortunate enough to be one of the three people from the original Nantucket production to be asked to join the New York company: Jerry Dempsey who played Professor Van Helsing, Gretchen Ayler who played the Maid, and myself. We had a kind of magical connection with each other and we brought that to New York.

It was very successful—everywhere. There was something about the Balderston-Deane play and its merging with the Edward Gorey stage sets and costumes which was a perfect match. The magic tricks, disappearances, turning into a bat, and breaking out in the last act, when you finally think Dracula's dead and his arm comes out of the coffin, was extremely well done.

We all took inspiration from Edward Gorey's scenery, in that it was so black and white; it was so one-dimensional, in a way, that it allowed us to embrace the cliché's of the day in a sort of truthful fashion, the way Gorey does in his cartoons— It gave us a springboard from which to start.

I know that I got my first clues about how to play Lucy when I was doing it on the little tiny stage in Nantucket. We placed the play in the nineteen-twenties which meant that we had very clear restrictions about what was acceptable for a young woman of those times. I was twenty-six, playing the little British virginal heroine—a girl very very protected by her British family. No mother in sight; and an overly protective father. I knew that this young woman had to keep her legs together because if her mother were alive she would make sure she was doing that—keep her knees together; and take very small steps.

I saw that Lucy's blooming sexuality had been stifled to such a degree that she almost didn't know it was there. At first, when she sees Dracula, she almost faints because of the eroticism that Dracula's presence awakens in her and which is of course completely forbidden. It's just too much for her system to bear.

That's all beautifully explored in the first sequence of the play, which is the dream lovers' sequence. Lucy doesn't know what's happening. There's something in the air when Dracula arrives. She's got this glass of red wine and she's toasting to her dream lover while Jeanette MacDonald is singing. She doesn't know what's come over her, but it's there fluttering right underneath the surface.

There's an interesting thing that happened when we were rehearsing *Dracula*, which is that at first there was a sort of iciness, a cold quality to their relationship, but as we were rehearsing it, and the presence of Dracula came closer and closer to awakening Lucy's sexuality, heat seemed to be generated. It was something the director liked and wanted me to explore.

At the end of the second act when Dracula comes in and seduces her in her bedroom, it was as if the heat was turned up as high as it could possibly go, consequently there is a relaxation, a melting away in the heat of Dracula's presence, of the icy cold, young heroine.

---

Frank [Langella}! Ah, Frank. He was perfect for *Dracula*. Frank has a natural distance from the world—outside the Dracula role. He always has a certain distance between where he is and where anyone else in proximity to him can be. They can't get too near, and I think that that distance is fascinating and it permeates his work. He is best when he is playing an off-putting character, someone that's pushing people away and distancing himself from them. That sense of distance worked beautifully for Dracula.

Frank was a dream to work with. He was completely committed to the moment; always connected to every person on the stage. He never in the whole year and a couple of months that I played it with him . . . he never was not present on the stage.

---

*L. Wolf: Why is the blood embrace erotic?*
I wish I knew. I wish I knew.
You know, I almost liked not knowing, because that sort of mystery, that sort of magic attraction that happened originally in Nantucket and that happened the whole year when were doing it in New York, was so real that my husband—my darling husband couldn't come near my neck for over a year. It took me a couple of years to get over. My neck was so sensitized that it was as if it was complete violation to have my husband kiss it.

*Frank Langella as Count Dracula (1979)*

I have spoken of two key performances. The second is Laurence Olivier as Dr. Van Helsing. Alas, what is memorable about Olivier's performance is not so much his muted interpretation of Van Helsing, as it is the sense that we have committed an intrusion of privacy by coming upon England's greatest actor at the moment when he has suddenly become an old man. His Van Helsing is profoundly tired, as I suspect Olivier was. Though it might be argued that his fatigue adds a poignancy to his role, it is hard to know whether we are feeling sympathy for Van Helsing or for a declining Olivier.

The years that followed saw the appearance of a motley series of Dracula films. *Old Dracula* (1974), starring David Niven, was meant to be a comic film, but did little to burnish either Niven's or Dracula's reputation.

There was a glimmer of light on the comic-Dracula horizon with the 1979 release of *Love at First Bite,* a film that deserves honorable comparison with Roman Polanski's splendid vampire spoof, *The Fearless Vampire Killers* (1967). In *Love at First Bite,* directed by Stan Dragoti, George Hamilton stars as Count Dracula. The Count has been forced to leave his ancestral home in Rumania because the Communist regime wants to use the castle as a training school for athletes. Attended by his faithful servant, Renfield, the Count makes his way to America, where he seeks out Cindy Sondheim, whose photograph he has seen and with whom he has fallen in love.

Cindy, a modern young woman whose worldview was shaped by the sexual revolution of the 1960s, thinks of herself as liberated, a believer in no commitment and in recreational sex, though her therapist, Dr. Jeff Rosenberg calls her promiscuous. Dr. Rosenberg, whose grandfather was Stoker's Dr. Van Helsing, is in love with Cindy, and much of the film's fun comes from the psychobabble these two exchange in the subplot.

Once Dracula enters Cindy's life, the screenplay assumes a brighter sparkle. When the Old World vampire Count appears in her bedroom, Cindy shocks him when she reassures him that she is quite willing to share a one-night stand with him:

*Cindy:* I just want to be honest.
*Dracula:* Don't be honest.
*Cindy:* What should I be?
*Dracula:* Be beautiful. Be romantic. Be mine.

Eventually, Cindy accepts Dracula's reasoning: "In a world without romance, it is better to be dead." Glad that she has finally met a man who knows who he is and what he wants, she willingly receives his third kiss, which will make her his bride. When last we see them, they are flying cheerfully off into the night to be undead forever.

It is all very sprightly and lighthearted. Knowing that he cannot be Bela Lugosi, George Hamilton imitates him with just the degree of exaggeration required for the spoof to work. He is droll and whimsical, a beguiling master of the riposte. Arte Johnson, who closely studied the Dwight Frye interpretation of Renfield, reposseses the role even as, by astute exaggeration, he trivializes it in the service of laughter. As Cindy, Susan St. James is brash, sexy and, like so many post-sixties young people, vaguely rootless and bewildered.

The year 1979 was also when *Nosferatu, the Vampire*, directed by the German director Werner Herzog, was released. That film has not fared well with critics, who have complained that Herzog too slavishly imitated F. W. Murnau's silent 1921 *Nosferatu*. They complain, too, that the film, though frequently beautiful, is in no way scary. Both criticisms are fair, and yet I find myself admiring the film precisely because it is so beautiful and because that beauty contrasts wonderfully with Herzog's unmatched rendering of the weariness that must be the lot of the vampire who gets to live forever in a world that is only rarely exhilarating. Klaus Kinski's performance, as I have suggested above, conveys the inert, almost boneless stillness of the immortal who can no longer be surprised by anything. Herzog's film reveals an unexpected truth: An appetite for life without enthusiasm for it is a curse.

More than a decade would pass before another Dracula film earned serious notice. Then, in 1992, *Bram Stoker's Dracula*, written by James V. Hart and directed by Francis Ford Coppola, was released by Columbia Pictures.

Before I go on, I must say that, to a degree, I was involved in the developmental process that produced this film. Hart writes:

> In 1977 with the help of a Texas partner, I began my attempt to bring *Dracula* to the screen. The first thing I did was to seek out Leonard Wolf . . . [at] San Francisco State University, and engage his services. . . . I knew that if I ever took a meeting with the devil, I wanted Wolf there to hold my hand. Born in Transylvania, he has

made extensive studies of Dracula and vampires in general, and his insights on their psychological appeal are acute. We vowed allegiance and toiled mightily, but never came up with the right screenplay to bring Dracula to life. But Leonard opened a window for me that would never close.[14]

Hart's passion to write the screenplay "that had been burning inside me since the day I read Stoker" remained unabated for more than fifteen years.[15] Then, in 1990, Coppola, who had been shown a copy of Hart's new screenplay by actress Winona Ryder, agreed to direct the film. A Rubicon was about to be crossed.

Though my name appears in the film credits as "Historical Consultant," I was brought into the filmmaking process only at the editing stage. With Coppola and Hart, I reviewed a nearly final print of the film and was pleased to see how scrupulous the filmmakers had been to be as historically accurate as possible. Beyond what I have just described, and whatever influence my published writings on *Dracula* may have had on Hart and Coppola, the screenplay and the film on which it is based were essentially shaped by them.

*Bram Stoker's Dracula* is a fascinating and complex movie. It is a stylish production. Above all, it is a Francis Ford Coppola film, which is to say that it is baroque, brilliant, wildly imaginative, supremely sensuous, and always self-indulgent. Surely, it is the most sumptuous and most erotic *Dracula* film ever made. And in the sense that it retains most of the elements of Stoker's plot, it is also the most "faithful."

However, what makes this film distinctive is the very contemporary slant that Hart has given Stoker's story. That slant and its thematic implications should be examined. To begin with, the Hart script fuses the historical Vlad Tepes with Stoker's Count Dracula. Here they are one and the same. With that bit of revision accomplished, Hart then gives Tepes-Dracula a romantic motivation for leaving Transylvania to go to England. Instead of the straightforward hunting trip for fresher and more abundant blood. Tepes-Dracula believes that in England he will find, in the person of Mina Murray, his reincarnated bride, Elizabeth, whom he lost in the fifteenth century. She committed suicide when she was misinformed that Tepes had been slain in battle.[16]

That rearrangement of the plot completely refracts the moral meaning of Stoker's story. Instead of being a Satanic blood drinker who breaks out of his Transylvanian fortress to batten on fresher,

*From Francis Ford Coppola's* Bram Stoker's Dracula *(1992)*

more plentiful game in England, Dracula is driven by the purest motivation of all: having endured centuries of loneliness, he is now on a pilgrimage of love. Once we accept that premise, Hart's *Dracula* becomes an inversion of Bram Stoker's. The Dracula who, in Stoker, is a threat to the lives and the souls of his victims is transformed here into a romantic tragic hero of love denied. There is still an air of religion permeating the film, but this time it is a secular religion. Instead of God or Christ as the source of redemption, earthly romantic love is the triumphant redeemer. Coppola tells us that what he wanted with this film was

> to do Dracula like a dark, passionate, erotic dream. Above all, it is a love story between Dracula and Mina . . . souls reaching out through a universe of horror and pathos. The counterforce to all this is Harker, the husband. And the subordinating characters: Van Helsing, Quincey, Seward and Lucy are all interacting as lovers and partners in the story.[17]

Coppola continues:

Blood is also the symbol of human passion, the source of all passion. I think that is the main subtext in our story. We've tried to depict feelings so strong they can survive across the centuries, like Dracula's love for Mina/Elizabeth. The idea that love can conquer death, or worse than death . . . that [Mina-Elizabeth] can actually give back to the vampire his lost soul.[18]

The key word in the first paragraph above is "counterforce," which tells us that the good guys in this film are Dracula and Mina and the bad guys are Van Helsing, Harker, Morris, Seward, and Godalming. Stoker's sanctified knights combating the Satanic dragon are nothing more than meddling fools who insist on standing in the way of love's redemption. This powerful idea drives the Coppola-Hart film and gives meaning to its otherwise-perplexing ending.

As we have seen from F. W. Murnau's time onward, filmmakers sensed—and exploited—the sexual implications of Stoker's story. One by one, and little by little, the films have grown more and more explicit. In *Nosferatu*, the heavy breathing is suggestive, but a filmgoer was saved from confronting male-female tension because Max Schreck's Count Orlok was so obviously repulsive. With the appearance of Bela Lugosi in the role, suavity and visual intensity stood in for passion. Though she spoke of them with heaving bosom Lucy's fantasies about the Count still had more to do with his accent and his ancestral castle in Transylvania than with sexual passion. But in the Hammer films, with their accent on beautiful interiors and female victims who lie in their beds waiting to be ravished or who, having been ravished, lie in those same beds looking spent, the message filtering down from the screen was increasingly overt.

Still, the Hammer films, though pulsatingly suggestive, maintained an air of British reserve. In *Bram Stoker's Dracula*, the sexual content of the story is anything but implicit. In that most lurid of Stoker's scenes in Dracula's castle, when Dracula's brides bend over Jonathan Harker, the sexual tension is as taut as can be precisely because Stoker will not name what is happening. In Coppola-Hart, the unabashedly naked women and Harker are entangled in a long, slow, languorous and bloody rape scene in which they coil over around and under him.

The screenplay reads:

We hear female gasps, erotic sighs, whispers in Roumanian. . . . He grows very sleepy. We see a young woman's (Youngest Bride) hands come out of the fabric; they start touching him and caressing him.

He joins in with his own hands. . . . Then suddenly the woman's hand slits his shirt with a fingernail, and her hands rip open his shirt to the waist . . . She works her way up his body, kissing his body, flicking her tongue up his stomach.

Middle Bride's mouth and tongue come into frame. She licks and caresses Harker's nipple. Suddenly her white teeth bite his tit. His blood spurts into her red lips like a water fountain.[19]

The scene ends: "The other Brides converge on Harker, their mouths finding each other in a torrid four-way kiss."[20]

When we first see Dracula and Lucy together, we are told:

She senses [his] presence and turns over. Her eyes brighten. We pull back as she smiles wantonly and reveals her body . . . We pan up her body as she arouses herself with her own caress. Her hands glide up her body, finding her breasts . . .[21]

When Dracula and Lucy have achieved their union, offscreen, we read: "Suddenly, Lucy's orgasmic wail echoes down the stairs . . ."[22]

The most startling and most audacious sequence in the film has a series of intercut scenes as the camera alternately watches Mina and Jonathan being married in a Rumanian convent and then Dracula in the form of a wolflike creature closing in on Lucy. The sequence ends with a nearly simultaneous glimpse of the wolf ravishing Lucy as Harker kisses his bride, Mina. We read:

*Mina and Harker*
    Harker lifts Mina's veil and they kiss. There is hope in Harker's face . . . and in Mina's. Rapid intercut of the kiss, growing more erotic, with the wolf Dracula ravaging Lucy.[23]

By the time the film has reached this point, it should be clear that Hart's characters' emotions are profoundly different from Stoker's. We have seen this Dracula shedding tears, then roaring with rage because his Mina has sent him a farewell letter: "My dear prince— forgive me . . ."; Mina, whose tears of regret have blurred that letter, regretfully marrying Jonathan in Rumania; and the dying Lucy, clasping the wolf's head passionately to her bosom. The lesson of the camera work is very clear: the bestial and the sacramental have been juxtaposed—and we are asked to give our pity to the beast.

# AN INTERVIEW WITH
# JAMES HART

*James V. Hart, a co-producer and screenwriter wrote the film script for the movie* Hook *and for* Bram Stoker's Dracula. *He is presently producing and writing the screenplay for a film on the Kent State University massacre.*

### ON THE WRITING OF THE "BRAM STOKER'S DRACULA" SCREENPLAY

I think the idea for writing a screenplay came to me around the same time that Anne Rice's book *Interview with the Vampire* hit it big: '76. Nobody had ever read anything like it or seen anything like it and I remember being fascinated by the book and becoming more curious about how this incredible experience can happen, because it drew on so much history, on so much stuff you never associated with vampires.

Most of the vampire movies we'd seen, at least where I grew up, had werewolves in them and cheerleaders. Billy the

Kid was in one; and the old Hammer films were just laughable. They were good, but they never scared us.

So I went back to the source. I went back and read the book, Bram Stoker's *Dracula*, and that one reading really changed my life. It changed my entire view of Victorian literature, of the sexual repression in Victorian England.

What a great novel it was! It floored me, how contemporary it felt in terms of the power of the blood and the power of the female sexuality, and also what a really wonderfully seductive man Dracula was. He wasn't a guy in a tuxedo running around going, "I want to bite your neck. I want to suck your blood." The novel was nothing like that.

My God, it had a Texan with a Bowie knife! And being from Texas I went, "Whoa. I've got to pay attention to this!" I was knocked out totally by Stoker's ability to paint this erotic image using the language of his period.

Then, one year when I was in Cannes at the Film Festival, one of my partners handed me your book! [*The Annotated Dracula*] I knew, after reading the novel and reading your annotations, that this had to be a movie; that there was a movie here that had never been discovered and had never been made on a large enough scale. This was not a cheap, low budget horror film: this was a grandiose, elegant movie.

So I set about to find you! I had some Texas money behind me at that point. The young man who was providing the money got this wild idea to do *Dracula* as a rock musical with Fleetwood Mac, with Nick Fleetwood as Dracula and Stevie Nicks as Mina. He actually took me to a concert. It wasn't a bad idea but it wasn't the movie I wanted to make, which was emblazoned in my soul. What I wanted to make was an elegant operatic, sexually charged version of *Dracula*. Years later, when Francis did it, it became an opera.

For the next ten years, 1978–1988 I made my living by writing screenplays. I mean, at every studio in town I worked with some major producer. None of my scripts got made, but I made a very nice living, but every year, my agents would say, "What do you want to do that you are really passionate about?" And I would say, "Dracula." And they would go,. "Forget it! It's been done. Nobody wants to see it!"

In 1988, my brother died, which had a very profound effect on me. We lost him to AIDS. I was with him the day before he died, and we had a long talk. Basically, what he was telling me to do was, "Get off your ass; stop talking about all the great things you're going to do and do them because you don't have as much time as you think."

In August of that year, I came away from my brother's death and I said, "I'm going to do two things. I'm going to do *Dracula*, and I'm going to do my version of *Peter Pan*, which turned out to be *Hook*. And I don't care what anybody tells me. This is what I'm going to do. And I'm going to hound people, I'm going to bug them. I'm going to get into their faces. And I'm going to get it done."

The Hart-Coppola film is wonderfully visual. Dracula's face takes many forms. In Transylvania, he is an old man with a strange pompadour; then, in London, rejuvenated by his intake of blood, we see him as a handsome young man. In his moments of rage or passion, we get to see his demonic, bestial features.

The women's gowns, and especially Lucy's death gown, created by the Japanese designer Eiko Ishioka, look more exquisite than wearable. Coppola wanted them splendid. He writes:

> It was clear from the beginning, that the script was envisaged for a group of very young actors. So I said, then let's spend our money not on the sets but on the costumes, because the costumes are the thing closest to the actors. Let's dress these young actors in beautiful, exotic, erotic costumes that have so much of the emotion right in the fabric.[24]

In that intention, we can discern the source of the film's major weakness. Coppola invested heavily in display, in effect and not in essence. A movie whose decor we remember more than its characters risks feeling superficial, as this one does. It is not true that we will have insights about Dracula just because, as here, he wears a robe whose design is borrowed from a Gustav Klimt painting. The same is true about Lucy's death gown, which Ms. Ishioka wanted to be "bizarre and haunting," but which turns out to be merely distracting at a moment in the action when the undead Lucy is trying to seduce Godalming, her fiancé. The situation we are watching is bizarre enough, and would be if she were wearing a cotton nightgown.

There are several outstanding performances in this film. Anthony Hopkins captures the essence of Van Helsing: a man with the temper of the ice brook, a scientist and a metaphysician who, on more than one occasion, is a tasteless boor. In giving us a profoundly agonized Renfield, Tom Waits makes us remember the phrase that tells us, "The poetry is in the pity." There has been no other movie Renfield who has plucked at one's heartstrings quite as effectively as Tom Waits's. Like Dwight Frye's mindless laughter in 1931, his sorrowful madness will linger long in the memories of all who see this film.

Gary Oldman does a valiant job trying to project three quite different men: the warrior Vlad Tepes of the film's opening; the weirdly mummified-looking count with his lacquered pompadour in Transylvania; and the dynamic, handsome young Victorian, *beau idéale*. It is a burden to be all these three, especially when in England he also has to compete with images of himself as a wolf and two or three kinds of ravening demons.

With Winona Ryder's performance, there is a different kind of problem. She is so successful at projecting onto the role of Mina a crystalline purity—she is so innocent, so fragile, so helplessly in thrall to love—that it is hard for me to believe that she would be drawn to a man who has spent the last five centuries drinking other people's blood. Whatever happened to a woman's intuition?

Sadie Frost's Lucy is superb. She is at once silly and sumptuously erotic. She is by turns calculatingly soft, whimsical, and cruelly hard. She shares, along with Tom Waits, the acting honors in this film.

The twentieth century will be over soon. It is very likely that *Bram Stoker's Dracula* will prove to be the last serious Dracula film made in this century. If we look back over the long parade of Draculas from Nosferatu to the present moment, two things are astonishing: the vast number of bloodthirsty Counts—*The Overlook Film Encyclopedia of Horror* lists some forty titles—and how few have stature: Murnau's *Nosferatu*, Browning's *Dracula*, Terence Fisher's *The Horror of Dracula*, John Badham's *Dracula*, Werner Herzog's *Nosferatu*, and now, despite all its faults, Francis Ford Coppola's *Bram Stoker's Dracula*.

What will the list look like in 2097?

# In Which a Thoughtful End and a Fairy Tale Come Together

"...such a castle as Jonathan tell of in his diary."

IS IT NOT A CAUSE FOR ASTONISHMENT THAT THIS SIMPLE IDEA DOES NOT FLASH INTO EVERYONE'S MIND: THAT PROGRESS (INSOFAR AS THERE IS PROGRESS) PERFECTS SORROW TO THE SAME EXTENT THAT IT REFINES PLEASURE.

——CHARLES BAUDELAIRE, BAUDELAIRE AS A LITERARY CRITIC

IT IS TIME FOR OUR CULTURE TO ABANDON DRACULA AND PASS BEYOND HIM, RELINQUISHING HIM TO SOCIAL HISTORY. THE LIMITS OF PROFITABLE REINTERPRETATION HAVE BEEN REACHED.
——ROBIN WOOD, "BURYING THE UNDEAD"

MICHAEL JACKSON IS OFTEN COMPARED TO PETER PAN, BUT PETER PAN IS RARELY ACKNOWLEDGED AS THE VARIATION ON DRACULA THAT HE IS.

——DAVID J. SKAL, THE MONSTER SHOW

**D**racula sucks!"

That's the name of a soft-porn movie and the message imprinted on T-shirts that teenagers wear. The film's audience is not left long in doubt about the meaning of the sentence. The T-shirt wearers displaying their message also have a raunchy intent in mind. Dracula sucks! Yes. He does. Once past the smile or the giggle the low-key joke induces, what is surprising is how much of the Dracula Matter, like a homunculus, is encapsulated in those two words.

In the twentieth century, the question of what Dracula really sucks: blood, power, psychic energy, identity is still a matter of perplexity. For the nineteenth-century reader, it was beyond discussion. He was a vampire in a long tradition in which the vampire sucked blood. In Stoker's novel — and not until then — the victim, in addition to blood, lost his or her immortal soul and joined the legion of the damned. I have suggested, too, that for Victorian readers — especially for the men — *Dracula* had the appeal of pornography disguised as adventure fiction. In the scene in which the lovely, loathsome ladies are gathered around the supine Harker, when the blonde licks her lips and bends "lower and lower" over his body, every Englishman who ever dreamed of — and was denied — oral sex, was hoping against hope that her lips would travel much farther south than his neck.

Now, at the end of the twentieth century, that's an easy judgment to make. Sexual repression was endemic in the Age of Victoria, when the Queen's view of the marital embrace was that she endured it patriotically. She is reported to have told her daughter the night before her wedding, "Just close your eyes and think of England."

Of course we have come a long way since then. Then why are

people in the more relaxed twentieth century still fascinated by Stoker's story?

Mostly, the answers turn on sex.

In America we have lived through the 1960s, in which the advent of the birth-control pill and the nearly simultaneous sexual revolution took place. In the glow of those years of liberation, enthusiasts proclaimed that if everyone in the world achieved orgasm, there would be no more wars. Leaving that wistful notion to one side, our sexual behavior, beginning with that decade, veered sharply away from its traditional restraints. Virginity lost its cachet, marriage its rock-solid permanence. Sex, which had been regarded with some awe because it was linked to procreation, cast off its serious mantle and became recreation.

However, it takes more than a hundred years to shake off the effects on our subconscious of thousands of years of acculturation. Over eons, we have burdened an instinct whose expression in nature is both simple and quick with an enormous weight of cultural, social, psychological, and personal meaning. The result is that in the recesses of the subconscious our shadowy hungers, lusts, fantasies, yearnings and fears have their hiding place. To this day, sex is the human wild card. Sex is still "a worrisome thing that leaves you to sing the blues in the night."

And then there is sexuality itself.

What a graceless thing is human coupling—hardly different at all from the mating of dogs. What was God thinking when He designed us? In a contest for gracefulness, a pas de deux wins anytime over the movements of a coupling couple. One notices how in novels written earlier in this century, when their characters reached the moment of lovemaking, authors always drew the curtain over the event with the word "Later." And how, even now, in today's more graphic movies, the couples are surrounded by distracting film-technology effects—constantly shifting camera angles, double exposures, changing foci, lighting effects, or camera angles, not to mention ridiculous surges of music meant to keep pace with the lovers through their moods as they roll about in the direction of their climax. Outside of hard-core porno films, screen love making turns something that, in the real world is ridiculously simple into a mishmash that is part wrestling match, part ballet exercise, part game of blindman's bluff. It's enough to make one yearn for the good old days when there was a fade-out at the critical moment in the film. What I suggested twenty-five years ago was that, given how overdetermined, how complicated a part of our lives sex had become, we ought not to be surprised that the vampire's embrace might seem to be, at least in fantasy, more attractive than the sexuality we know. In it

> any number of sexual dilemmas are outwitted. His [the vampire's] kiss permits all unions: men and women; men and men; women and women; fathers and daughters; mother and sons. Moreover, his is an easy love that evades the usual failures of the flesh. It is the triumph of passivity, unembarrassing, sensuous, throbbing, [silently] violent, and cruel.[1]

For the most part, I stand by those words, but what I overlooked then—and what needs emphasis now—is the mysterious attraction of the silence that is a critical element of vampire imagery. That stillness emphasizes the passivity of the victim, who therefore cannot be held responsible for being victimized.

In *Dracula Rising* (1992), a recent Roger Corman film, that languorous sweetness is reflected in the following dialogue. The character speaking is Alec, the "bad" vampire in this film, which has two vampires, one good and one bad. He says: "Life is about controlling, grasping. Death is about letting go. No more struggle. It's a liberation." The scriptwriters may have remembered Emily Dickinson's poem, "After great pain a formal feeling comes," which ends with the lines about death: "First chill, then stupor, then the letting go."[2] When Lawrence Durrell writes about that languor in *The Alexandria Quartet*, the passivity has a silken charm: "Until you have experienced it, you have no idea what it is like. To have one's blood sucked in darkness by someone one adores."[3] When a similar sentiment was expressed by the blood-drinking Alex in my living room in 1971 there was no literary distance I could put between myself and him. Alex, it will be remembered, said, "Beautiful! If somebody cares enough for you to suck your blood . . . I can't think of much more to ask."

The stillness I'm talking about usually reflects despair. It is in the deep submission that a deer gives when it is seized in the death grip of a wolf's jaws. Its muscles relax in acknowledgment that its struggle has failed. From that point of view, it is very like the silence that surrounds suicides who are about to cut their veins and then lie in warm bathtubs, waiting for their lives to end with the ebbing of their blood. We find such languorous sweetness in Anne Rice's novel, *The Vampire Lestat,* in the scene where Lestat vampirizes his mother:

> All the memories of my life surrounded us; they wove their shroud around us and closed us off from the world, the soft poems and songs of childhood, and the sense of her before words when there had only been the flicker of light on the ceiling above her pillows and the smell of her all around me . . .[4]

The same mesmerizing silence suffuses the Keats's poem "Bright Star":

> *Pillow'd upon my fair love's ripening breast,*
> *To feel for ever its soft fall and swell,*
> *Awake for ever in a sweet unrest,*
> *Still, still to hear her tender-taken breath,*
> *And so live ever—or else swoon to death.*[5]

Related to the appeal of the silent embrace is the way that vampirism celebrates an ecstatic inertia. In no film that I have ever seen do we see a victim embracing the vampire at the moment that he or she takes blood. Except for the tiny wince that the bite produces, the blood-taking scenes become almost immediately dreamlike and soothing for those who have grown weary of the tugging and hauling that is part of the contemporary dating scene.

In that connection, in recent years I have wondered whether one of the attractions of vampire coupling might not be the nonphallic nature of the lovemaking. In 1972 I wrote: "His [the vampire's] is an easy love that evades the usual failures of the flesh."[6] The failures I had in mind were, for men, the possibility of impotence and, for women, the need to pretend orgasm where there might not have been one. Though I think I was right in 1972, I think now that the way the vampire makes love must seem attractive to people for whom sex involving the phallus is invasive actually or symbolically.

Finally, we ought to notice how the slow, sleepy drifting away I've been talking about is also part of the attraction of the drug scene: the opiates, marijuana, LSD. I am thinking, too, of drug users who inject their drug of choice intravenously, and the sorts of associations that the vampiric coupling must set off in them. Before the vampire takes blood, there is tension, expectation, anxiety.

Afterward, satiety, fulfillment, and sleep. In short, a familiar scene-let in the addict's life.

The meaning of Renfield's observation that "the blood is the life" has acquired a bizarre new meaning in the light of the AIDS epidemic, in which the contagion is passed from person to person by means of blood exchanges and transfers. Though at first identified with the sexuality of homosexual men, it is by now evident that the disease is a universal scourge. It is a grim irony that sexuality, which has been feared for any number of psychological and religious reasons, can now be feared in the real world as a life-threatening event. It has reinvested blood and sex with dangerous meaning, and it makes reading Stoker's novel in the light of this plague a newly terrifying experience.

So far, my focus has been on the sexual implications of vampire imagery. But there is more to it than that. *Dracula* has been read as a social, psychological, anthropological, and political document. In 1972, when I was considering the Dracula matter first, I, too, risked making global comments about what Dracula might represent:

> We wanted to blame the machine. It drew us, promising power and plenty, but as the century wore on, the dynamo proved an insufficient symbol. We hated it for being impersonal, but it was also innocent. We despised its impartial power, but it served us without complaint. At its best, the machine did what we asked of it; at its worse, it was a pile of junk. . . . We could hate it, but we could not make of it a sufficient symbol for a moral dilemma. For that, we needed a force like ourselves, made of flesh, and capable of evil; a force that could entice, and destroy us; a force, moreover, that we could destroy.[7]

It seemed to me that Dracula could stand as a sufficient symbol for a moral dilemma: how to use power without losing humanity.

> [Dracula is] our eidolon, the willing representative of the temptations, and the crimes, of the Age of Energy. He is huge, and we admire size; strong, and we admire strength. He moves with the confidence of a creature that has energy, power, and will. Granted that he has energy without grace, power without responsibility, and that his will is an exercise in death . . . with only a moderate intake of blood, he can stay young.[8]

In the Age of Information and as a consequence of what has become a cottage industry of Dracula scholarship and theorizing, our eidolon has acquired more meanings. In *Our Vampires, Ourselves,* Nina Auerbach says that "there are many Draculas," and she is right. Dracula has become the monster in the eye of the beholder.

Maurice Richardson, a Freudian writing in 1959, insisted that Dracula was "a kind of incestuous, necrophilious, oral-anal-sadistic all-in wrestling match . . . in a sort of homicidal lunatic's brothel in a crypt."[9] Later, in another Freudian reading, James Twitchell noted: "If *Dracula*'s claim on our attention is not artistic, it must be psychological." He writes:

> The story is of incest, of the primal horde, and of the establishment of social and sexual taboos.[10]

David Skal cites approvingly Bram Dijkstra's summary of *Dracula* as a misogynist fiction.

> "[Stoker] . . . had a remarkably coherent sociological imagination and a brilliant talent for fluid, natural-sounding, visually descriptive prose. Together, these qualities made it possible for him to write, perhaps without ever completely realizing what he had done, a narrative destined to become the twentieth century's basic commonplace book of the anti-feminine obsession."[11]

In his own voice, Skal adds:

> *Dracula* can be read—in our time, at least—as an almost transparent metaphor for the Victorian confusion, guilt, and anger over the "proper" role of women. The attack of the vampire—a male's act of oral, infantile rage—succeeds in sexualizing women, who, according to the double standard of the time must then be punished through more sex and violence (penetrated by stakes, etc.).[12]

There is no question in my mind that Stoker's novel reflects a fear of women, but I think it is ascribing too much consciousness on his part to charge him with being a misogynist. If we were not in the midst of an era in which male-female relationships are being reshaped and politicized, we might notice that Mina Harker is the most intelligent person in *Dracula*. Mina is indeed "loaded . . . with the virtues of a schoolmarm, typist, doormat, and mother—everything an insensitive man could want in the way of a help-mate," but beyond all that, Stoker, influenced undoubtedly by his affection for his mother, cannot hide his admiration for Mina. "[Mina can] out-think and out-intuit any of them, including the redoubtable Van Helsing. While the men make one blunder after another . . . it is her sagacity and sensitivity that brings them back to the right path."[13]

Andrea Dworkin would disagree resolutely with my judgment. She characterizes *Dracula* as being:

> beyond metaphor in its intuitive rendering of an oncoming century filled with sexual horror: the throat as a female genital; sex and death as synonyms; killing as a sex act; slow dying as sensuality; . . . mutilation of the female body as a male heroism and adventure; cal-lous, ruthless, predatory lust as the one-note meaning of sexual desire; intercourse itself needing blood . . . to count as a sex act in a world excited by sadomasochism, bored by the dull thud of the lit-eral fuck.[14]

On the other hand, Nina Auerbach derives comfort from the novel. In *The Women and the Demon*, she sees women as being empowered by the Count. As they grow stronger, Dracula himself grows weaker.

*Dracula* has been seen as an anti-Semitic document and as a Christian allegory. In recent years, Christopher Craft has written a persuasive study of *Dracula*, in which its concealed homoeroticism plays a dynamic part.[15] And some anthropologists have even found a way of seeing Dracula as representing the liberating power of the menses in women:

> Before they [the women] were bitten, they were chlorotic weak creatures with vapors, dressed in stiff constricting corseted gar-ments, who spoke in faint and genteel voices expressing deep frus-tration. After their blood had been shed for the vampire, though (and it is always from the neck; as we say neck or cervix of the womb), and they had suffered their first death into their new lives as vampires—why, what creatures they became! The corsets were replaced by practical white unhampering shrouds, very free and easy, sometimes a little blood-stained to show the red on the white, with the black hair and the bright glances tossing above very low-cut shrouds displaying a great deal of rosy bosom. . . . At last there seemed some point in becoming a vampire! Dracula opened the per-

missive sixties with his chorus of happily bleeding women, with broad hints about sexual menstruation.[16]

Finally, there is the appeal of the vampire as exile. To those who feel that they are living in an era of personal dislocation, Dracula — or vampirism — has become an admirable symbol of the solitary exile, despite the fact that Stoker's Dracula in no way resembles the Byronic hero who is "the wandering outlaw of his own dark mind."[17] Norine Dresser, who has given fans of vampirism questionnaires about what attracts them to Dracula reports that "they are sympathetic to his plight as a loner" and quotes Anne Rice as saying the vampire is "a metaphor for the outsider, the alienated 'who feel like monsters deep inside . . .' "[18] Responding to Michael Riley's question about the vampire Lestat, Rice says:

> That's how *The Vampire Lestat* was born in my mind — wanting to give the strong, independent, atheistic, child-of-nobody point of view . . .[19]

The child-of-nobody, surging with the energy of the exile, glories in the solitude of the night life to which he is condemned.

In a film called *The Addiction* (1995), blood becomes the drug of choice itself. It starts off at once by straining to be profound, as it bandies about the names of the philosophers associated with the existentialist movement of the 1950s: Heidegger, Husserl, Kierkegaard, Sartre. We are shown scenes of My Lai and Auschwitz, after which we watch what happens to Kathy, a young philosophy graduate student at New York University, who becomes the victim one day of a modishly dressed female vampire, whose parting words to her are, "It was your decision."

The victim discovers that she has herself been infected with the thirst for human blood. The rest of the film shows our young Ph.D. candidate vampirizing a number of people. Meanwhile, the film's theme is virtually spray-painted on a wall for us: "In the light of this century's many bloodlettings, personal vampirism is hardly a matter of much concern." For most of its running time, the film — and its theme — ask to be taken seriously. We get "heavy" observations like, "The entire world's a graveyard and we're like the birds picking at the bones," "Kierkegaard is right: there is an awful precipice before us," and, "We are not evil because of the evil we do but because we are evil." Then, as the film approaches the end and Kathy gets her degree, the film veers off into the ridiculous as she makes her thank-you speech to her committee, various academic panjandrums, and her former victims who just happen to be there. Suddenly she departs from the thank-you clichés she has prepared as she and her previous victims leap about vampirizing everyone in sight who is not already a vampire.

All of which leaves us without Husserl or Kierkegaard or Sartre but very much in the presence of a sophomore chortling somewhere in the audience, "Ha, ha, ha! The entire NYU philosophy department is nothing but a bunch of vampires. Ha, ha, ha."

It does seem to be true that the *Dracula* we read now is a much different one than the one Stoker thought he wrote. It has turned into a porcupine, all of whose quills are symbols. That does not mean that we have rewritten his fiction or that we have got it wrong. The hallmark of a work of art is that it transforms itself to become newly visible to each successive generation.

Still, in all this talk about sex and fantasy and gender confusion, of AIDS, of feminist readings, of homosexuality, menstrual liberation, and power struggles in love—there is in all of this a real danger that we may lose Bram Stoker's *Dracula,* that we may overlay the novel with the debris of our wisdom. One would do well to remember Ezra Pound's observation that the thing itself is a sufficiently adequate symbol. In this case, the thing itself is Bram Stoker's story as he wrote it. That story has a very wicked monster out of Transylvania pursuing some beautiful and good Englishwomen because he wants to drink their blood, thereby turning them into creatures like himself. To prevent him from succeeding in his goal, there is a band of good guys led by the wise counselor, Dr. Van Helsing. The saga is about the quarrel over the women between the monster and the men. How to destroy the ogre. How to get back home alive and well.

As a sheer exercise in right reason, let us try something else. In spite of what we know about gender confusion, about psychosexual symbols, about the hunger for youth or the fear of death, let us, Jack or Jill, get into that coach. Our driver turns the horses' heads toward the upland slope, and we ride through a dense forest. We hear the howling of wolves. Emerging from the trees, we glimpse ahead of us a vast ruined castle. Without warning, the driver pulls up the horses in the castle courtyard. Jack or Jill dismounts from the coach and, hearing a heavy step, turns toward a massive door. There is the sound of rattling chains and the clanking of bolts drawn back. A huge door swings open.

Within, there stands a tall old man, clean shaven save for a long white mustache, and clad in black from head to foot, without a single speck of color about him anywhere.

It is the ogre. Somewhere deep in his castle, he heard us arrive and raised his massive head. First he sniffed and then he growled:

> *"Fee, fi, fo, fum,*
> *I smell the blood*
> *Of an English one."*

And now he is here, holding in his hand an antique silver lamp whose flame throws long quivering shadows as it flickers.

The tall old man waits for Jack or Jill to step over the threshold of his castle. Then, bowing in a courtly way, he says, "I am Dracula; and I bid you welcome to my house. . . ."

Into the fable, then. You and I.

But you go first.

# Notes

*". . . but before our very eyes, and almost in the drawing of a breath, the whole body crumbled into dust and passed from our sight."*

## INTRODUCTION

1. James Twitchell, *Dreadful Pleasures: An Anatomy of Modern Horror* (New York: Oxford University Press, 1985), 140.

2. Leonard Wolf, *A Dream of Dracula* (Boston-Toronto: Little, Brown and Company, 1972).

3. Barbara Belford, *Bram Stoker: A Biography of the Author of Dracula* (New York: Knopf, 1996).

4. From the introduction to James Malcolm Rymer, *Varney the Vampyre* or *The Feast of Blood* (1845) (New York: Dover, 1970), xxvii.

5. Christopher Craft, *Another Kind of Love: Male Homosexual Desire in English Discourse* (Berkeley: University of California Press, 1994), 73.

6. Ibid., 73.


## CHAPTER 1

1. *Hamlet*, 5.1.150–159.

2. Paul Barber, *Vampires, Burial and Death: Folklore and Reality* (New Haven: Yale University Press, 1990), 108.

3. Ibid., 112.

4. Ibid., 113

5. Albert Ponsold, *Lehrbuch der gerichtlichen* (*Manual of Medical Jurisprudence*), 2nd ed. (Stuttgart: Georg Thieme Verlag, 1957), 292.

6. Baudelaire, Charles, "Une Charogne (The Carcass)." Citations translated from the French by L. W.

7. John Glaister and Edgar Rentoul, *Medical Jurisprudence and Toxicology*, 12th ed. (Edinburgh: E. & M. S. Livingston, 1966), as cited in Barber, *Vampires*, 106.

8. Barber, *Vampires*, 115.

9. See P. V. Glob, *The Bog People: Iron Age Man Preserved*, translated by Rupert Bruce-Mitford (New York: Ballantine Books, 1969).

10. Stephen Peithman, ed., *The Annotated Tales of Edgar Allan Poe* (Garden City, NY: Doubleday, 1981), 77.

11. Augustine Calmet, *The Phantom World* (London: Richard Bentley, 1850).

12. Montague Summers, *The Vampire: His Kith and Kin* (1928) (New Hyde Park, NY: University Books, 1960).

13. Ibid., 1.

14. Emily Gerard, *The Land Beyond the Forest* (New York: Harper and Bros., 1888).

15. Ibid., 185–86.

16. Tony Faivre, *Les vampires: essai historique, critique et littèraire* (Paris: E. Losfeld, 1962), 105–106.

17. Ibid., 98.

18. Werner U. Spitz and Russell S. Fisher, eds. *Medicolegal Investigation of Death*, 2nd ed. (Springfield, IL: Charles C. Thomas, 1980), 349.

19. Summers, *Vampire*, 208.

20. Summers, *Vampire*, 238.

21. Otto-Wilhelm von Vacano, *Etruscans in the Ancient World* (London: Edward Arnold, 1960), 6.

22. James G. Frazer, *The Golden Bough* (New York: Macmillan, 1951), 223.

23. See page 83 of this book.

24. Leonard Wolf, ed., *The Essential Dracula* (New York: Plume, 1991), xxiii.

25. Summers, *Vampire*, 174.

26. Wolf, *Essential Dracula*, 262.

27. Summers, *Vampire*, 204.

28. Wolf, *Essential Dracula*, 255.

29. Summers, *Vampire*, 203.

30. In Joyce Carol Oates, *Bellefleur* (New York: E. P. Dutton, 1980), 374.

## CHAPTER 2

1. Wolf, *Essential Dracula*, 376.

2. Richard Noll, *Vampires, Werewolves, and Demons* (New York: Brunner/Mazel, 1992), 65.

3. Wolf, *Dream*, 269.

4. Ibid., 272.

5. Ibid., 273–74.

6. From an article by Frank Bruni, *New York Times* (Metro Section), August 10, 1996.

7. Jean Paul Roux, *Le Sang: Mythes, Symboles, et Realités (Blood: Myths, Symbols, and Realities)* (Paris: Fayard, 1988), 333. Citation translated from the French by L. W.

8. Ibid., 334.

9. Leo Kirschbaum, ed., *Plays of Christopher Marlow* (New York: Meridian Books, 1962), 120.

10. Henry Hogg, *Cannibalism and Human Sacrifice* (New York: Citadel Press, 1966), 15.

11. Genesis 37:18–34.

12. Isabel Burton, ed., Richard F. Burton, transl., *Vikram and the Vampire* or *Tales of Hindu Devilry* (New York: Dover Publications, 1969), 240.

13. *Macbeth* 5.1.25–61.

14. "The Prioress's Tale." Geoffrey Chaucer, *The Canterbury Tales*, Oxford World Classics Edition (New York: Avenel Books, 1985), 165. All excerpts translated from the Middle English by L. W.

15. Ibid., 166.

16. Ibid., 165.

17. Genesis 9:4.

18. Deuteronomy 12:23–25.

19. Acts 15:29.

20. *Koran.* Translated by George Sale (New York: Garland Publishing, Inc., 1984). Facsimile of 1734 edition, 25.

21. Thomas Buckley and Alma Gottlieb, eds., *Blood Magic: The Anthropology of Menstruation* (Berkeley, CA: University of California Press), 1988).

22. Wolf, *Dream*, 9.

23. Penelope Shuttle and Peter Redgrove, *The Wise Wound: Myths, Realities, and Meanings of Menstruation* (New York: Bantam, 1990), 295.

24. See pages 131 of this book.

## CHAPTER 3

1. Wolf, *Essential Dracula*, 125.

2. Ibid., 143.

3. Ibid., 182.

4. Ibid., 191.

5. Ibid., 293.

6. Summers, *Vampire*, 18.

7. Beatriz Villa and Maria Canela, "Man, Gods, and Legendary Vampire Bats." From Arthur Greenhall and Uwe Schmidt, eds., *Natural History of Vampire Bats* (Elkins Park, PA: Franklin Book Company, 1988), 239.

8. Dennis C. Turner, *The Vampire Bat* (Baltimore, MD: Johns Hopkins University Press, 1975), 1–2.

9. William A. Wimsatt, "Portrait of a Vampire." *Ward's Natural Science Bulletin* 32:2 (Spring 1959):13–39, 62–63.

10. Greenhall and Schmidt, *Natural History*, 114.

11. Clayton E. Ray, Omar J. Linares, and Gary S. Morgan, "Paleontology." In Greenhall and Schmidt, *Natural History*, 29.

12. Wallace Stevens, "Sunday Morning" (1915).

## CHAPTER 4

1. Wolf, *Essential Dracula*, 39.

2. Ibid., 41–42.

3. Ibid., 42.

4. Belford, *Bram Stoker*, 260.

5. Radu Florescu and Raymond T. McNally, *Dracula: Prince of Many Faces* (New York: Little Brown, and Company, 1989), 55–56.

6. Radu Florescu and Raymond T. McNally, *In Search of Dracula* (Greenwich, CT: New York Graphic Society, 1972), 22.

7. This account is based on the chronology made by Constantin Rezachevici in Kurt Treptow, ed., *Dracula: Essays on the Life and Times of Vlad Tepes* (New York: Columbia University Press, 1991). Florescu and McNally have Dracula meeting Vladislav II in combat near Tirgoviste. They write: "He had the satisfaction of killing his mortal enemy and his father's assassin in hand-to-hand combat." (Florescu and McNally, *Dracula*, 81).

8. Florescu and McNally, *Dracula*, 163.

9. Constantin Rezachevici, "Vlad Tepes—Chronology and Historical Bibliography." In Kurt, *Dracula*, 263.

10. Denys Hays, *Europe in the Fourteenth and Fifteenth Centuries* (London: Longmans, Green and Co., Ltd., 1966), 43–44.

11. Florescu and McNally, *Dracula*, 104.

12. Lord Eversley and Sir Valentine Chirol, *The Turkish Empire from 1288 to 1914* (London: T. Fisher Unwin, Ltd., 1923), 95–96.

13. Quoted in Treptow, *Dracula*, 190.

14. Florescu and McNally, *Dracula*, 104.

15. Wolf, *Dream*, 49.

16. Ibid., 59.

17. Georges Bataille, *The Trial of Gilles de Rais: Documents*, transl. by Richard Robinson (Los Angeles, CA: Amok, 1991).

18. Colonel Jean Lamouche, *Histoire de Turquie* (Paris: Payot, 1953), 69–70.

19. Florescu and McNally, *Dracula,* 101–102. The lengthy quotation here and below reflect both my astonishment and my desire to be fair.

20. Florescu and McNally, *In Search*, 27.

21. Ibid., 91.

## CHAPTER 5

1. Judges, 4–5, passim.
2. David Grene and Richard Lattimore, eds., *Greek Tragedies*, vol. 1 (Chicago: University of Chicago Press, 1960), 166.
3. David R. Slavitt, transl., *Seneca: The Tragedies* (Baltimore: The Johns Hopkins University Press, 1992), 72.
4. Ibid., 72.
5. Ibid., 72.
6. "The Knight's Tale." Chaucer, *Canterbury Tales*, 52.
7. *King Lear*. 3.4.83.
8. *Titus Andronicus*. 5.4.
9. Wolf, Leonard, *New York Times Review of Books*, January 14, 1973, 2.
10. Horace Walpole, *The Castle of Otranto*. In E. F. Bleiler, ed., *Three Gothic Novels* (New York: Dover Publications, 1966), 34–35.
11. From John Berryman's introduction to Matthew Gregory Lewis, *The Monk* (New York: Grove Press, 1952), 13.
12. Wolf, *Dream*, 153.
13. Lewis, *Monk*, 65.
14. Ibid., 81.
15. Ibid., 85.
16. Ibid., 14.
17. Ibid., 179.
18. Ibid., 237.
19. Ibid., 268–69.
20. Ibid., 195.
21. Ibid., 195.
22. Ibid., 363–64.
23. Ibid., 366.
24. Ibid., 367.
25. Ibid., 369.
26. Ibid., 369.
27. Ibid., 407.
28. Ibid., 418.
29. Ibid., 420.
30. Charles Robert Maturin, *Melmoth the Wanderer* (Oxford University Press, 1979), 160.
31. Ibid., 173.
32. Ibid., 213.
33. Maturin, *Melmoth*, 244.
34. W. H. Auden, "The Wanderer" (1933).
35. Maturin, *Melmoth*, 252.
36. Ibid., 302.
37. Ibid., 409.

38. Ibid., 410.

39. From William Wordsworth, "Lines Composed a Few Miles Above Tintern Abbey" (1798).

40. Charles Brockden Brown, *Wieland* or *The Transformation* (New York: Harcourt Brace Jovanovich, 1926), 61.

## CHAPTER 6

1. I am aware that Shelley's drama *The Cenci* is often cited as an influence — particularly by James Twitchell, but I think the connection is too tenuous. The incestuous Count Cenci fantasizes drinking blood, but does not do so.

2. Samuel Taylor Coleridge, "Rime of the Ancient Mariner" (1798), part 3, stanza 11.

3. From the introduction to Mary Shelley, *Frankenstein* (London: H. Delburn & R. Bentley, 1831).

4. Wolf, Leonard, ed., *The Essential Frankenstein: The Complete Annotated Edition of Mary Shelley's Classic Novel* (New York: Plume, 1993), xxii.

5. In Lord Byron, *The Complete Works of Lord Byron* (Paris: Baudry's European Library, 1835), 234.

6. From E. F. Bleiler's introduction to John Polidori, *The Vampyre* (1819). In Bleiler, *Three Gothic Novels*, xxxix.

7. Polidori, *Vampyre*, in Bleiler, *Three Gothic Novels, 274.*

8. Johan Ludwig Tieck, "Wake Not the Dead." Quoted in Wolf, *Dream*, 167.

9. Ibid., 167.

10. Ibid., 168.

11. Ibid., 168.

12. Peithman, *The Annotated Tales*, 49.

13. Théophile Gautier, "La Morte Amoureuse." In Francis Lancassin, *Vampires de Paris* (Paris: Christian de Bartillat, 1995), 143.

14. Ibid., 145.

15. Ibid., 146.

16. Ibid., 146.

17. Ibid, 145.

18. Ibid., 150.

19. Ibid., 161–62.

20. Ibid., 163.

21. Ibid., 173.

22. Ibid., 175.

23. Ibid., 177.

24. Ibid., 180.

25. Ibid., 180.

26. Ibid., 180.

27. Ibid., 180.

28. Ibid., 181.

29. Ibid., 181.

30. Ibid., 181.

31. Aleksei Tolstoi, "The Vourdalak Family." In Lacassin, *Vampires*, 237.

32. Ibid., 260.

33. Ibid., 262.

34. Ibid., 262.

35. Ibid., 263.

36. Ibid., 299.

37. In Jack Sullivan, ed., *The Penguin Encyclopedia of Horror and the Supernatural* (New York: Viking, 1986), 365.

38. Wolf, *Dream*, 169.

39. Rymer, *Varney*, 824–25.

40. Wolf, Leonard, ed., *Carmilla* (New York: Signet, 1996), 271.

41. Ibid., 272.

42. Ibid., 287.

43. Ibid,. 287.

44. Ibid., 289.

45. Ibid., 290–91.

46. E. F. Bleiler, ed., *Supernatural Fiction Writers* (New York: Charles Scribner's Sons, 1985), 229.

47. Wolf, *Essential Dracula*, 425.

48. Ibid., 455.

49. Ibid., 455.

## CHAPTER 7

1. Ludlam, Harry, *A Biography of Dracula: The Life Story of Bram Stoker* (London: Foulsham, 1962).

2. Daniel Farson, *The Man Who Wrote Dracula* (London: Michael Joseph, 1975).

3. Belford, *Bram Stoker*, xi.

4. Ibid., xi.

5. Ibid., 17.

6. Ibid., 33.

7. Ludlam, *Biography*, 32.

8. Belford, *Bram Stoker*, 53.

9. Ibid., 57.

10. Ibid., 57.

11. Ibid., 56.

12. Ibid., 72.

13. Ludlam, *Biography*, 43.

14. Thomas Hood, "Eugene Aram" (1931).

15. Bram Stoker, *Personal Reminiscences of Henry Irving*, vol. 1 (London: Heinemann, 1906), 28–30.

16. Laurence Irving, *Henry Irving: The Actor and His World* (London: Faber and Faber, 1951), 278–79.

17. Stoker, *Personal Reminiscences*, 31–32.

18. Ibid., 33.

19. Wolf, *Dream*, 252.

20. Belford, *Bram Stoker*, 40.

21. Ibid., 42.

22. Ibid., 41–42.

23. Ibid., 44.

24. Ibid., 83.

25. David J. Skal, *Hollywood Gothic* (New York: W. W. Norton, 1990), 35.

26. Belford, *Bram Stoker*, 94.

27. Stoker, *Personal Reminiscences*, 62.

28. Frances Donaldson, *The Actor Managers* (London: Heineman, 1906), 31–32.

29. Irving, *Henry Irving*, 200.

30. Ibid., 200.

31. Ibid., 209.

32. Skal, *Hollywood Gothic*, 18.

33. Farson, *Man Who Wrote Dracula*, 213–14.

34. Belford, *Bram Stoker*, 60.

35. Horace Wildham, *The Nineteen Hundreds* (New York: T. Seltzer, 1923), 118–19.

36. Stoker, *Personal Reminiscences*, 160.

37. Roger Manville, *Ellen Terry* (London: Heinemann, 1968).

38. Belford, *Bram Stoker*, 160.

39. Stoker, *Personal Reminiscences*, 5.

40. Wolf, *Dream*, 254.

41. Belford, *Bram Stoker*, 196.

42. Ludlam, *Biography*, 140.

43. Bram Stoker, *Lair of the White Worm* (London: Rider, 1911), 29.

44. Ibid., 118.

45. Ibid., 118–19.

46. Ibid., 117.

47. Ibid., 135.

48. Ibid., 143–44.

49. Ibid., 186.

50. Belford, *Bram Stoker*, 268.

51. Peter Haining, ed., *Midnight Tales by Bram Stoker* (London: Peter Owen, 1990), 48.

52. Ibid., 51.

53. Ibid., 54.

54. Ibid., 57.

55. Ibid., 58.

56. Bram Stoker, "The Squaw." In *The Bram Stoker Bedside Companion* (London: Victor Gollancz, Ltd., 1973), 127.

57. Gerard, *Land Beyond*.

58. Leonard Wolf, ed., *The Annotated Dracula* (New York: Ballantine Books, 1975), 65.

59. Belford, *Bram Stoker*, 226–27.

60. Ibid., 264.

61. Ibid., 228.

62. Review quotations are from Carol A. Senf, ed., *The Critical Response to Bram Stoker* (Westport, CT: Greenwood Press, 1993), 59–60.

63. Ibid., 61.

64. Belford, *Bram Stoker*, 274.

65. Iriving, *Henry Irving*, 68.

66. Belford, *Bram Stoker*, 51.

67. Ibid., 270.

68. Stoker, *Personal Reminiscences*, 34.

69. Belford, *Bram Stoker*, 316.

70. Ibid., 319–20.

71. Ibid., 320.

72. Ibid., 320.

### CHAPTER 8

1. Unless otherwise indicated, all quotes in this chapter are from Wolf, *Essential Dracula*. Page numbers in parentheses follow each quote.

2. See Craft, *Another Kind of Love*.

3. Dom Gaspar Lefebvre, O.S.B., *St. Andrew's Daily Missal* (St. Paul, MN: E. M. Lohmann, Co., 1949), 1046.

### CHAPTER 9

1. Hans Heinz Ewers, *Vampir*. Quoted in Wolf, *Dream*, 235.

2. Genesis 30:14–17.

3. Stephen King, *Salem's Lot* (New York: Plume, 1975), 302.

4. Ibid., 303.

5. Chelsea Quinn Yarbro, *Hotel Transylvania* (New York: St. Martin's Press, 1978), 116.

6. Ibid., 269.

7. Chelsea Quinn Yarbro, *Tempting Fate* (New York: St. Martin's Press, 1982), 477.

8. Katherine Ramsland, *The Vampire Companion* (New York, Ballantine Books, 1993), 195.

9. Ibid., 196.

10. Ibid., 64.

11. Anne Rice, *The Vampire Lestat* (New York: Ballantine Books, 1985), 3.

12. Anne Rice, *The Tale of the Body Thief* (New York: Alfred A. Knopf, 1992), 3.

13. Anne Rice, *The Queen of the Damned* (New York: Alfred A. Knopf, 1988), 3.

14. Anne Rice, *Memnoch the Devil* (New York: Ballantine Books, 1995), 4.

15. Rice, *Queen*, 3.

16. Rice, *Memnoch*, 306–307.

17. Anne Rice, *Interview with the Vampire* (New York: Alfred A. Knopf, 1985), 157.

18. Rice, *Memnoch*, 329.

19. Ibid., 407.

20. F. Marion Crawford, "For the Blood Is the Life." In Alan Ryan, *The Penguin Book of Vampire Stories* (New York: Penguin Books, 1988), 196.

21. Ibid., 198.

22. Ibid., 201.

23. Ibid., 202.

24. Mary Wilkins Freeman, "Luella Miller." In Mary Wilkins Freeman, *The Wind in the Rosebush and Other Stories of the Supernatural* (New York: Garrett Press, Inc., 1969), 83.

25. Fritz Leiber, "The Girl with the Hungry Eyes." In Ellen Datlow, ed., *Blood Is Not Enough* (New York: W. Morrow, 1989), 195.

26. Ibid., 195.

27. Suzy McKee Charnas, "Unicorn Tapestry." In Ryan, *Vampire Stories*, 561.

28. Hans Heinz Ewers, "The Spider." In Leonard Wolf, ed. and transl., *Wolf's Complete Book of Terror* (New York: Newmarket Press, 1994), 173.

29. Ray Bradbury, "Homecoming." In Tom Shippey, ed., *The Oxford Book of Fantasy Stories* (New York: Oxford University Press, 1994), 145.

30. Robert Devereaux, "A Slow Red Whisper of Sand." In Poppy Z. Brite, ed., *Love in Vein* (New York: HarperPrism, 1994), 371.

## CHAPTER 10

1. *Bloodsuckers*, a film by Lucinda-Titan International.

2. Wolf, *Dream*, 282.

3. Skal, *Hollywood Gothic*, 115.

4. David Skal suggests that the armadillos were there because of an idiosyncratic decision on Browning's part. In Skal, *Hollywood Gothic*, 131.

5. Wolf, *Dream*, 284–85.

6. Skal, *Hollywood Gothic*, 126.

7. Wolf, *Essential Dracula*, 147.

8. Skal, *Hollywood Gothic*, 160.

9. Ibid., 169.

10. In the prologue to the Spanish *Dracula*, Universal Studios, Monster Collection.

11. Wolf, *Dream*, 178.

12. Phil Hardy, ed., *The Overlook Film Encyclopedia, Science Fiction* (Woodstock, NY: Overlook Press, 1994), 225.

13. Leonard Wolf, *Horror: A Connoisseur's Guide to Literature and Film* (New York: Facts on File, 1990), 67,

14. James V. Hart, in Francis Ford Coppola and James V. Hart, *Bram Stoker's Dracula: The Film and the Legend* (New York: New Market Press, 1992), 7.

15. Ibid., 7.

16. Radu Florescu and Raymond T. McNally tell a version of this story. According to their account, one of Vlad Tepes's relatives, a slave in the Turkish camp bivouacked beneath Dracula's castle, climbed to the top of a nearby hill and sent an arrow around which was wrapped a message urging Dracula to make good his getaway while he could. They write: "Dracula's mistress apprised her husband of the ominous content of the message. She told him that she would 'rather have her body rot and be eaten by the fish of the Arges than be led into captivity by the Turks.' She then hurled herself from the upper battlements." (Florescu and McNally, *Dracula*, 154.)

17. Copola and Hart, *Bram Stoker's Dracula*, 5.

18. Ibid., 5.

19. Ibid., 56–57.

20. Ibid., 57.

21. Ibid., 90.

22. Ibid., 90.

23. Ibid., 112.

24. Ibid., 126.

25. The richly gilded pattern of the cloak was based on a Gustav Klimt painting (Ibid., 127).

## CONCLUSION

1. Wolf, *Dream*, 4.

2. Emily Dickinson, poem #122 (Johnson, *Final Harvest*, 73).

3. Lawrence Durrell, *Balthazar* (London: Faber and Faber, 1958), 196–98.

4. Rice, *Vampire Lestat*, 157.

5. John Keats, "Bright Star! Would I Were Steadfast as Thou Art" (1819).

6. Wolf, *Dream*, 303.

7. Ibid., 269.

8. Ibid., 302.

9. Maurice Richardson, "The Psychoanalysis of Ghost Stories," *Twentieth Century 166* (1959): 419–31, 427.

10. Twitchell, *Dreadful Pleasures*, 127.

11. Bram Dijkstra, *Idols of Perversity: Fantasies of Evil in Fin de Siècle Culture* (New York: Oxford University Press, 1986), 342.

12. Skal, *Hollywood Gothic*, 31.

13. Wolf, *Dream*, 216.

14. Andrea Dworkin, *Sexual Intercourse* (New York: Free Press, 1987), 119.

15. See Craft, *Another Kind of Love*.

16. Shuttle and Redgrove, *Wise Wound*, 296.

17. Lord Byron, "Childe Harold's Pilgrimage" (1812).

18. Norine Dresser, *American Vampires: Fans, Victims, Practitioners* (New York: Vintage Books, 1984), 161.

19. Michael Riley, *Conversations with Anne Rice* (New York: Ballantine Books, 1996), 15.

# BIBLIOGRAPHY

Adler, Michael H. *The Writing Machine*. London: George Allen & Unwin, Ltd., 1974.

Allen, Glover Morrill. *Bats*. New York: Dover Publications, 1939.

Ambrose, Gordon and Newbold, George. *A Handbook of Medical Hypnosis*. London: Baillere, Tindall and Cox, 1959.

Ariès, Philippe. *The Hour of Our Death*. Translated by Helen Weaver. New York: Alfred A. Knopf, 1981. [Orig. pub. *L'homme devant la mort*. Paris: Editions du Seuil, 1977.]

Auden, W. H., ed. *Poets of the English Language*, Volume IV. New York: Viking Press, 1950.

Auerbach, Nina. *Ellen Terry: Player in Her Time*. New York: Norton, 1987.

———. *Our Vampires, Ourselves*. Chicago: University of Chicago Press, 1995.

———. *Woman and the Demon: The Life of a Victorian Myth*. Cambridge: Cambridge University Press, 1982.

Babinger, Franz. *Mehmed der Eroberer: Seine Zeit. (Mehmed the Conqueror: His Times)* Munich: F. Bruckmann, 1959.

Balys, Jonas. *Dvasios ir zmones: Ghosts and Men: Lithuanian Folk Legends about the Dead*. Bloomington: Indiana University Press, 1951.

Barber, Paul. *Vampires, Burial and Death: Folklore and Reality*. New Haven: Yale University Press, 1990.

Baring-Gould, Rev. Sabine. *A Book of Folklore*. London: Collins's Clear Type Press, n.d.

Bataille, Georges. *The Trial of Gilles de Rais: Documents*. Translated by Richard Robinson. Los Angeles, CA: AMOK, 1991.

Bayer-Berenbaum, Linda. *The Gothic Imagination*. London: Associated University Press, 1982.

Beahm, George. *The Stephen King Companion*. Kansas City: Andrews and McMeel, 1995.

———. *The Unauthorized Anne Rice Companion*. Kansas City: Andrews and McMeel, 1996.

Belford, Barbara. *Bram Stoker: A Biography of the Author of Dracula.* New York: Knopf, 1996.

Bentley, C. F. "The Monster in the Bedroom: Sexual Symbolism in Dracula." *Literature and Psychology* 22 (1972): 27–34.

Bierman, Joseph S. "Dracula: Prolonged Childhood Illness and the Oral Triad." *American Image* 29 (1972): 186–98.

Binding, G. J. *Everything You Want to Know about Garlic.* New York: Pyramid Books, 1970.

Birkhead, Edith. *The Tale of Terror.* London: Russell and Russell, 1963.

Bleiler, E. F., ed. *Best Ghost Stories of J. S. LeFanu.* New York: Dover Publications, 1964.

— — —. *Supernatural Fiction Writers.* New York: Charles Scribner's Sons, 1985.

Blodgett, Harold W. and Sculley Bradley, eds. *Leaves of Grass.* New York: New York University Press, 1965.

Bojarski, Richard. *The Films of Bela Lugosi.* Secaucus, NJ: Citadel Press, 1980.

Bouvier, M. and J.-L. Letrat. *Nosferatu.* Paris: Cahiers du Cinéma/Gallimard, 1981.

Brustein, Robert. "Reflections on Horror Movies." *Partisan Review* 25 (1988): 296–99.

Buckley, Thomas and Alma Gottlieb, eds. *Blood Magic: The Anthropology of Menstruation.* Berkeley, CA: University of California Press, 1988.

Budge, Sir E. A. Wallis (translator). *The Book of the Dead.* New York: Dover Publications, 1969.

Buican, Denis. *Les Métamorphoses de Dracula: L'Histoire et la Légende.* Paris: Éditions du Félin, 1993.

Bunson, Matthew. *The Vampire Encyclopedia.* New York: Crown Publishers, 1993.

Burton, Isabel, ed. *Vikram the Vampire; or, Tales of Hindu Diety.* Translated by Richard F. Burton. New York: Dover Publications, 1969.

Byron, Lord (George Gordon). *The Complete Works of Lord Byron.* Paris: Baudry's European Library, 1835.

— — —. "The Vampire" [a fragment]. In *Three Gothic Novels,* edited by E. F. Bleiler. New York: Dover Publications, 1977.

Calmet, Augustine. *The Phantom World.* London: Richard Bentley, 1850.

Calverton, V. F. and S. D. Schmalhausen, eds. *Sex in Civilization.* Garden City, New York: Garden City Publishing Co., 1929.

Camporesi, Piero. *Juice of Life: The Symbolic and Magic Significance of Blood.* Translated by Robert R. Barr. New York: Continuum, 1995.

Cardin, Philip and Ken Mann. *Vampirism: A Sexual Study.* San Diego, CA: Late-Hour Library/Phoenix Publishers, 1969.

Carter, Margaret L., ed. *Dracula: The Vampire and the Critics.* Ann Arbor: UMI Research Press, 1988.

———. *Shadow of a Shade: A Survey of Vampirism in Literature.* New York: Gordon Press, 1977.

———. *The Vampire in Literature.* Ann Arbor: UMI Research Press, 1989.

Chaucer, Geoffrey. *The Canterbury Tales.* Oxford World Classics Edition. New York: Avenel Books, 1985.

Clarens, Carlos. *An Illustrated History of the Horror Film.* New York: G. P. Putnam's Sons, 1967.

Cohen, Daniel. *A Modern Look at Monsters.* New York: Dodd, Mead & Co., 1970.

Coles, Paul. *The Ottoman Impact on Europe.* London: Thames and Hudson, 1968.

Collins, Charles M., ed. *A Feast of Blood.* New York: Avon Books, 1967.

Copper, Basil. *The Vampire in Legend, Fact and Art.* London: Hale, 1973.

Coppola, Francis Ford and James V. Hart. *Bram Stoker's Dracula: the Film and Legend.* New York: Newmarket Press, 1992.

Craft, Christopher, ed. *Another Kind of Love: Male Homosexual Desire in English Discourse.* Berkeley: University of California Press, 1994.

———. " 'Kiss Me with Those Red Lips': Gender and Inversion in Bram Stoker's *Dracula.*" *Representations* 8 (1984): 107–33.

Cremer, Robert. *Lugosi: The Man Behind the Cape.* Chicago: Henry Regnery, 1977.

Cunningham, Gail. *The New Woman and the Victorian Novel.* New York: Barnes and Noble, 1978.

Dalby, Richard. *Bram Stoker: A Bibliography of First Editions.* London: Dracula Press, 1978.

Daniels, Les. *Living in Fear: A History of Horror in the Mass Media.* New York: Charles Scribner's Sons, 1975.

Datlow, Ellen, ed. *Blood Is Not Enough.* New York: W. Morrow, 1989.

Deane, Hamilton. *Dracula.* In Skal, *Dracula.*

——— and John L. Balderston. *Dracula, the Vampire Play.* New York: David Lewis, 1970.

Demetrakopoulos, Stephanie. "Feminism, Sex Roles Exchanges, and Other Subliminal Fantasies in Bram Stoker's *Dracula.*" *Frontiers: A Journal of Women's Studies* 2 (1977): 104–13.

Derry, Charles. *Dark Dreams: A Psychological History of the Modern Horror Film.* New York: A. S. Barnes, 1977.

Dickstein, Morris. "The Aesthetics of Fright." *American Film* 5 (1980): 32–37, 56–59.

Dijkstra, Bram. *Idols of Perversity: Fantasies of Evil in Fin de Siècle Culture.* New York: Oxford University Press, 1986.

Dömötör, Tekla. *Volksglaube und Aberglaube der Ungarn (Folk Beliefs and Superstitions of Hungary).* Budapest: Corvina Kiadó, 1981.

Donaldson, Frances. *The Actor-Managers.* London: Weidenfeld & Nicholson, 1970.

Dresser, Norine. *American Vampires: Fans, Victims, Practitioners*. New York: Vintage Books, 1984.

Dreyer, Carl Theodor. *Vampyr, in Four Screenplays*. Bloomington: Indiana University Press, 1970.

Durham, Edith. "Of Magic, Witches and Vampires in the Balkans." *Man* 23 (1923): 189–92.

Durrell, Lawrence. *Balthazar*. London: Faber and Faber, 1958.

Dworkin, Andrea. *Sexual Intercourse*. New York: Free Press, 1987.

Eisner, Lotte H. *The Haunted Screen: Expressionism in the German Cinema and the Influence of Max Reinhardt*. Berkeley: University of California Press, 1969.

— — —. *Murnau*. Berkeley: University of California Press, 1973.

Ellis, Havelock. *Studies in the Psychology of Sex*, 2d ed., vol. 3. Philadelphia: F. A. Davis Co., 1927.

Eversley, Lord and Sir Valentine Chirol. *The Turkish Empire from 1288 to 1914*. London: T. Fisher Unwin, Ltd., 1923.

Ewers, Hans Heinz. *Vampir. Ein verwilderter Roman (Vampir. A Savage Novel)*. Munich: George Müller Verlag, 1921.

Faivre, Tony. *Les Vampires; essai historique, critique et littéraire*. Paris: E. Losfeld, 1962.

Farson, Daniel. *The Man Who Wrote Dracula: A Biography of Bram Stoker*. London: Michael Joseph, 1975.

Florescu, Radu and Raymond T. McNally. *Dracula: Prince of Many Faces*. New York: Little, Brown and Company, 1989.

— — —. *Dracula: A Biography of Vlad the Impaler*. New York: Hawthorn Books, 1973.

— — —. *The Essential Dracula*. New York: Mayflower Books, 1979.

— — —. *In Search of Dracula*. Greenwich, Connecticut: New York Graphic Society, 1972.

Frayling, Christopher. *Vampires: Lord Byron to Count Dracula*. London: Faber, 1991.

Frazer, James G. *The Golden Bough*. New York: Macmillan, 1951.

Freud, Sigmund. *General Psychological Theories*. Edited by Philip Rieff. New York: Crowell Collier, 1963.

Gerard, Emily. *The Land Beyond the Forest*. New York: Harper and Bros., 1888.

Gifford, Denis. *Movie Monsters*. London: Dutton, 1969.

Glob, P. V. *The Bog People. Iron Age Man Preserved*. Translated by Rupert Bruce-Mitford. New York: Ballantine Books, 1969.

Glut, Donald. *The Dracula Book*. Metuchen, NJ: Scarecrow Press, 1975.

Goens, Jean. *Loups-garous, vampires et autres monstres (Werewolves, Vampires, and Other Monsters)*. Paris: CNRS Éditions, 1993.

Greenhall, Arthur, M. Artois and M. Fekadu. *Bats and Rabies*. Lyon, France: Fondation Marcel Mérieux, 1993.

Greenhall, Arthur and Uwe Schmidt, eds. *Natural History of Vampire Bats*. Boca Raton, FL: CRC Press, 1988.

Grene, David and Richmond Lattimore, ed. *Greek Tragedies*, Volume I. Chicago: The University of Chicago Press, 1960.

Griffin, Gail B. " 'Your Girls That You All Love Are Mine': Dracula and the Victorian Male Sexual Imagination." *International Journal of Women's Studies* 5 (1980): 454–65.

Gussow, Mel. "Gorey Goes Batty." [An extended discussion of the 1977 Broadway production of "Dracula."] *New York Times Magazine*, October 16, 1977, 40–42, 71, 74–76.

Haining, Peter. *The Dracula Scrapbook*. London: New English Library, 1976.

— — —, ed. *Shades of Dracula. The Uncollected Stories of Bram Stoker*. London: Kimber, 1982.

— — —. *The Midnight People*. New York: Popular Library, 1968.

— — —, ed. *Midnight Tales/Bram Stoker*. London: Owen, 1990.

Hardy, Phil, ed. *Encyclopedia of Horror Movies*. Cambridge: Harper and Row, 1986.

— — —, ed. *The Overlook Film Encyclopedia: Horror*. Woodstock, NY: Overlook Press, 1994.

Hartmann, Franz. *Premature Burial*. London, 1896.

Hay, Denys. *Europe in the Fourteenth and Fifteenth Centuries*. London: Longmans, Green and Co., Ltd., 1966.

Hicks, Arthur C. and R. Milton Clarke. *A Stage Version of Shelley's Cenci*. Caldwell, Ohio: The Caxton Printers, Ltd., 1945.

Hogg, Henry. *Cannibalism and Human Sacrifice*. New York: Citadel Press, 1966.

Hole, Christina. *English Folklore*, 2d ed. London: B.T. Batsford, Ltd., 1945.

*Horne's Guide to Whitby*, 5th ed. Whitby: Horne and Son, 1897.

Howes, Marjorie. "The Mediation of the Feminine: Bisexuality, Homoerotic Desire, and Self-Expression in Bram Stoker's *Dracula*." *Texas Studies in Literature and Language* 30 (spring 1988): 104–19.

Hutchinson, Tom and Roy Pickard. *Horrors: A History of Horror Movies*. Seacaucus, NJ: Chartwell Books, 1984.

Hutchinson, Thomas, ed. *The Poetical Works of Wordsworth*. London: Oxford University Press, 1939.

Hyde, Mongomery, ed. *The Annotated Oscar Wilde*. New York: Clarkson N. Potter, Inc., 1982.

Hyslop, Lois Boe and Francis E. Hyslop, eds. *Baudelaire as a Literary Critic*. University Park, PA: Pennsylvania State University Press, 1964.

Irving, Laurence. *Henry Irving, The Actor and His World*. London: Faber and Faber, 1951.

Johnson, Thomas, ed. *Final Harvest: Emily Dickinson's Poems*. Boston: Little, Brown and Company, 1961.

Jones, Ernest. *On the Nightmare.* New York: Liveright, 1971.

Jung, C. G. *Modern Man in Search of a Soul.* Translated by W. S. Dell and Cary F. Baynes. New York: Harcourt, Brace and World, 1933.

Katz, Leon. *Dracula: Sabbat.* Copyright by Leon Katz, 1970.

Kendrick, Walter. *The Thrill of Fear: 250 years of Scary Entertainment.* New York: Grove Weidenfield, 1991.

Kenny, M. G. "Multiple Personality and Spirit Possession." *Psychiatry* 44 (1981): 337–58.

King, Stephen. *Salem's Lot.* New York: Plume, 1975.

Kirschbaum, Leo, ed. *Plays of Christopher Marlow.* New York: Meridian Books, 1962.

Kline, Salli J. *The Degeneration of Women: Bram Stoker's Dracula as Allegorical Criticism of the Fin de Siècle.* Rheinbach, Germany: CMZ-Verlag, 1992.

Knight, Chris. *Blood Relations: Menstruation and the Origins of Culture.* New Haven, CT: Yale University Press, 1991.

*Koran.* Translated by George Sale. New York: Garland Publishing, Inc., 1984. (Facsimile of 1734 edition).

Kracauer, Siegfried. *From Caligari to Hitler: A Psychological History of the German Film.* Princeton, NJ: Princeton University Press, 1966.

Lacassin, Francis. *Vampires: Anthologie.* Paris: Christian de Bartillat, 1995.

Lamouche, Colonel Jean. *Histoire de la Turquie.* Paris: Payot, 1953.

Lapin, Daniel. *The Vampire, Dracula and Incest.* San Francisco: Gargoyle Publishers, 1995.

Leatherdale, Clive. *Dracula: The Novel and the Legend.* Wellingborough, Northamptonshire: The Aquarian Press, 1985.

———. *The Origins of Dracula.* London: William Kimber, 1987.

Lefebvre, Dom Gaspar O.S.B. *St. Andrew Daily Missal.* St. Paul, MN: E.M. Lohmann Co., 1949.

Lennig, Arthur. *The Count: The Life and Times of Bela "Dracula" Lugosi.* New York: G. P. Putnam's Sons, 1974.

Lévy-Bruhl, Lucien. *Les Fonctions mentales dans les sociétés inférieures (Mental Functioning in Primitive Societies).* 1910; reprint, Paris, 1951.

Lewis, Matthew Gregory. *The Monk.* New York: Grove Press, 1952.

Lucas, C. J., P. Saintsbury, and J. G. Collins. "A Social and Clinical Study of Delusions in Schizophrenia." *Journal of Mental Science* 108 (1962): 747–58.

Ludlam, Harry. *A Biography of Dracula: The Life Story of Bram Stoker.* London: Foulsham, 1962.

MacAndrew, Elizabeth. *The Gothic Tradition in Fiction.* New York: Columbia University Press, 1979.

MacGillivray, Royce. "*Dracula:* Bram Stoker's Spoiled Masterpiece." *Queen's Quarterly* 79 (1972): 518–27.

MagicImage Filmbooks. *Dracula* (The Original 1931 Shooting Script). Hollywood, CA: MagicImage Filmbooks, 1990.

Manville, Roger. *Ellen Terry.* London: Heinemann, 1968.

Marcus, Stephen. *The Other Victorians: A Study of Sexuality and Pornography in Mid-Nineteenth-Century England.* New York: Basic Books, 1974.

Marrero, Robert. *Vampire Movies.* Key West, FL: Fantasma Books, 1994.

Masters, Anthony. *The Natural History of the Vampire.* New York: G. P. Putnam's Sons, 1972.

Maturin, Charles Robert. *Melmoth the Wanderer.* Lincoln: University of Nebraska Press, 1961.

McCormack, W. J. *Sheridan Le Fanu and Victorian Ireland.* Dublin: The Lilliput Press, 1991.

Melton, Gordon J. *The Vampire Book.* Detroit: Visible Ink Press, 1994.

Murgoçi, Agnes. "The Vampire in Roumania." *Folklore* 37 (1926): 320–49.

Murphy, Michael J. *The Celluloid Vampires: A History and Filmography, 1897–1979.* Ann Arbor: Pierian Press, 1979.

Nandris, Grigore. "The Historical Dracula: The Theme of His Legend in the Western and in the Eastern Literatures of Europe." *Comparative Literature Studies* 3 (1966): 367–96.

Noll, Richard. *Vampires, Werewolves and Demons.* New York: Bruno-Mazel, 1992.

Oates, Joyce Carol. *Bellefleur.* New York: E. P. Dutton, 1980.

O'Clair, Robert, ed. *The Norton Anthology of Modern Poetry.* New York: W. W. Norton, 1973.

O'Donnell, Elliott. *Werewolves.* New York: Longvue Press, 1965.

Oesterreich, T. K. *Possession, Demoniacal and Other Among Primitive Races.* Translated by D. Ibberson. New Hyde Park, N.Y.: University Books, 1966.

Osborne, Charles, ed. *The Bram Stoker Bedside Companion.* London: Quartet, 1974.

Paget, John. *Hungary and Transylvania.* Philadelphia: Lea and Blanchard, 1850.

Peithman, Stephen, ed. *The Annotated Tales of Edgar Allan Poe.* Garden City, NY: Doubleday, 1981.

Pirie, David. *A Heritage of Horror: The English Gothic Cinema, 1946–1972.* New York: Avon Books, 1973.

— — —. *The Vampire Cinema.* New York: Crescent, 1977.

Polidori, John. *The Vampyre* (1819). In *Three Gothic Novels,* edited by E. F. Bleiler, New York: Dover, 1966.

Ponsold, Albert. *Lehrbuch der gerichtlichen Medizin (Textbook of Forensic Medicine),* 2d ed. Stuttgart: Georg Thieme Verlag, 1957.

Prawer, S. S. *Caligari's Children: The Film as Tale of Terror.* Oxford: Oxford University Press, 1980.

Praz, Mario. *The Romantic Agony.* London: Oxford University Press, 1933.

Radcliffe, Ann. *The Italian.* New York: Russell & Russell, 1968.

— — —. *The Mysteries of Udolpho.* London, New York: J. M. Dent & Sons, Ltd., E. P. Dutton & Inc., 1931.

Ramsland, Katherine. *The Vampire Companion.* New York: Ballantine Books, 1993.

Raschka, L. B. "The Incubus Syndrome: A Variant of Erotomania." *Canadian Journal of Psychiatry* 24 (1979): 549–53.

Reed, Donald. *The Vampire on the Screen.* Inglewood, CA: Wagon and Star Publishers, 1965.

Rice, Anne. *Interview with the Vampire.* New York: Alfred A. Knopf, 1985.

— — —. *Memnoch the Devil.* New York: Ballantine Books, 1995.

— — —. *The Queen of the Damned.* New York: Alfred A. Knopf, 1988.

— — —. *The Tale of the Body Thief.* New York: Alfred A. Knopf, 1992.

— — —. *The Vampire Lestat.* New York: Ballantine Books, 1985.

Richardson, Maurice. "The Psychoanalysis of Ghost Stories." *Twentieth Century* 166 (1959): 419–31.

Riley, Michael. *Conversations with Anne Rice.* New York: Ballantine Books, 1996.

Roberts, Bette B. *The Gothic Romance: Its Appeal to Women Writers and Readers in Late Eighteenth-Century England.* New York: Arno Press, 1980.

Rogers, Robert. *A Psychoanalytic Study of the Double in Literature.* Detroit, MI: Wayne State University Press, 1970.

Ronay, Gabriel. *The Truth About Dracula.* New York: Stein & Day, 1974.

Roth, Phyllis A. *Bram Stoker.* Boston: Twayne Publishers, 1982.

— — —. "Suddenly Sexual Women in Bram Stoker's *Dracula.*" *Literature and Psychology* 27. (1977): 113–21.

Roux, Jean-Paul. *Le Sang, Mythes, Symboles et Realités (Blood: Myths, Symbols and Realities).* Paris: Fayard, 1988.

Russell, Sharon A. *Stephen King: A Critical Companion.* Westport, CT: Greenwood Press, 1996.

Ryan, Alan, ed. *The Penguin Book of Vampire Stories.* New York: Penguin Books, 1988.

Rymer, James Malcolm. *Varney the Vampyre, or The Feast of Blood* (1845). New York: Dover, 1870.

Schaffer, Talia. "A Wilde Desire to Look at Me: The Homoerotic History of *Dracula.*" *ELH* (summer 1993): 381–425.

Schiff, Gert. *Images of Horror and Fantasy.* New York: Harry N. Abrams, Inc., 1978.

Schroeder, Aribert. *Vampirismus.* Frankfurt am Main: Akademische Verlagsgesellschaft, 1973.

Senf, Carol A, ed. *The Critical Response to Bram Stoker.* Westport, CT: Greenwood Press, 1993.

— — —. *"Dracula:* Stoker's Response to the New Woman." *Victorian Studies* 2 (1982): 33–49.

— — —. "Dracula: The Unseen Face in the Mirror." *Journal of Narrative Technique* 9 (1979): 160–70.

— — —. "Polidori's *The Vampyre:* Combining the Gothic with Realism." *North Dakota Quarterly* 56 (1988): 179–208.

— — —. *The Vampire in Nineteenth-Century Literature.* Bowling Green, OH: Bowling Green State University Popular Press, 1988.

Shippey, Tom, ed. *The Oxford Book of Fantasy Stories.* New York: Oxford University Press, 1994.

Showalter, Elaine. *Sexual Anarchy: Gender and Culture at the Fin de Siècle.* New York: Viking, 1990.

Shuttle, Penelope and Peter Redgrove. *The Wise Wound: Myths, Realities, and Meanings of Menstruation.* New York: Bantam Books, 1990.

Skal, David J. *Dracula: the Ultimate, Illustrated Edition of the World-Famous Vampire Play.* New York: St. Martin's Press, 1993.

— — —. *Hollywood Gothic.* New York: W. W. Norton, 1990.

— — —. *Monster Show: A Cultural History of Horror.* New York: W. W. Norton & Co., 1993.

— — —. *V is for Vampire.* New York: Plume, 1996.

Slavitt, David R., ed. *Seneca: The Tragedies,* Vol. I. Baltimore: Johns Hopkins University Press, 1992.

Smith, Wayland. *Eros Denied.* New York: Grove Press, 1964.

Spitz, Werner U. and Russell S. Fisher, eds. *Medicolegal Investigation of Death,* 2d ed. Springfield, IL: Charles C. Thomas, 1980.

Stoker, Bram. *Dracula.* London: Constable, 1897.

— — —. *Dracula's Guest—And Other Weird Stories.* London: Sidgwick & Jackson, 1910.

— — —. *The Duties of Clerks of Petty Sessions in Ireland.* Dublin: John Falconer, 1879.

— — —. *Famous Impostors.* London: Sidgwick & Jackson, 1910.

— — —. *A Glimpse of America.* London: Sampson Low, Marston & Co., 1886.

— — —. *The Jewel of the Seven Stars.* London: Heinemann, 1903.

— — —. *Lady Athlyne.* London: Heinemann, 1908.

— — —. *The Lady of the Shroud.* London: Heinemann, 1909.

— — —. *The Lair of the White Worm.* London: Rider, 1911.

— — —. *The Man.* London: Heinemann, 1905.

— — —. *Miss Betty.* London: Pearson, 1898.

— — —. *The Mystery of the Sea.* London: Heinemann, 1902.

— — —. *Personal Reminiscences of Henry Irving,* 2 vols. London: Heinemann, 1906.

— — —. *The Shoulder of Shasta.* London: Constable, 1895.

———. *The Snake's Pass.* London: Sampson Low, Marston, Searle & Rivington, 1890.

———. *Snowbound: The Record of a Theatrical Touring Party.* London: Collier, 1908.

———. *Under the Sunset.* London: Sampson Low, Marston, Searle & Rivington, 1881.

———. *The Watter's Mou.* London: Constable, 1895.

Stuart, Roxana. *Stage Blood: Vampires of the Nineteenth-Century Stage.* Bowling Green, OH: Bowling Green State University Popular Press, 1994.

Sturgeon, Theodore. *Some of Your Blood.* London: Sphere Books, Ltd., 1961.

Sullivan, Jack, ed. *The Penguin Encyclopedia of Horror and the Supernatural.* New York: Viking, 1986.

Summers, Montague. *The Gothic Quest.* London: Russell and Russell, 1964.

———. *The Vampire: His Kith and Kin* (1928). New Hyde Park: New York University Books, 1960.

———. *The Vampire in Europe* (1929). New Hyde Park: New York University Books, 1961.

Symonds, John Addington and Havelock Ellis. *Sexual Inversion.* London: Wilson and Macmillan, 1897.

Tolstoi, Aleksei. *Vampires.* Translated by Fedor Nikanov. New York: Hawthorne Books, 1969.

Treptow, Kurt W., ed. *Dracula: Essays on the Life and Times of Vlad Tepes.* New York: Columbia University Press, 1991.

Turgenev, Ivan. *Dream Tales and Prose Poems.* Translated by Fedor Nikanov. New York: Hawthorne Books, 1969.

Turner, Dennis C. *The Vampire Bat.* Baltimore: The Johns Hopkins University Press, 1975.

Twitchell, James B. *Dreadful Pleasures: An Anatomy of Modern Horror.* New York: Oxford University Press, 1985.

———. *The Living Dead: A Study of the Vampire in Romantic Literature.* Durham, NC: Duke University Press, 1981.

Tymn, Marshall B. *Horror Literature.* New York: R. R. Bowker Company, 1981.

Tyson, Donald. *How to Make and Use a Magic Mirror.* Custer, WA: Phoenix Publishing, Inc., 1995.

Vacano, Otto-Wilhelm von. *Etruscans in the Ancient World.* London: Edward Arnold, 1960.

Van Gennep, Arnold. *The Rites of Passage* (1908). Translated by Monika B. Vizedom and Gabrielle L. Caffee. Chicago: University of Chicago Press, 1960.

Varma, Devendra P. *The Gothic Flame.* London: Arthur Barker, Ltd. 1957.

Walpole, Horace. *The Castle of Otranto.* Edited by E. F. Beiler. New York: Dover Publications, 1966.

Watt, William W. *Chilling Shockers of the Gothic School: A Study of Chapbook Gothic Romances.* Cambridge, MA: Harvard University Press, 1932.

Weinstein, Donald. *Savonarola and Florence; prophecy and patriotism in the Renaissance.* Princeton, N.J.: Princeton University Press, 1970.

Weintraub, Stanley. *Victoria.* New York: E.P. Dutton, 1987.

Weissman, Judith. "Women and Vampires: *Dracula* as a Victorian Novel." *Midwest Quarterly* 18 (1977): 392–405.

Wilkins Freeman, Mary. *The Wind in the Rosebush and Other Stories of the Supernatural.* New York: Garrett Press, Inc., 1963.

Wimsatt, William A. "Portrait of a Vampire." *Ward's Natural Science Bulletin* 32:2 (Spring 1959): 13–39.

Wolf, Leonard, ed. *The Annotated Dracula.* New York: Ballantine Books, 1975.

— — —, ed. *Carmilla and 12 Other Classic Tales of Mystery.* New York: Signet, 1996.

— — —, ed. *Doubles, Dummies, and Dolls.* New York: Newmarket Press, 1995.

— — —. *A Dream of Dracula.* Boston-Toronto: Little, Brown and Company, 1972.

— — —, ed. *The Essential Dracula.* New York: Plume, 1991.

— — —, ed. *The Essential Frankenstein: The Complete Annotated Edition of Mary Shelley's Classic Novel.* New York: Plume, 1993.

— — —, ed. *The Essential Jekyll & Mr. Hyde.* New York: Plume, 1995.

— — —, ed. *The Essential Phantom of the Opera.* New York: Plume, 1996.

— — —. *Horror: A Connoisseur's Guide to Literature & Film.* New York: Facts on File, 1990.

— — —. *Monsters.* San Francisco: Straight Arrow Books, 1974.

— — —, ed. *Wolf's Complete Book of Terror.* New York: New Market Press, 1994.

Wood, Robin. "Burying the Undead." *Mosaic* 16 (Winter/Spring 1983): 175–86.

Wyndham, Horace. *The Nineteen Hundreds.* New York: T. Seltzer, 1923.

Yarbro, Chelsea Quinn. *Hotel Transylvania.* New York: St. Martin's Press, 1978.

— — —. *Tempting Fate.* New York: St. Martin's Press, 1982.

# FILMOGRAPHY

*The films below have been listed not because they are the best Dracula films that have been made, but because they seem to me to have contributed to the still-emerging film lore of Dracula.*

**Nosferatu, Eine Symphonie Des Grauens** (A Symphony of Terror)
(1922 — B/W) 72 Min.
Production Company: Prana Films (Germany)
Director: F. W. Murnau
Screenplay: Henrik Galeen
Photography: Fritz Arno Wagner and Gunther Krampf
Editor: Simon Gould
Special Effects: Albin Grau (set design)

Cast: Max Schreck (Graf Orlok, Nosferatu), Alexander Granach
(Knock), Gustav Von Wandenheim (Hutter), Greta Schroder-Matry
(Ellen), Ruth Landshoff (Annie), John Gottowt (Professor Bulwer).

**Dracula**
(1931 — B/W) 85 Min.
Production Company: Universal (USA)
Director: Todd Browning
Producer: Carl Laemmle, Jr.
Screenplay: Garrett Fort and Dudley Murphy
Photography: Karl Freund
Editor: Milton Carruth
Music: Peter Tchaikovsky

Cast: Bela Lugosi (Count Dracula), Helen Chandler (Mina), David Man-
ners (John Harker), Dwight Frye (Renfield), Edward Van Sloan
(Professor Van Helsing), Herbert Bunston (Dr. Seward), Frances
Dade (Lucy).

**Dracula's Daughter**
(1936 — B/W) 72 Min.
Production Company: Universal (USA)
Director: Lambert Hillyer
Producer: E. M. Asher
Screenplay: Garrett Fort
Editor: Milton Carruth
Photography: George Robinson
Special Effects: John F. Fulton
Music: Heinz Roemheld

Cast: Otto Kruger (Jeffrey Garth), Gloria Holden (Countess Marya Zaleska), Edward Van Sloan (Dr. Van Helsing), Irving Pichel (Sandor).

**Son of Dracula**
(1943 — B/W) 90 Min.
Production Company: Universal (USA)
Director: Robert Siodmak
Producer: Jack Gross
Screenplay: Eric Taylor
Photography: George Robinson
Editor: Saul Goodkind
Special Effects: John P. Fulton
Music: Hans J. Salter

Cast: Lon Chaney (Count Dracula), Louise Allbritton (Katherine Caldwell), Robert Paige (Frank Stanley), Evelyn Ankers (Claire Caldwell), Frank Craven (Dr. Harry Brewster), J. Edward Bromberg (Professor Laszlo), Adelaide De Walt (Queen Zimba).

**House of Dracula**
(1945 — B/W) 67 Min.
Production Company: Universal (USA)
Director: Erle C. Kenton
Producer: Paul Malvern
Screenplay: Edward T. Lowe
Photography: George Robinson

Cast: John Carradine (Count Dracula), Lon Chaney, Jr. (Werewolf), Onslow Stevens (Mad Scientist), Glenn Strange (Frankenstein Creature).

**Abbott and Costello Meet Frankenstein**
(1948 — B/W) 83 Min.

Production Company: Universal International (USA)
Director: Charles T. Barton
Producer: Robert Arthur
Screenplay: Robert Lees, Frederic Rinaldo, and John Grant
Photography: Charles Van Enger
Special Effects: David S. Horsley
Music: Frank Skinner

Cast: Bud Abbott, Lou Costello, Bela Lugosi (Count Dracula), Lon
  Chaney, Jr. (Wolfman), Glenn Strange (The Frankenstein Creature),
  Lenore Aubert (Sandra Morney), Vincent Price (The Invisible Man).

**The Horror of Dracula**
(1958 — Color) 82 Min.
Production Company: Hammer Films (Great Britain)
Director: Terence Fisher
Producer: Anthony Hinds
Screenplay: Jimmy Sangster (Based on the novel by Bram Stoker)
Photography: Jack Asher

Starring: Christopher Lee (Count Dracula), John Van Eyssen (Jonathan
  Harker), Peter Cushing (Professor Van Helsing), Melissa Stribling
  (Mina), Carol Marsh (Lucy).

**Return of Dracula**
(1958 — B/W) 73 Min.
Production Company: United Artists (USA)
Director: Paul Landres
Producers: Jules V. Levy and Arthur Gardner
Screenplay: Pat Fielder
Photography: Jack McKenzie

Starring: Francis Lederer (Count Dracula), Norma Eberhardt, Ray
  Stricklyn, Jimmie Baird, John Wengraf, Virginia Vincent.

**Brides of Dracula**
(1960 — Color) 85 Min.
Production Company: Hammer Films (Great Britain)
Director: Terence Fisher
Producer: Anthony Hinds
Screenplay: Jimmy Sangster, Edward Percy, and Peter Bryan
Photography: Jack Asher

Cast: David Peel (Baron Meinster), Martita Hunt (Baroness Meinster),
  Peter Cushing (Professor Van Helsing), Yvonne Monlaur (Marianne).

## Dracula—Prince of Darkness
(1965—Color) 90 Min.
Production Company: Hammer Films (Great Britain)
Director: Terence Fisher
Producer: Anthony Nelson Keys
Screenplay: Jimmy Sangster (as John Samson)
Photography: Michael Reed

Cast: Christopher Lee (Count Dracula), Barbara Shelley (Wife), Francis
Matthews, Susan Farmer, Andrew Keir (Father Sandor).

## Billy the Kid Versus Dracula
(1965—Color) 84 Min.
Production Company: Circle Productions
Director: William Beaudine
Producer: Carroll Case
Screenplay: Carl Hittleman
Photography: Lothrop Worth
Editor: Roy Livingston
Special Effects: Cinema Research
Music: Raoul Kraushaar

Cast: John Carradine (Count Dracula), Chuck Courtney (Billy the Kid),
Melinda Plowman (Betty Bentley), Virginia Christine (Eva Oster),
Olive Carey (Doc), Harry Carey, Jr. (Ben), Marjorie Bennett (Mrs.
Bentley).

## Dracula Has Risen from the Grave
(1968—Color) 92 Min.
Production Company: Hammer Films (Great Britain)
Director: Freddie Francis
Producer: Aida Young
Screenplay: Anthony Hinds (as John Elder)
Photography: Arthur Grant
Music: James Bernard

Cast: Christopher Lee (Count Dracula), Ewan Hooper (enslaved priest),
Veronica Carlson (Maria), Barry Andrews (Paul).

## Blood of Dracula's Castle
(1969—Color) 84 Min.
Production Company: Crown International (USA)
Director: Al Adamson
Producer: Al Adamson
Screenplay: Rex Carlton

Photography: Lazlo Kovacs
Editors: Ewing Brown and Peter Perry
Music: Lincoln Mayorage

Cast: John Carradine (George), Paula Raymond (Countess
Townsend/Countess Dracula), Alex d'Arcy (Count Townsend/Count
Dracula), Robert Dix (Johnny), Gene O'Shane (Glen Cannon), Bar-
bara Bishop (Liz Arden).

**Dracula—The Dirty Old Man**
(1969—Color) 82 Min.
Production Company: Boyd Productions/Art Films (USA)
Director: William Edward
Producer: William Edward
Screenplay: William Edward

Starring: Vince Kelly (Count Dracula)

**Count Dracula**
(1970—Color) 98 Min.
Production Company: World (Spain/Italy/Great Britain/West Germany)
Director: Jesus Franco
Producer: Harry Alan Towers
Screenplay: Jesus Franco, Harry Alan Towers, August Finochi, Milo G.
Ciccia, and Dietmar Behnke.

Starring: Christopher Lee (Count Dracula), Herbert Lom (Professor Van
Helsing), Klaus Kinski (Renfield), Maria Rohm, Soledad Miranda,
Teresa Gimpera.

**Countess Dracula**
(1970—Color) 93 Min.
Production Company: Fox/Rank (USA)
Director: Peter Sasdy
Producer: Alexander Paal
Screenplay: Jeremy Paul
Photography: Kenneth Talbot
Special Effects: Bery Luxford

Starring: Ingrid Pitt (Elisabeth Nadsdy), Sandor Eles (Toth), Lesley-
Anne Down (Ilona), Nike Arrighi, Charles Farrell.

**Scars of Dracula**
(1970—Color) 96 Min.
Production Company: Hammer Films (Great Britain)

Director: Roy Ward Baker
Producer: Aida Young
Screenplay: Anthony Hinds (as John Elder)
Camera: Maray Grant

Starring: Christopher Lee (Count Dracula), Jenny Hanley, Dennis
Waterman, Christopher Matthews, Anoushka Hempel, Patrick
Troughton, Michael Gwynn, Wendy Hamilton, Delia Lindsay,
Michael Ripper.

## Taste the Blood of Dracula
(1970 — Color) 95 Min.
Production Company: Hammer Films (Great Britain)
Producer: Aida Young
Screenplay: Anthony Hinds (as John Elder)
Photography: Arthur Grant
Editor: Chris Batnes
Special Effects: Brian Johcock
Music: James Bernard

Cast: Christopher Lee (Count Dracula), Geoffrey Keen (William Hargood), Gwen Watford (Martha Hargood), Linda Hayden (Alice Hargood), Peter Sallis (Samuel Paxton), John Anthony Corlan (Paul
Paxton), Isla Behr (Lucy Paxton), John Carson (Jonathan Secker),
Martin Jarvis (Jeremy Secker).

## Blacula
(1972 — Color) 92 Min.
Production Company: American International (USA)
Director: William Crane
Producer: Joseph T. Naar
Screenplay: Joan Torres and Raymond Koenig
Photography: John M. Stevens
Editor: Allan Jacobs
Special Effects: Roger George
Music: Gene Page

Cast: William Marshall (Mumawalde/Blacula), Vonetta McGee (Tina),
Denise Nichols (Michelle), Gordon Pinsent (Lt. Peters), Thalmus
Rasulala (Gordon Thomas), Emily Yancy (Nancy).

## Blood for Dracula
(1973 — Color) 103 Min.
Production Company: Bryarson (Italy/France)
Director: Paul Morrissey
Producer: Andrew Braunsberg

Screenplay: Paul Morrissey
Photography: Luigi Kuveiller

Starring: Udo Keir (Count Dracula), Vittorio de Sica, Roman Polanski, Stefania Casini, Silvia Dioniso, Milena Vukotic, Joe Dallesandro.

## The Legend of the Seven Golden Vampires
(1973 — Color) 110 Min.
Production Company: Hammer/Shaw Brothers (Great Britain and Hong Kong)
Director: Roy Ward Baker
Producer: Don Houghton and Vee King Shaw
Screenplay: Don Houghton
Photography: John Wilcox and Roy Ford

Cast: John Forbes-Robinson (Count Dracula), Peter Cushing, David Chiang, Julie Ege, Shih Szu, Robin Stewart, Robert Hanna, Chan Shen, James Ma.

## Dracula A.D.
(1972 — Color) 95 Min.
Production Company: Hammer Films
Director: Alan Gibson
Producer: Josephine Douglas
Screenplay: Don Houghton
Photography: Richard Bush

Cast: Christopher Lee (Count Dracula), Peter Cushing (Van Helsing), Christopher Neame (Johnny Alucard), Marsha Hunt, Caroline Munro, Janet Key.

## The Satanic Rites of Dracula
(1973 — Color) 87 Min.
Production Company: Hammer Films/Warner (Great Britain)
Director: Alan Gibson
Producer: Roy Skeggs
Screenplay: Don Houghton
Photography: Brian Probyn

Starring: Christopher Lee (Count Dracula), Peter Cushing (Professor Van Helsing), Joanna Lumley, Michael Coles, Freddie Jones, William Franklyn, Richard Vernon, Patrick Barr, Barbara Yu Ling.

## Old Dracula
(1974 — Color) 88 Min.
Production Company: American International Pictures (Great Britain)

Director: Clive Donner
Screenplay: Jeremy Lloyd
Photography: Tony Richmond
Music: David Whitaker, Anthony Newley

Starring: David Niven (Vladimir Dracula), Theresa Graves (Vampira),
Jennie Linden, Veronica Carlson, Nicky Henson (the writer), Linda
Hayden, Bernard Bresslaw.

## Dracula's Dog
(1977—Color) 88 Min.
Production Company: Crown International (USA)
Director: Albert Band
Producers: Charles Band and Frank Ray Perilli
Screenplay: Frank Ray Perilli

Starring: Michael Pataki (Dracula), José Ferrer (Inspector Branco),
Reggie Nalder, Jan Shutan (Dracula's wife), Libbie Chase.

## Dracula
(1979—Color) 112 Min.
Production Company: Universal (USA)
Director: John Badham
Producer: Walter Mirisch
Screenplay: W. D. Richter from the novel *Dracula*, by Bram Stoker
Photography: Gilbert Taylor
Music: John Williams

Cast: Frank Langella (Count Dracula), Kate Nelligan (Lucy), Laurence
Olivier (Van Helsing), Trevor Eve (Jonathan Harkes), Tony Hay
Garth (Renfield), Donald Pleasance (Jack Seward).

## Nosferatu: Phantom der Nacht *(Nosferatu—the Vampire)*
(1979—Color) 107 Min.
Production Company: Gaumont/Fox (Germany)
Director: Werner Herzog
Screenplay: Werner Herzog from the 1922 film, *Nosferatu*
Photography: Jorg Schmidt—Reitwein

Starring: Klaus Kinski (Count Dracula) and Isabelle Adjani (Lucy
Harker).

## Dracula Sucks (soft porn)
(1979—Color) 90 Min.
Production Company: M.H.E. (USA)
Director: Philip Marshak

Starring: Jamie Gillis (Count Dracula).

**Bram Stoker's Dracula**
(1992—Color) 123 Min.
Production Company: Columbia/Zoetrope
Director: Francis Ford Coppola
Producer: Francis Ford Coppola, Fred Fuchs, and Charles Mulvehill
Screenplay: James V. Hart based on the novel *Dracula,* by Bram Stoker
Photography: Michael Ballhaus

Cast: Gary Oldman (Count Dracula), Sadie Frost (Lucy), Keanu Reeves
(Jonathan Harker), Winona Ryder (Mina), and Anthony Hopkins
(Professor Van Helsing), Tom Waits (Renfield).

# THEATER PRODUCTIONS

*May 18, 1897    Lyceum Theatre (London)*
This is the staged reading of Stoker's novel to protect his dramatic rights
to his story. The play, divided into five acts, took four hours to read and
was never performed afterward. Asked by Stoker how he liked the play,
Henry Irving is said to have replied, "Dreadful."

### Cast of Characters

| | |
|---|---|
| Dracula | Mr. Jones |
| Jonathan Harker | Mr. Passmore |
| John Seward | Mr. Rivington |
| Professor Van Helsing | Mr. T. Reynolds |
| Quincey Morris | Mr. Widdicombe |
| Arthur Holmwood | Mr. Innes |
| Renfield | Mr. Howard |
| Lucy | Miss Gurney |
| Mina | Miss Craig |

*February 14, 1927    Little Theatre (London), Hamilton Deane Adaptation*

### Cast of Characters

| | |
|---|---|
| Dracula | Raymond Huntley |
| Van Helsing | Hamilton Deane |
| Seward | Stuart Lomath |
| Harker | Bernard Guest |
| Quincey Morris | Frieda Hearn |
| Lord Godalming | Peter Jackson |
| Renfield | Bernard Jukes |
| Mina | Dora Mary Patrick |
| The Maid | Betty Murgatroyd |

*October 4, 1927    Fulton Theater (New York), Hamilton Deane–John*
  *Balderston Adaptation*

| | |
|---|---|
| Dracula | Bela Lugosi |
| The Maid | Nedda Harrigan |
| Harker | Terrence Neill |
| Seward | Herbert Bunston |
| Van Helsing | Edward Van Sloan |
| Renfield | Bernard Jukes |
| Lucy Seward | Dorothy Peterson |

*October 15, 1977    Martin Beck Theater (New York), Hamilton Deane–John*
  *Balderston Adaptation*

| | |
|---|---|
| Dracula | Frank Langella |
| Lucy Seward | Ann Sachs |
| Harker | Alan Coates |
| Renfield | Richard Kavanaugh |
| Seward | Dillon Evans |
| Van Helsing | Jerome Dempsey |
| Wells (The Maid) | Gretchen Oehler |

# MAY

● *New Moon*  ◐ *First Quarter*  ○ *Full Moon*  ◑ *Last Quarter*

| Sunday | Monday | Tuesday | Wednesday | Thursday | Friday | Saturday |
|---|---|---|---|---|---|---|
| **1** Jonathan Harker departs Munich 8:35 P.M. <br> SR: 4:49 SS: 7:04 † ● | **2** Harker arrives in Klausenburg; stays the night. <br> SR: 4:48 SS: 7:04 † ● | **3** Harker arrives in Bistrita; stays at Golden Krone Hotel; makes first journal entry. <br> SR: 4:46 SS: 7:07 † ◐ | **4** Harker leaves by coach for Castle Dracula; arrives at 2 A.M. (?) the following morning. <br> SR: 4:44 SS: 7:10 † ◐ | **5** St. George's Day. Harker becomes acquainted with Dracula. <br> SR: 4:44 SS: 7:10 † ◐ | **6** <br> SR: 4:44 SS: 7:10 † ◐ | **7** <br> SR: 4:40 SS: 7:13 † ◑ |
| **8** Harker realizes he is a prisoner. <br> SR: 4:40 SS: 7:13 † ◑ | **9** Mina Murray's first communication to Lucy Westenra. <br> SR: 4:15 SS: 7:37 ♦ ◑ | **10** <br> SR: 4:37 SS: 7:16 † ◑ | **11** Harker watches Dracula crawl facedown over the castle wall. <br> SR: 4:37 SS: 7:16 † ○ | **12** <br> SR: 4:33 SS: 7:19 † ○ | **13** <br> SR: 4:33 SS: 7:19 † ○ | **14** <br> SR: 4:31 SS: 7:22 † ○ |
| **15** Harker enters the forbidden room and encounters the three beautiful vampires. <br> SR: 4:31 SS: 7:22 † ○ | **16** <br> SR: 4:31 SS: 7:22 † ○ | **17** <br> SR: 4:29 SS: 7:25 † ○ | **18** Dracula asks Harker to write three misleading letters to England dated June 12, June 19, and June 29. <br> SR: 4:29 SS: 7:25 † ◑ | **19** <br> SR: 4:26 SS: 7:28 † ◑ | **20** <br> SR: 4:26 SS: 7:28 † ◑ | **21** <br> SR: 4:26 SS: 7:28 † ◑ |
| **22** <br> SR: 4:23 SS: 7:30 † ◑ | **23** <br> SR: 4:21 SS: 7:33 † ◑ | **24** Lucy is proposed to three times in one day, and accepts Arthur Holmwood. <br> SR: 3:53 SS: 8:02 ♦ ◑ | **25** Dr. Seward makes his first entry on Renfield, the madman. <br> SR: 3:53 SS: 8:02 ♦ ◑ | **26** <br> SR: 4:21 SS: 7:33 † ● | **27** <br> SR: 4:21 SS: 7:33 † ● | **28** Harker tries to smuggle letters out with the gypsies. <br> SR: 4:18 SS: 7:38 † ● |
| **29** <br> SR: 4:18 SS: 7:38 † ● | **30** <br> SR: 4:18 SS: 7:38 † ● | **31** Harker discovers his personal effects are gone. <br> SR: 4:18 SS: 7:38 † ● | | | | |

## CALENDAR OF EVENTS · 1887

1887 is a probable date for the events in this book, but a reader is cautioned not to believe in it to precisely. Any five-year period before or after 1887 will do to account for the phases of the moon as Stoker has given them to us. **Note:** The sunrise and sunset times, accurate within ± 2½ minutes, are based on the latitude either of Castle Dracula (45°0'), indicated by a cross (†), or of London (51°30'), indicated by a diamond (♦). In other places where there is action, the local sunrise and sunset times are given.

# JUNE

| Sunday | Monday | Tuesday | Wednesday | Thursday | Friday | Saturday |
|---|---|---|---|---|---|---|
| | | | | | **1** † ◑ SR: 3:43 SS: 8:21 | **2** † ◑ SR: 3:44 SS: 8:21 |
| **3** ◆ ◑ Renfield begins to catch and eat flies. SR: 3:45 SS: 8:22 | **4** † ◑ SR: 3:46 SS: 8:22 | **5** † ◑ SR: 3:46 SS: 8:22 | **6** † ● SR: 4:09 SS: 7:38 | **7** † ◑ SR: 3:49 SS: 8:21 | **8** † ○ SR: 3:51 SS: 8:20 | **9** † ○ SR: 3:51 SS: 8:19 |
| **10** † ○ SR: 3:52 SS: 8:19 | **11** † ○ SR: 4:40 SS: 7:30 | **12** † ○ SR: 4:40 SS: 7:30 | **13** † ○ SR: 4:58 SS: 7:17 | **14** † ○ SR: 3:56 SS: 8:15 | **15** † ○ Slovaks deliver large empty boxes to Castle Dracula. SR: 3:57 SS: 8:14 | **16** † ◆ Renfield turns his attention to spiders. SR: 4:58 SS: 7:14 |
| **17** † ◑ SR: 4:58 SS: 7:13 | **18** † ◑ SR: 4:01 SS: 8:10 | **19** † ◑ SR: 4:03 SS: 8:09 | **20** † ● SR: 4:04 SS: 8:08 | **21** † ● Dracula leaves the castle dressed in Harker's clothes and returns with a child for the three beautiful vampire women. SR: 4:05 SS: 8:06 | **22** † ● The bereft mother is killed by wolves in the courtyard of Castle Dracula. SR: 5:05 SS: 7:10 | **23** † ● Harker climbs along the castle wall to Dracula's room, thence to the cellar where he finds Dracula inert in a box. SR: 4:07 SS: 8:04 |
| **24** Whitby Bay of Biscay SR: 4:00 SS: 8:12 SR: 4:36 SS: 7:36 † ● | **25** † ● SR: 4:11 SS: 8:02 | **26** † ● SR: 4:02 SS: 8:10 | **27** † ● SR: 4:05 SS: 8:06 | **28** † ● Harker again seeks out Dracula in his box and gashes Dracula's forehead with a spade. SR: 4:40 SS: 7:33 | **29** ● SR: 5:05 SS: 7:10 | **30** SR: 4:43 SS: 7:36 |
| **31** SR: 4:21 SS: 7:51 | | | | | | |

# JULY

| Sunday | Monday | Tuesday | Wednesday | Thursday | Friday | Saturday |
|--------|--------|---------|-----------|----------|--------|----------|
| | | | **1** ◑<br>SR: 4:18<br>SS: 7:38 | **2**<br>SR: 4:17<br>SS: 7:38 | **3** ●<br>Renfield eats a blowfly.<br>SR: 4:15<br>SS: 7:42 | **4** ◑<br>SR: 4:15<br>SS: 7:42 |
| **5** ◑<br>SR: 3:44<br>SS: 8:13 | **6** ◑<br>SR: 4:15<br>SS: 7:42 | **7** ◑<br>SR: 4:13<br>SS: 7:45 | **8** ◑<br>The Schooner *Demeter* departs Varna.<br>SR: 4:13<br>SS: 7:45 | **9** ◑<br>SR: 4:13<br>SS: 7:45 | **10** ◑<br>Renfield captures a sparrow, to which he feeds flies and spiders. He begins to collect a colony of birds.<br>SR: 4:13<br>SS: 7:45 | **11** ◑<br>SR: 4:13<br>SS: 7:45 |
| **12** ◑<br>SR: 4:13<br>SS: 7:48 | **13** ○<br>The *Demeter* enters the Bosphorus.<br>SR: 4:13<br>SS: 7:48 | **14**<br>The *Demeter* clears the Dardanelles.<br>SR: 4:13<br>SS: 7:48 | **15** ○<br>The *Demeter* passes Cape Matapan.<br>SR: 4:13<br>SS: 7:48 | **16**<br>SR: 4:13<br>SS: 7:48 | **17** ○<br>SR: 4:13<br>SS: 7:50 | **18** ○<br>A man disappears from the *Demeter*.<br>SR: 3:39<br>SS: 8:23 |
| **19** ◑<br>A tall, thin man is seen on board.<br>SR: 4:13<br>SS: 7:50 | **20** ◑<br>SR: 4:13<br>SS: 7:50 | **21** ◑<br>Renfield asks Dr. Seward for a kitten and is refused.<br>SR: 4:13<br>SS: 7:50 | **22** ◑<br>Renfield eats his colony of sparrows.<br>SR: 4:14<br>SS: 7:51 | **23** ◑<br>SR: 4:14<br>SS: 7:51 | **24** ◑<br>The *Demeter* passes Gibraltar.<br>SR: 4:14<br>SS: 7:51 | **25** ●<br>SR: 4:14<br>SS: 7:51 |
| **26** ●<br>Mina arrives in Whitby. Another sailor is lost.<br>SR: 4:14<br>SS: 7:51 | **27** ●<br>SR: 4:16<br>SS: 7:51 | **28** ●<br>Mina receives the false letter written by Jonathan on May 18. Lucy begins walking in her sleep.<br>SR: 4:16<br>SS: 7:51 | **29** ●<br>Lucy walks in her sleep.<br>SR: 4:16<br>SS: 7:51 | **30** ●<br>The *Demeter* weathers heavy storms; the men are exhausted.<br>SR: 4:16<br>SS: 7:51 | | |

# AUGUST

| Sunday | Monday | Tuesday | Wednesday | Thursday | Friday | Saturday |
|---|---|---|---|---|---|---|
| | **1** Whitby. Old Mr. Swales discusses death with Mina and Lucy. *Demeter* in English Channel. ◗ SR: 4:10 SS: 8:06 | **2** The *Demeter* passes the Strait of Dover. A sixth crew member disappears. ◗ SR: 4:23 SS: 7:48 | **3** Aboard the *Demeter* a seventh sailor disappears. Later this day, the mate jumps overboard. ◗ SR: 4:24 SS: 7:47 | **4** Last entry log of the *Demeter*. Captain ties himself to the wheel, prepared to die like a man. ◆ SR: 4:25 SS: 7:43 | **5** ◗ SR: 4:27 SS: 7:44 | **6** The *Demeter* is sighted off Whitby. ◗ SR: 4:21 SS: 7:50 |
| **7** A great storm strikes Whitby. The *Demeter* is beached. A dog is seen leaping from the ship. Dracula takes refuge in the suicide's grave. ◗ SR: 4:25 SS: 7:47 | **8** ◆ SR: 4:32 SS: 7:38 | **9** ◆ SR: 4:34 SS: 7:36 | **10** Whitby. The captain of the *Demeter* is buried. Mr. Swales dies of a broken neck, the result of a fall. He is Dracula's first British victim. ○ SR: 4:28 SS: 7:43 | **11** Whitby. Lucy sleepwalks to the "suicide's seat" on the East Cliff. Dracula drinks her blood for the first time. ○ SR: 4:30 SS: 7:40 | **12** ○ SR: 4:38 SS: 7:30 | **13** ◆ SR: 4:40 SS: 7:28 |
| **14** Whitby. Dracula, in the form of a bat, takes Lucy's blood again. ○ SR: 4:36 SS: 7:33 | **15** ◆ SR: 4:42 SS: 7:24 | **16** ◆ SR: 4:44 SS: 7:22 | **17** ◗ SR: 4:46 SS: 7:20 | **18** Fifty boxes of earth from the *Demeter* are delivered to Carfax, Purfleet, near London. ◗ SR: 4:48 SS: 7:18 | **19** Whitby. Mina receives word of Jonathan from Sister Agatha in Budapest. ◗ SR: 4:46 SS: 7:24 | **20** Purfleet. Renfield escapes for the first time. He is peculiarly agitated and runs toward Carfax before being captured. ◗ SR: 4:50 SS: 7:13 |
| **21** ◆ SR: 4:52 SS: 7:11 | **22** ◆ SR: 4:54 SS: 7:09 | **23** Purfleet. Renfield escapes again. ● SR: 4:56 SS: 7:08 | **24** Mina and Jonathan married in Budapest. ● SR: 5:09 SS: 7:57 | **25** ● SR: 4:54 SS: 7:05 | **26** ● SR: 5:01 SS: 7:03 | **27** ● SR: 5:03 SS: 7:00 |
| **28** ● SR: 5:05 SS: 6:57 | **29** ◆ SR: 5:07 SS: 6:55 | **30** ◆ SR: 5:08 SS: 6:52 | **31** Hillingham. Arthur Holmwood asks Dr. Seward to examine Lucy. ◆ SR: 5:10 SS: 6:50 | | | |

# SEPTEMBER

● New Moon  ◐ First Quarter  ○ Full Moon  ◑ Last Quarter

| Sunday | Monday | Tuesday | Wednesday | Thursday | Friday | Saturday |
|---|---|---|---|---|---|---|
| | | | | **1** SR: 5:12 SS: 6:48 | **2** Dr. Seward writes to Dr. Van Helsing requesting help in his treatment of Lucy. SR: 5:13 SS: 6:46 | **3** Van Helsing arrives, examines Lucy, and leaves. SR: 5:15 SS: 6:44 |
| **4** Lucy appears to improve. SR: 5:16 SS: 6:42 | **5** SR: 5:17 SS: 6:39 | **6** Lucy suddenly becomes worse. SR: 5:19 SS: 6:37 | **7** Van Helsing supervises the first transfusion to Lucy. (Donor: Arthur Holmwood.) SR: 5:21 SS: 6:34 | **8** SR: 5:23 SS: 6:31 | **9** SR: 5:24 SS: 6:29 | **10** Lucy receives the second transfusion. (Donor: John Seward.) SR: 5:26 SS: 6:27 |
| **11** SR: 5:28 SS: 6:25 | **12** SR: 5:29 SS: 6:23 | **13** Lucy receives the third transfusion. (Donor: Dr. Van Helsing.) SR: 5:30 SS: 6:20 | **14** SR: 5:31 SS: 6:18 | **15** SR: 5:33 SS: 6:16 | **16** SR: 5:35 SS: 6:14 | **17** The wolf Berserker escapes from the zoo. Later, he breaks a window at Hillingham, frightening Mrs. Westenra to death and providing Dracula with entry to Lucy. Renfield attacks Seward and licks his spilled blood. SR: 5:37 SS: 6:11 |
| **18** Lucy receives the fourth transfusion. (Donor: Quincey Morris.) Mr. Hawkins dies. SR: 5:39 SS: 6:09 | **19** Lord Godalming, Arthur's father, dies; Arthur assumes the title. SR: 5:41 SS: 6:06 | **20** Lucy dies 6:30 A.M. (?) Renfield escapes and attacks workmen removing two boxes of earth from Carfax. SR: 5:42 SS: 6:04 | **21** Arthur's father is buried. SR: 5:43 SS: 6:01 | **22** Dracula, looking younger, is seen in Hyde Park by the Harkers. Lucy is buried in a churchyard near Hampstead Heath. SR: 5:45 SS: 5:59 | **23** On Hampstead Heath children are lured and bitten by the beautiful "Bloofer" lady. Mina reads Jonathan's journal. SR: 5:47 SS: 5:56 | **24** SR: 5:48 SS: 5:54 |
| **25** Van Helsing meets Mina and reads Jonathan's journal. SR: 5:50 SS: 5:51 | **26** Van Helsing and Seward visit Lucy's tomb at night and find it empty. Van Helsing meets Jonathan Harker. SR: 5:52 SS: 5:49 | **27** Van Helsing and Seward visit the tomb by daylight and find Lucy "more radiantly beautiful than ever" in her coffin. SR: 5:54 SS: 5:47 | **28** Van Helsing, Seward, Godalming, and Morris visit the tomb at night. They see Lucy walking with a child. Lucy and Arthur were to have been married today. SR: 5:56 SS: 5:45 | **29** Van Helsing, Seward, Godalming, and Morris visit the tomb at night. Godalming drives stake through Lucy's heart. Mina meets Seward; they exchange diaries. SR: 5:57 SS: 5:43 | **30** Dracula take first blood from Mina, who believes she has had only a bad dream. SR: 5:59 SS: 5:40 | |

# OCTOBER

| Sunday | Monday | Tuesday | Wednesday | Thursday | Friday | Saturday |
|---|---|---|---|---|---|---|
| | | | | | | **1** Renfield astounds Mina, Jonathan, Morris, Van Helsing, and Seward by his apparent sanity. The men break into Carfax and search the chapel. ◆● SR: 6:00 SS: 5:38 |
| **2** Dracula breaks Renfield's back: crushes skull. Van Helsing operates. Renfield dies. Mina and Dracula drink each other's blood. Mark on Mina's forehead. ◆◑ SR: 6:02 SS: 5:36 | **3** Van Helsing, Seward, Harker, Godalming, and Morris confront Dracula at 347 Piccadilly. Dracula escapes. ◆◑ SR: 6:04 SS: 5:34 | **4** ◆◑ SR: 6:06 SS: 5:31 | **5** Dracula leaves for Varna on the *Czarina Catherine* at high tide, at 12:55 A.M. ◆◑ SR: 6:08 SS: 5:28 | **6** SR: 6:04 SS: 5:31 | **7** SR: 6:05 SS: 5:30 | **8** ○ SR: 6:06 SS: 5:28 |
| **9** † ○ SR: 6:07 SS: 5:26 | **10** SR: 6:09 SS: 5:24 | **11** † ○ SR: 6:10 SS: 5:22 | **12** The Harkers, Morris, Godalming, Seward, and Van Helsing leave London in pursuit of Dracula. They board the Orient Express in Paris and arrive in Varna three days later. ○ SR: 6:10 SS: 5:23 | **13** † ◑ SR: 6:12 SS: 5:19 | **14** † ◑ SR: 6:14 SS: 5:17 | **15** The group arrives in Varna. They wait for news of Dracula. ◑ SR: 6:10 SS: 5:02 |
| **16** † ◑ SR: 6:17 SS: 5:13 | **17** † ◑ SR: 6:18 SS: 5:12 | **18** † ◑ SR: 6:19 SS: 5:10 | **19** † ● SR: 6:21 SS: 5:08 | **20** † ● SR: 6:22 SS: 5:06 | **21** † ● SR: 6:23 SS: 5:05 | **22** ● SR: 6:25 SS: 5:04 |
| **23** † ● They arrive in Galatz. Godalming and Harker set off upriver in a steam launch. Morris SR: 6:26 SS: 5:02 | **24** † Mina and Van Helsing arrive at Veresci. Van Helsing buys a carriage and horses. SR: 6:27 SS: 5:00 | **25** † ◑ SR: 6:29 SS: 4:58 | **26** † ◑ SR: 6:30 SS: 4:57 | **27** SR: 6:31 SS: 4:56 | **28** They learn that the *Czarina Catherine* has been diverted to Galatz. ◑ SR: 6:27 SS: 4:59 | **29** They travel by train from Varna to Galatz. SR: 6:28 SS: 4:59 |
| **30** and Seward set out on horseback. Mina and Van Helsing leave by train for Veresci. ◑ SR: 6:35 SS: 4:51 | **31** SR: 6:36 SS: 4:50 | | | | | |

# NOVEMBER

● New Moon  ◐ First Quarter  ○ Full Moon  ◑ Last Quarter

| Sunday | Monday | Tuesday | Wednesday | Thursday | Friday | Saturday |
|---|---|---|---|---|---|---|
| | | **1**<br><br>SR: 6:38<br>SS: 4:49 ✝ ● | **2**<br><br>SR: 6:39<br>SS: 4:47 ✝ ● | **3**<br><br>SR: 6:40<br>SS: 4:46 ✝ ● | **4**<br><br>SR: 6:42<br>SS: 4:45 ✝ ○ | **5** Mina and Van Helsing reach the Borgo Pass.<br><br>SR: 6:43<br>SS: 4:43 ✝ ○ |
| **6** Their launch being disabled. Harker and Godalming take up the pursuit on horseback.<br><br>SR: 6:45<br>SS: 4:42 ✝ ○ | **7** Mina and Van Helsing arrive in the vicinity of Castle Dracula. Van Helsing encloses Mina in a holy circle. The three female vampires appear and invite Mina to follow. Later: Van Helsing drives stakes through their hearts.<br>SR: 6:47<br>SS: 4:41 ✝ ○ | **8** The wagon bearing Dracula approaches the castle, pursued by Seward, Morris, Jonathan, Harker, and Godalming. After a fight in which Morris dies, Jonathan kills Dracula at 4:42 P.M.—sunset!<br>SR: 6:48<br>SS: 4:40 ✝ ○ | **9** | **10** | **11** | **12** |
| **13** | **14** | **15** | **16** | **17** | **18** | **19** |
| **20** | **21** | **22** | **23** | **24** | **25** | **26** |
| **27** | **28** | **29** | **30** | | | |

# INDEX